KU-404-317

EDDIE SHAH AND THE NEWSPAPER
REVOLUTION

About the Authors

David Goodhart read History and Politics at York University. He worked for the *Yorkshire Evening Press* before joining the *Financial Times*, first as a labour reporter and now on the City desk.

Patrick Wintour read History at Oxford. He then worked for the *New Statesman* and is now Labour Correspondent for the *Guardian*.

Eddie Shah and the Newspaper Revolution

David Goodhart and Patrick Wintour

CORONET BOOKS
Hodder and Stoughton

Copyright © 1986 by David Goodhart and
Patrick Wintour

First published in Great Britain in 1986
by Coronet Books

British Library C.I.P.

Goodhart, David
    Eddie Shah and the newspaper revolution.
    1. Newspaper publishing – Great Britain
    I. Title
    338.4'7072   PN5118

    ISBN 0-340-39263-0

This book is sold subject to the condition that
it shall not, by way of trade or otherwise, be
lent, re-sold, hired out or otherwise circulated
without the publisher's prior consent in any
form of binding or cover other than that in
which it is published and without a similar
condition including this condition being
imposed on the subsequent purchaser.

Printed and bound in Great Britain for
Hodder and Stoughton Paperbacks, a
division of Hodder and Stoughton Ltd.,
Mill Road, Dunton Green, Sevenoaks,
Kent (Editorial Office: 47 Bedford
Square, London, WC1 3DP) by
Cox and Wyman Ltd., Reading, Berks.
Photoset by Rowland Phototypesetting Ltd.,
Bury St Edmunds, Suffolk.

Contents

Acknowledgements

This book is a snapshot of a set of events that have been moving at high speed. We are painfully aware that by the time of publication, there will already be much that proves to be out of focus and much that should have been in the picture that is out of view.

We thank the many people who helped in the research and writing of this book, in particular Lionel Barber, Sally Anderson and Philippa Thomson for patience and advice; Jane Birkett who expertly copy edited the manuscript on the run; Claire Gristwood for emergency typing; Ian Chapman and Amanda Stewart at Coronet for tolerance and a sense of direction; our work colleagues for bearing with our distractedness. While we have shamelessly plagiarised from many sources, one book on the Messenger dispute by Mark Dickinson, *To Break a Union*, has been an especially valuable aid. Thanks also to Eddie Shah who gave generously of his time in the knowledge that he might not like a good deal of what we wrote. Finally, for the mistakes, and the original idea, we blame each other.

'It is only a few months since I reproached Mrs Thatcher on this score: "You have done nothing for Fleet Street. I am putting my trust solely in Eddie Shah." "Ooh," she said fervently, "so am I, so am I!"'

Paul Johnson, The Spectator, 21 December 1985

'It was going to happen anyway. I was just the lucky guy who got in first.'

Eddie Shah, October 1985

Introduction

For the three out of five adults in Britain who regularly read, or glance at, a national daily newspaper, something important is happening. The industry which produces their familiar 'window' on the world is in the throes of transformation.

1986 has been billed as year zero of the Fleet Street revolution. It opened momentously. In the course of just one week at the end of January, Eddie Shah successfully concluded the first dummy run of his new colour daily, *Today*; Robert Maxwell, having reduced the workforce at Mirror Group Newspapers by 2,000, told advertisers they could expect cuts of up to half in his paper's advertising rates; United Newspapers formally confirmed that it wanted a one-third reduction in manning at the Express group; and most dramatic of all, Rupert Murdoch's News International produced its four titles – the *Times*, *Sunday Times*, *Sun* and *News of the World* – from behind barbed wire at a new printing plant in Wapping while, in effect, locking out 5,000 members of the traditional print unions.

It will also be a record year for new launches. In the past few months no less than six national titles have been planned in an industry which has become a by-word for stagnation. Apart from Shah's *Today* there is Maxwell's proposed new entertainment daily *Good Day*; the left-wing *News on Sunday*; a new quality daily planned by former Telegraph journalists; a racing daily to be launched by the Dubai-based Maktoun brothers; a soft-porn paper, *Sunday Sport*, planned by sex shop millionaire David Sullivan; and a rising tide of rumours about new financial, sports and other specialist papers.

The speed of change has been bewildering and, as the battle for Wapping has shown, the transition will not be smooth or painless. Vested interests on all sides continue to resist the process but in five years time the industry will be barely recognisable.

The upheaval is centred on radical changes to a geriatric Fleet Street production cycle which each night converts several tonnes of pulped tree into many millions of individual newspapers. These papers will soon be produced using modern, computer-based, electronic equipment cutting out the traditional resetting of journalist's copy by skilled print workers, in many cases still using 60-year-old Linotype machines. Instead of being printed in one claustrophobic part of London the electronic pages and pictures will be beamed to printing plants all over Britain, incidentally uprooting the present mainline railway-based distribution system.

It is quite possible that the men and women engaged in this new production process will belong to different trade unions from those which have dominated the printing industry for the past century; they could even be in no trade union at all. Additionally, many of them will be employed by a new breed of businessmen.

Britons are unusually avid readers of newspapers and, at their best, internationally admired writers and designers of them; but for decades Central London's last manufacturing centre has been an industry in suspended animation, a vivid microcosm of Britain's wider industrial decline.

Everyone has heard half-truths about £1,000-a-week Fleet Street printers working on museum-piece machines, or astonishing acts of incompetence by employers still, significantly, known as proprietors. Yet, like the worst of the nationalised industries, the inefficiency of the national newspaper business has been able to defy the textbook laws of the market: it has faced no foreign competition and the threat of bankruptcy has had no sway so long as rich men have queued to buy their way into 'the Street'.

But in the *Daily Mirror*'s now famous phrase: 'The gravy train has hit the buffers.' This most belated modernisation in British industry is, in part, the expression of slowly unwinding technological and political trends. In most other industrialised countries over the past fifteen years newspapers have been in the vanguard of the information revolution, exploiting the new electronic technology to phase out the 'hot metal' composing room.

In Britain the power of the unions in Fleet Street, and to a lesser extent in the provincial press, has been able to delay this re-equipping. Where the new technology has been introduced its application has often been twisted to fit the unions job-preserving imperative, thus negating most of the hoped-for savings in time and money.

The political and legal changes since 1979 have seriously curtailed that union power and transferred the whip hand to radically emboldened employers. The shift has taken longer to percolate through to Fleet Street than elsewhere in British industry, but the shake-out now gathering pace in the national newspaper industry marked by the shedding of labour, the introduction of new processes and the smashing of the old conventions of industrial relations, is in a line of descent from the disputes in the steel industry (1980), British Leyland (1981), British Telecom (1983) and the mining industry (1984–5).

Yet, to a quite remarkable extent, the speed of change is a consequence of the catalytic effect of one man – Eddie Shah; a man who two-and-a-half years ago was an impatient, unknown, south-Manchester-based free newspaper owner. At a time when economic and industrial life seems increasingly dominated by huge impersonal forces, such as US interest rates or the strength of sterling, Shah is a throwback to the 'romantic' industrial innovators of the nineteenth century. He has reasserted the role of the individual in industrial history.

This is in part thanks to his self-promotional skills, exploiting the opportunity provided by his victory over the National Graphical Association (NGA) at Warrington in 1983. He has also, alongside men such as Sir Freddie Laker, been helped by the media's hunger to promote flamboyant capitalists, particularly those in highly visible industries like travel or newspapers. Even more important, his timing has been perfect. Shah has slipped through an opening created by Margaret Thatcher and in so doing has himself become a symbol of the Thatcher era.

Fleet Street has always been theoretically vulnerable to undercutting by an outsider. But the print union veto that has barred internal reform has also blocked such an interloper; until, that is, the technical, political, and legal changes of the 1970s and early 1980s combined to provide the impetus for one man to unlock the door to the newspaper of the future.

The nimble outsider has a significant advantage for the moment, but it will probably only be for a short time. After years stuck in the doldrums the Fleet Street crew, now skippered by Captain Bob Maxwell and Rupert Murdoch, have eased themselves into Shah's slipstream with a cheery wave of thanks and every intention of scuttling him as soon as practicable. The recent changes of ownership at Express Newspapers and the *Telegraph* have also ushered in two more aggressive management strategists intent on the dismantling of the old Fleet Street.

Murdoch's rupture with the past has followed the Shah model: a militaristic confrontation with the old print unions; the use of the Tory Government's employment laws; and, in all likelihood, a single-union and no-strike arrangement with the Electricians Union (EETPU). The result has been a fall in his production workforce from 5,000 to about 1,000. Most of the other Fleet Street employers look set to achieve rather smaller, but nonetheless considerable manning reductions with the acquiescence of the shell-shocked print unions.

Shah's own paper, *Today*, is the newspaper revolution in practice, with printing at three separate plants around the country and the complete absence of an old composing room. For the first time in seventy years it has put a British newspaper in the technological top dozen of the world. *Today*'s reception as a newspaper will be fascinating to watch over the next few months but in five years the paper will probably seem of only minor significance to the revolution. Even if it fails, it represents the future and is already prompting others to follow. The question now is not whether the industry will be revolutionised but who will play the bigger part in it: Shah and the other outsiders, or Fleet Street's newly galvanised corporate giants?

Why should a new product such as *Today* cause such interest? Why, indeed, should the shake-out of the national newspaper industry itself be of any note? It directly employs less than 25,000 people and its exports are minimal. The foundry industry, for example, is more significant to the British economy on both counts, but no books are being written about its own equally profound restructuring in recent years.

Newspapers, however, unlike moulded iron, influence people. The extent to which they do so is hotly contested but their reporting and analysis are inevitably part of the democratic equation. In large, complex societies the citizen cannot possibly know from direct experience what is being done by his local or national rulers and is becoming ever more dependent on the 'media' for his daily information and entertainment.

The degree of choice available and the extent of pollution in these channels of communication is much more than an industrial matter. The imminent revolution in newspapers, as with cable TV, promises at least to open up more channels.

The past few years have shown however that more may not mean better. As Paul Foot recently wrote: 'The more national newspapers there are the more difficult it is to tell them apart.' Yet here too the newspaper revolutionaries make bold promises. Not only, they claim, will the editorial service be enhanced by later deadlines and greater use of colour, but the lower cost of entry into the industry will allow an explosion of political and special-interest-group diversity in the British press. Their thesis is now set for the test.

1

Battle at Winwick Quay

'The miners should have learnt from our experience with the police.'

Tony Burke, president of the Stockport branch of the NGA.

1

Battle at Winwick Quay

The story of *Today*, Britain's first fully electronic newspaper, can be traced back to the freezing early hours of Tuesday, 29 November 1983.

It was 5 a.m. when Eddie Shah arrived outside his factory unit on the modern Winwick Quay industrial estate north of Warrington in Lancashire. He flicked a V-sign, almost affectionately, towards the two faces watching him from inside the NGA's ever-present 'battle-wagon' parked thirty yards away.

Shah walked upstairs to the room above the printing presses. It had been turned into an industrial warfare survival base – bunk beds, a cooker, a freezer full of food, television sets, video games, packs of cards, cans of beer; everything that the past three weeks had taught Shah he would need to satisfy his twelve staff and five security guards for the next two days until his print-run was complete and the mass pickets had dispersed.

He reflected on how odd it was to be producing something as homely as a local weekly newspaper under siege conditions. Winwick Quay estate, built in the late 1970s, was a neat, if appropriately desolate, setting for this miserable drama; with its well-kept grass verges and flower-beds hugging the rather flimsy-looking, flat-roofed units, it was a small part of Warrington's struggle against industrial decline.

Shah went back downstairs to let in the early arrivals among his young staff. Their mood was a mixture of apprehension and high spirits, like sailors returning to ship after leave. Inside, the cramped conditions felt more like a submarine. Squashed into the print room next to the press were four three-ton box vans parked bumper to bumper, their windows covered by steel grilles, their wing mirrors and bumpers greased, ready to run the blockade.

Two of the Special Security Services guards, with their dogs, arrived with the morning papers. Shah joked with them about the descriptions of him in the press but complained about a less than flattering photograph. It depicted a man of six foot and seventeen stone whose wide frame had puffed out and run to fat. It was the physique of a former sportsman who had spent the last fifteen years eating too much and exercising too little.

In the past month this 39-year-old small businessman had become a public figure. His stooping figure and boyish features constantly filled the TV screens, vowing that he would not give in to mob rule. 'My staff must have the right to join or not to join a union, it's as simple as that,' he was always insisting in pained, defensive tones.

Like many major conflicts, it had begun as a local dispute. Shah had portentously launched his first free paper (paid for entirely by advertising) during the 'three-day week' of 1974, and by 1982 was running a moderately successful group publishing five Messenger titles pushed through letter boxes along the south-Manchester belt. He had also become embroiled in almost daily rows with his NGA employees.

To claim back his 'right to manage' he rejected the print industry's customary closed shop when he opened a new typesetting subsidiary in Bury. In a vigorous – and occasionally violent – attempt to press him back into line, the NGA had begun to organise unlawful mass-picketing at the end of October 1983. Crowds of between two hundred and twelve hundred had gathered at Warrington on Tuesday and Wednesday nights when Shah printed the papers and distributed them to a small army of school children for delivery.

More than most serious industrial disputes, this had become an intensely personal conflict – driven by a clash of temperament and personality. Many of the local and national union officials whom Shah had grown to despise over the past three months – or in some cases three years – would be out with the pickets in the courtyard that night, as would the striking 'Stockport Six' – the NGA members at Messenger who had been called out by the union in July.

The confrontation had not been confined to that courtyard. Leaders of both camps received abusive midnight phone calls. In the previous week Shah had had four coffins delivered to his front door – one for his wife and one for each of his three children. He invested in two ferocious Rhodesian ridgeback guard dogs. Alan Royston, the NGA father of the chapel (shop steward), had also had several unwanted deliveries of gas cylinders and double glazing.

Most of Shah's staff had closed ranks around him. Only eight employees were ever in NGA grades and the rest, mainly advertising, administrative and management staff, had a strong bond with Messenger and its chairman. The past few weeks of fear and physical violence had drawn them even closer together. 'It was what the Blitz must have felt like,' said Steve Hart, one of Shah's managers.

Nevertheless, it was a bruising period for Shah. The dispute began only a few months after his wife, Jennifer, was found to have a recurrence of cervical cancer. At one point she was given only five months to live. Yet as the pressure escalated he remained unusually composed, planning his tactics like a clear-headed army

5

officer. 'We feel cold and lonely out at the front but we happen to believe in this country and what it's about,' he said. Part of him relished the struggle. In any case the mass picket had so far had little effect beyond delaying his deliveries slightly on two occasions. But that night of the 29th, a big turnout was expected.

At the centre of the maelstrom Shah sat alone in the upstairs room. He must have smiled to himself as he contemplated the stir he had caused: the arguments in the High Court, the questions in Parliament, rows of pundits in TV studios – all discussing him. He imagined all those schoolteachers and employers who had dismissed him as a petulant failure gasping in astonishment when they saw him on TV.

As the trains and coachloads of NGA members made their way towards Warrington they found little to smile about. They talked about this 'maverick' and 'spiv' who had unilaterally broken the industry's carefully constructed code of conduct. The middle-aged members of possibly the strongest union in Britain were not used to demonstrations; they usually applied industrial pressure in more subtle ways.

Around midday, ACAS, the Government funded industrial conciliation body, tried and failed to restart talks to head off the anticipated clash. Dennis Boyd, the ACAS Chief Conciliator, rang Shah and told him that Tony Dubbins, the NGA leader, had offered to call off the pickets if he would talk again. Shah said he would not leave his staff and suggested Helen Graham, the Messenger managing director, as his representative. Dubbins declined the offer.

In the early afternoon Shah called a press conference in the cluttered printing room. His handling of the media through the dispute had been adroit – as befitted a newspaper proprietor with a background in theatre and TV. Reporters and camera crew stood between vans or sat on huge reels of newsprint while Shah announced he would seek a third writ for contempt against the NGA arising from last week's picket. He said: 'It's a military situation. The pickets would need three armoured tanks, a couple of helicopters with machine guns and about 600 men from 2 Para to stop the newspapers leaving.'

He showed a flash of irritation when asked if he had considered suspending publication. 'You make it sound like a crime to publish. That is our business, that is what we will do, regardless of how many people are out there breaking the law. If pilots in the Battle of Britain had given up just because they were outnumbered, we would not be here today.'

Two hundred miles to the south, in London, the dispute was aired for the first time that afternoon in the House of Commons. Neil Kinnock, in one of his most difficult exchanges since becoming Labour leader in October, said the confrontation had been caused by the Government's new legislation. John Biffen, Leader of the House, replied that the Labour leader was clearly embarrassed by the tactics being used in the dispute.

Down the road at the High Court in the Strand, seven national papers applied for injunctions against a repeat of the previous weekend's action when the NGA had called up its heavy artillery in Fleet Street and unlawfully halted the production of all national papers on Saturday and Sunday. The aim – to build employer-pressure on Shah – was misjudged. He was not part of the print employer club and therefore out of range of the traditional weaponry.

Another group of national paper employers, who had stuck to the hard line agreed at the Newspaper Publishers Association (NPA) and locked out their staff on Monday, had by Tuesday resentfully acknowledged their isolation and started printing again. The absence of any collective will to sit out a prolonged dispute with the NGA surprised no one; Shah liked to call Fleet Street the 'yellow press' – the double meaning was immediately understood.

But the Government's legal straitjacket was effectively closing round the union. In the previous ten days the courts had fined the NGA a total of £150,000 for ignoring injunctions against mass 'secondary' picketing. Subsequently the union's entire £11m. assets were seized. Despite its right-wing craft roots, the militant rhetoric of resistance to the new Tory anti-union laws was taken seriously by the NGA, the union with most to lose from them. For Government, courts, police, and trade union movement, Warrington had become the long-awaited trial of strength over the new legal framework, like the challenge mounted to the Heath Government twelve years before by the Pentonville Five.

In Bedford, that same afternoon, the forty-two-man ruling body of the National Council of the NGA decided that the dispute could only be won by drawing on the whole trade union movement's qualified commitment to fight the laws. After the meeting, the members boarded the coach for Warrington, swapping stories about how the court-appointed sequestrators had frozen even the bank accounts opened for retired members' Christmas parties.

Joe Wade, the general secretary, and Tony Dubbins, the general secretary elect who had already in practice taken the lead role, took a train to London and presented their case to the TUC's important employment committee. They asked for financial assistance and full moral and physical support in line with the commitment from the special TUC conference on the new law at Wembley in 1982.

Len Murray, TUC general secretary, was markedly cool, however, and in the light of legal advice he recommended unions to give only lawful support. Dubbins and Wade left the evening meeting less than happy, as did several left-wingers on the committee. But when news of TUC support reached the gradually filling courtyard on Winwick Quay it was greeted with cheers and the qualifications were forgotten.

8

George Jerrom, the NGA's national newspaper official and leading Communist Party activist, had established a regular spot as master of ceremonies on the picket line. With a microphone in front of the battle-wagon, he kept pickets (and policemen) amused with his stream of news, humour and political diatribe – fuelled by his hip-flask. It was real soap-box oratory and earned him the nickname Lord Haw Haw from the senior police officers.

From about 4.30 p.m. he had begun welcoming contingents of pickets from Liverpool NGA, Scottish miners, London dockers. As in the Grunwick dispute six years before, it had become 'like a left-wing Ascot', as one NGA picket put it.

Inside the plant an edge of tension had crept into the banter as the printing plates were fitted on to the presses in readiness for the first run. The sound of the growing crowd outside was barely muted by the thin walls of the factory unit. The confidence Shah had felt earlier in the day began to drain away. Why were the police not stopping them getting on to the forecourt?

The war chant of the trade union Left started up: 'The workers united will never be defeated.' Shah peered out of one of the small grille windows: 'They're not workers, they're fucking animals,' he said. It sounded like two thousand people baying for his blood.

But they had not got in before and there was no reason why they should now. Most of the pickets, especially the moderate skilled workers of the NGA, had come as a gesture of support – to take part in a demonstration and, if possible, stop the papers coming out through sheer weight of numbers. Occupation of the plant or physical violence was a long way from their minds.

In any case the police had not been idly sipping tea in the Warrington station canteen. After the first 'surprise' mass picket at Winwick Quay on 9 November – when they had been caught unawares – word reached the chief constable of Cheshire, George Fenn, from the Home

Office (prompted by local Tory MPs) that no expense must be spared in protecting Shah.

The chief constable immediately began making requests for Police Support Units (thirty men, three sergeants and an inspector) from neighbouring forces following the informal practice that had grown up in the 1970s. There was to be no repeat of Saltley Gate – that traumatic symbol of defeat for both the Tory Government and the police, when Arthur Scargill's miners' pickets aided by local engineers closed the Birmingham coke depot in 1972.

Preparations for the night of the 29th were especially careful. Police intelligence suggested that the relatively well-behaved NGA members were sure to be supported by a higher than usual proportion of groups such as students, far-leftists and even local hoodlums, less averse to a punch-up. In case of serious violence, Greater Manchester's élite Tactical Aid Group were on stand-by. Like the Met's Special Patrol Group, they were usually reserved for anti-terrorism duties or riots.

The Cheshire constabulary had rented one of the empty factory units a hundred yards behind Shah's for use as a command centre. The space was dominated by a large canteen and rest area, staffed by chefs in full regalia, able to feed up to two thousand policemen. There was also a first-aid unit and rows of shields, helmets, shin pads, night sticks, and amongst the pickets rumours were spreading about CS gas cylinders.

By 8.00 p.m. the yard had filled up with about fifteen hundred pickets. More were arriving every minute. The narrow entrances to the estate and to Shah's forecourt provided favourable terrain for a blockade. Just past eight, however, the police seized the initiative. Several hundred of them emptied the forecourt by pressing the pickets back on three sides and clearing them away from the front of the plant.

It made an eerie sight. TV and police floodlights lit up an empty forecourt littered with leaflets and discarded

Socialist Workers Party placards; circling the edge of the vacant stage was a three-deep line of police holding back two thousand pickets. A large crowd was pushed round to an opening at the right of the plant. Several hundred people were cordoned off to the left, and this group started pushing back more vigorously, urged on by speakers from the battle-wagon.

By about 9.30 p.m. a section of them had pushed all the way to the entrance to Shah's unit and were pressing the police back against the steel shuttered door. At one point the door began to buckle slightly. Feeling a mixture of fear and anger Shah decided to telephone Andrew Neil, the young Scot who, two months before, had become editor of the *Sunday Times*. He was one of the few men of national influence who had offered Shah support and sympathy over the past weeks.

Shah described to Neil how dangerous the situation had become. Neil was outraged and immediately rang Leon Brittan, then Home Secretary, at home, and demanded that something more be done. Neil remembers that Brittan 'behaved like a lawyer', saying he could not interfere in operational matters and 'I told him that unless something was done I would be reproducing this conversation in the *Sunday Times*.'

While these agitated conversations had been flowing between Winwick Quay and Central London, David Graham, the deputy chief constable in charge of the operation, had gone on to the offensive. The exits from the nearby M62 were blocked off, stopping any more pickets swelling the crowd of up to four thousand that had gathered.

The police snatch squads, with helmets and batons, had also started to move into aggressive parts of the crowd and haul people out. Around midnight the NGA's battle-wagon was peremptorily closed down by the police and the PA system's wires cut. Jerrom was angrily accused of incitement by senior police officers. To many

11

pickets the loss of the van was deeply offensive, like the taking of their 'flag'.

The 2,000-strong crowd to the right of the plant continued to block the exit from the forecourt and spread out over a small mound that became known as the 'Kop'. For the newspaper vans to get out, this body of people had to be moved.

The Tactical Aid Group were called to the ready. But the senior officers were wary of using their most powerful weapon. Just before 1.00 a.m. they took up the suggestion of several NGA officials and asked Shah if he would delay printing by a few hours to let tempers cool and the crowd disperse. There was, after all, no particular need for the papers to leave in the early hours of the morning. Shah immediately thought that having come so far he could not concede to the enemy even this minor symbolic victory. Never a man to miss his theatrical cue, he declined to delay. The senior police officers were not too unhappy with the decision. They knew they could win. The Saltley humiliation could be avenged.

The Tactical Aid Group were finally sent in, and cut through the crowd with their batons flailing. Soon the road round the back of the plant looked like an Ulster riot, with burning barricades, felled telegraph poles, and groups of riot police chasing after pickets. There were excesses on both sides. Some members of the Tactical Aid Group in full riot gear clearly enjoyed the night out. But individual acts of police thuggery were in part provoked by the impersonal violence of the missiles which hailed down from the Kop.

Most of the pickets were stunned by the efficiency and ruthlessness of the police-clearing operation and started to hurry away. John Ibbotson, later the NGA's deputy general secretary, said the next day: 'A large number of our members, middle-aged blokes who've never been in that kind of scene, were horrified. They're the sort of people who have always been supportive of law and order but they changed their views about the police last night.' It had been one of those rare, but uncomfortable, reminders that even in a mature democracy the struggle for industrial power can still involve a literal battle, and that the law remains ultimately underpinned by physical force.

At 4.45 in the morning the vans finally screeched out of the plant with their load of weekly papers. Only a few die-hards were left to impotently shout 'scab'. It was the end of an era in trade union history, an end too for the effective use of a tactic that for the past ten years had come to represent the high watermark of trade union power. Tony Burke, the NGA Stockport branch president, admitted: 'Flying pickets were born at Saltley Gate and died at Warrington.' As the pickets, police and Messenger staff stumbled wearily home to catch a few hours' sleep, most people sensed it was the beginning of the end of the Messenger dispute. What they could not have predicted was that Winwick Quay had become the symbolic birthplace of a project which two-and-a-half years later was to help transform the national newspaper industry and directly inspire Rupert Murdoch's Wapping escapade.

2

An Idea Whose Time Has Come

'If we are not prepared to embrace new technology . . . then competition from alternative sources in this country, or from abroad, will spell the death knell of the newspaper industry as we have known it.'

Joe Wade, former general secretary of the NGA, addressing his union's conference in 1982

2

An Idea Whose Time Has Come

Two weeks after the disturbing scenes in Warrington, Len (now Lord) Murray, the TUC general secretary, stepped out of Congress House to make one of the most controversial pronouncements in postwar trade union history. Murray told the TV cameras that the TUC could not support its own employment committee's nine to seven vote – taken just minutes before – to adopt a 'sympathetic and supportive' attitude to the NGA's unlawful one-day national print strike planned for two days hence on 14 December. Five-and-a-half months after it had begun, the Messenger dispute – a classic confrontation between free enterprise and trade union solidarity – was effectively over. Eddie Shah had won a famous victory over the powerful print union.

When, two days later, the full TUC General Council backed Murray's stand by thirty-one votes to twenty it also marked a turning point in British industrial relations, foreshadowing the 1984–5 miners' strike which was to rerun many of the same arguments about the role of the unions, the law, the courts and the police.

The Messenger crisis brought a large part of the trade union movement, excluding the National Union of Mineworkers' leadership, down to earth with a rude jolt. The NGA, which on 9 December had suffered the largest contempt fine in British legal history (£375,000), had argued that the one-day strike would increase the pressure on Shah unbearably. But faced with the realities of a challenge to the law and an elected government which logically led to a general strike or some similar conflagration, the TUC leadership acknowledged that it couldn't – and many believed shouldn't – win such a fight. The day after the General Council decision, the NGA called off the one-day strike and in early January purged its contempt of court to unfreeze its assets. The dispute had cost it about £2m.

The dispute also ripped away a thick veil of illusion which had wrapped itself around many of the Labour movement's leaders and activists since 1979. By providing 'new realism' with its first uncomfortable victory, it seemed to confirm a belated rejection of a form of British Syndicalism which had taken root in the late sixties. The moderate, low-key strategy of new realism was a recognition that mass unemployment had produced fear not militancy. It was to be temporarily blown off-course first by the ban on unions at GCHQ and then by the miners' strike – but it had passed its major challenge. The price was a shattering and very public trauma for the Labour movement.

Shah, too, suffered his own more private trauma after the dispute. Despite his impulsive, volatile nature, he had remained in an almost trance-like state of calm determination for the past two months. But now the waters would be held back no longer. He was in his Bury office the afternoon after Murray's renunciation of the employment committee: 'I remember I was sitting at my desk and it suddenly hit me – we've actually done it – we've come through – and I just started shaking uncontrollably. Helen Graham came in – I think she thought I was going to have a heart attack or something – but I didn't want anyone else to see.'

The description of his minor breakdown sounds like the effect of accumulated delayed shock – similar to

18

that sometimes recalled by soldiers who have just seen action. In Shah's own self-analysis, it illustrates the extent to which he acts on impulse, rationalising only later: like the cartoon character happily walking on air until he looks down, realises the impossibility of his position, and drops.

As the normally teetotal Shah calmed himself with a small brandy in his Bury office that December afternoon, something gradually dawned on him. He realised his life had been permanently changed by the dispute; what's more, he knew he did not want to return to 'civilian' life. Shah had found his brief taste of the big time exhilarating. He had also become even more fascinated by the high politics of the newspaper industry, a fascination that was enhanced by formal and informal contacts with some of its leading figures.

As the Messenger dispute gathered steam he began to recognise what all the commentators were later to alight upon: that this struggle was merely a vivid and violent symptom of a deeper shift within the industry. When the din of battle had reverberated into history, he began to talk less about human rights and the closed shop and would say, rather conspiratorially, 'You know, the dispute is really all about new technology.'

The new electronic and computerised printing technology had, over the previous decade, started to displace thousands of craft jobs, and was beginning to seriously hurt the NGA. The Messenger Group itself underlined the technological point. During and after the dispute the papers were being set, in the absence of the NGA staff, by four young women straight out of secretarial college who had been trained by Steve Hart for only two weeks. Several experienced craftsmen with four-year apprenticeships behind them could no doubt have done a better job, but not that much better, and would have cost an employer a good deal more.

Shah, who often pointed out that he had only ever known the 'new' technology, was coming increasingly to place his own battle for the right to manage in this technological context. His grand Fleet Street supporters, locked into the most archaic methods almost anywhere in the world, encouraged this thinking, perhaps playing out their own dreams through him. As it happened, he found that he knew as much about the power struggle in the industry as they did and that they were indeed looking to him for inspiration.

Reflecting on his changed perspective, he recalls: 'It was odd really, a lot of these people – especially the union people like Joe Wade and Bill Keys – were just famous names to be held rather in awe. And then you see them at ACAS surrounded by a sea of empty wine bottles and overflowing ashtrays, someone in the corner with his shoes and socks off, picking his toe-nails. You lose your awe quite quickly.'

Shah had handled the transition from nobody to national figure with apparent ease. For the man who had once earned a living raising the curtain at the Adelphi Theatre, the national stage now held little fear. As his friend and accountant Ian Templeton puts it: 'The strike revealed to him that he had got a lot more in him than he thought.' Shah also knew the dispute had given him a reputation, an image he could exploit providing he struck quickly, while his entrance could still send a ripple of whispers through any restaurant or bar in the country. Messenger would undoubtedly need some hard work on it to get it back into shape after the disruption of the dispute. But he couldn't face that and anyway he knew his colleague Helen Graham would do a better job if he was not breathing down her neck.

Shah began daydreaming. He had always been strong on ideas, less good on application. It had earned him a reputation as something of a Walter Mitty with a few of his past business partners. It was some time early in January 1984 that he first began toying with the idea of launching a national paper. The logical next step would have been a free daily in Manchester – which he also

20

considered. But he was immediately attracted to the romance – the sheer bravado – of going national. After all, wasn't bypassing the bloated and lethargic Fleet Street one of the last great entrepreneurial opportunities that Britain had to offer in the latter part of the twentieth century? He had defied the critics and doubters once already in his defeat of the NGA. What fun to do it all over again by aiming at Fleet Street – 'an industry ripe for the taking' as he is fond of saying – with a high-tech, non-union paper.

He rang an old friend – and chief doubter – Chris Bullivant. Bullivant is chief executive of the *Daily News* in Birmingham, Britain's first daily free paper. He is in his own right another important figure in the newspaper revolution and particularly the free newspaper revolution which he helped to promote with his unusual insistence (back in 1970) on strong editorial in the frees. Shah, who was building up his chain in south Manchester while Bullivant was doing the same in south Birmingham, indirectly learned that important editorial lesson from him.

But Bullivant had stuck closer to the textbooks than Shah. 'I suppose I'm more of a traditional Brit who prefers doing things by compromise.' Shah, on the other hand, he sees in 'that great tradition of enterprising foreigners – like Murdoch and Maxwell – who come over here and teach us how to do it.'

When Shah first rang him to tell him about the Messenger dispute it was several months before the strike had even begun. 'He said he was going to take them on and described what would happen – as it turned out he was uncannily accurate.' Bullivant had advised against taking on the NGA. He now said he thought the national paper was a non-starter. 'Shah feeds me ideas and if I disagree he knows they will work,' he jokes. 'He said he was going to exploit the credibility given by the strike to take on Fleet Street – and I just said I don't think it's possible,' recalls Bullivant.

The seed had been planted – but the notion remained more fantasy than serious project until a crucial meeting on 7 February 1984. If *Today* has a date of birth, it must be Shah's meeting on that day with Andrew Neil in the Savoy Hotel.

The two men had agreed during one of their long telephone chats that it would be nice to meet when it was all over. Shah now also wanted to bounce the idea of the national paper off him. He respected Neil, and was impressed by his sharp mind and confident overviews.

Neil had first contacted Shah the Friday night before the climactic Winwick Quay confrontation when it had become clear there would be no *Sunday Times* that week because of the Messenger dispute. Shah had been rather apologetic about the non-appearance of his paper but Neil said he would far rather not have a paper than see Shah give in. He also warned him to expect the great weight of the Establishment to bear down upon him to force compromise.

The big-jowled Scot had now been editing the *Sunday Times* for six months. He was still something of a media prodigy, although he looked a good deal older than his thirty-five years. He is a committed Tory but, despite considerable admiration for Mrs Thatcher, is on the Peter Walker wing of the Party and is indeed a close friend and former research assistant to Walker.

A period as labour correspondent on *The Economist* during the *Times* shut-down of 1978–9 had taught him a deep dislike for Fleet Street's peculiar ways. It was a dislike confirmed by his next posting in the US where he experienced the benefits of the unfettered use of new technology. Now, as editor of the *Sunday Times*, he found himself struggling with the unions every week to get the paper out in the face of what he described as the 'six o'clock stitch up.'

The Messenger story appealed to him enormously and he seized the opportunity to run a four-page 'Battle for Britain' centre spread on Sunday 4 December, explaining the background to the dispute. Under the same Battle for Britain heading he also penned one of the most damning leader articles on Fleet Street ever written, sparing neither unions nor management. A framed copy of it now hangs in Shah's study.

Shah recalls twitches of nerves coming so close to Fleet Street on that day; on one of his visits to the High Court he found himself caught in a Fleet Street traffic jam with an aggressive group of print workers peering through the car windows.

They met at about 2.30 p.m. Neil was, like many people when they first meet Shah, struck by the size of the man. After a few minutes of small talk and reminiscing about the great victory they sank into forty minutes' intense conversation, with Neil doing most of the talking. When they both had to leave they realised they hadn't even remembered to order a drink.

Shah confided that he found it difficult to slot back into Messenger life and was looking around for a role. What should he do with himself and his business? Where should he go from here? As it happened, Shah didn't even have to raise the idea of a new-technology, non-union, national paper; Neil went straight to it: 'I said, "Look, I don't know how rich you are but the next thing that should be done is to do what you have just done, only this time to Fleet Street."' Neil ran through an argument he had tripped out many times before: 'The Fleet Street unions have not only blocked the rational use of technology, they have also been allowed to win the most chronic over-pay and overmanning – particularly in the publishing and distribution areas. And in the composing area it's still a nightmare even though we've transferred from the old hot metal to the newer photo-composition. Most of those guys are working against you, not working with you to bring out a paper.'

He went on: 'Fleet Street can only be reformed by an outsider. It will never solve its own problems because as long as each proprietor shares the same cost base they have no incentive to change and can just pass on their absurd labour costs to the reader and the advertiser.

'The great pity of English newspapers is that the Japanese don't make them. What we really need is a newspaper Toyota. That could give us a paper that is journalist-led rather than production-led – a paper which gives the readers what they want.'

Neil also suggested he should go and see that great beacon of the technological revolution – *USA Today* – the paper owned by the Gannett Corporation which, through satellite printing at seven plants in the USA, has become the country's first national newspaper. He said there was no good reason, with the new Tory laws and the new technology, why the UK could not now have a greenfield site, non-union, national paper printed – similarly – in several places around the country. Like *USA Today* it should be in colour, and should aim at the middle-market, the area worst hit by TV. 'You should aim to bring the *News at Ten* viewer back to print with a mix of tabloid pezzaz and serious news reporting,' Neil counselled Shah.

Unusually for him, Shah had sat quietly soaking it all in, asking the occasional question. It was, of course, just what he had wanted to hear. Neil's endorsement had taken the idea out of the realm of fantasy and on to the drawing board. Or at least on to the back of a cigar pack where Shah says he did his first crude calculations about circulation, revenue and production costs, while flying back to Manchester.

Neil himself remembers thinking that taking on the Fleet Street problem was all probably a bit big for Shah.

24

3

Fleet Street: The History of a Problem

'A poet writing in the silence of his study may or may not have an intellectual right to despise the journalist. But I greatly doubt that he would not be morally the better if he saw the great lights burning on through darkness until dawn and heard the roar of the printing wheels weaving the destinies of another day. Here at least is a school of labour and of some rough humility, the largest work ever published anonymously since the great Christian Cathedrals.'

G. K. Chesterton

3

Fleet Street: The History of a Problem

It seems appropriate that a story as bizarre as how the British national newspaper industry came to be jointly run by the heads of three media conglomerates and 350 union chapels should begin with a man whose life ended in a hut on the roof of the Duke of Devonshire's home, as he uttered blasphemous obscenities and convinced himself he was the victim of a German plot to poison him with icecream.

Lord Northcliffe died in 1922, an insane millionaire, at the age of fifty-six. His life had been devoted to the invention of the mass-circulation paper in Britain. To a remarkable degree the contemporary form of the national newspaper industry, into which Eddie Shah is entering, is still shaped by Northcliffe's career.

Born in 1865, the son of an undistinguished barrister, Alfred Harmsworth (later Lord Northcliffe) with his inquiring, if unstable, mind collected facts like others collect stamps. He had an all-encompassing, child-like inquisitiveness that was reflected in the spirit of his papers. From his earliest days he wanted to be a news-paper man, editing at the age of twenty-one a cycling magazine and two years later launching *Answers to Correspondents*, a magazine firmly modelled on the already successful *Titbits*. *Answers* contained competitions, unusual facts, interesting snippets such as 'Narrow Escapes from Burial Alive', 'Strange Things Found in Tunnels', 'What the Queen Eats (game she cannot bear)' and 'Remarkable Arrests'. Many of the commercial strengths of *Answers* – brevity, inconsequentiality and exploitation of the growth of working-class literacy, following the Education Act in 1870 – were to stand Harmsworth in good stead throughout his career. In his most successful stunt with *Answers*, Harmsworth asked his readers to guess the value of the gold and silver lying in the Bank of England on a particular day. He offered a prize – a pound a week for life. Over 700,000 people entered. Soon afterwards, Harmsworth, with his accountant brother Harold (later Lord Rothermere), opened a string of other magazines – *Comic Cuts* (motto: 'Amusing, but not Vulgar'), *Home Chat, Forget-Me-Not, Home Sweet Home, Half Penny Marvel* and *Union Jack*. Harmsworth admitted, 'I saw it as our policy to launch paper after paper on the public and thus raise our prestige and block competition.' Total sales of his magazines topped 1.5 million.

With the profits, Harmsworth bought the ailing London newspaper, the *Evening News*, for £25,000, quickly turning it into a form of 'Evening Answers' with news added. A mixture of crime and bellicose anti-German news stories was laced with Harmsworth's fascination with brief 'items of knowledge'. In 1896 he used the *Evening News* as the means to launch the novel *Daily Mail*, pronouncing, 'Four leading articles, a page of parliament and columns of speeches will *not* be found in the *Daily Mail* on May 4.' The papers used sub-editors, bold headlines and linotype machines, an invention capable of setting and spacing a line of uniform lead type that Harmsworth claimed cut costs by a third and allowed the paper 'to be sold for half the price of our contemporaries''. Equally important to the paper's success was the acceptance for the first time by a British pressman that women were able not only to read, but also happy to buy papers, if feature material aimed at their interests was included. On the day of the *Daily Mail*'s launch, Harmsworth wondered aloud: 'bankruptcy or Berkeley Square?' He publicly forecast a sale of 100,000 but secretly hoped he might touch 150,000. The first day's sale of the 'busy man's paper' in fact totalled 397,215. An entirely new readership had been unearthed, revealing in the national character a peculiar penchant for newspapers that survives to this day. 'We've struck a gold-mine,' exclaimed Harmsworth. The cost of launching the paper had been only £150,000.

Before the *Mail*'s arrival, the newspaper industry had effectively catered only for the one million readers to be found among the Victorian middle-class. Papers such as the *Daily Telegraph*, *The Times*, and the *Morning Post* displayed the great Victorian values of comprehensiveness, public duty, high morals and solid dullness. The *Daily Mail* lacked a social conscience and any strict party political affinity, but nevertheless the success of the paper allowed Harmsworth to develop a news team beyond the resources of his rivals. By 1889 the paper was selling a million copies a day, almost more than the rest of the press put together. Harmsworth explained the revolution he had engineered: 'Before the *Daily Mail* was published, journalism dealt with only a few aspects of life. What we did was to extend its view to life as a whole. We don't direct the ordinary man's opinion. We reflect it.' He himself admitted that in his papers, 'everything counted, but nothing mattered'.

By 1921 Lord Northcliffe owned *The Times*, the *Daily Mail*, the *Weekly Dispatch* and the London *Evening News*. His brother was responsible for the *Daily Mirror*, the *Sunday Pictorial*, the *Daily Record*, the *Glasgow Evening News* and the *Sunday Mail*. The size of their joint empire allowed them to take financial setbacks in their stride. The *Daily Mirror*, for instance, had started disastrously in 1903. It has been intended as a 'gentlewomen's newspaper', written by women for women, but as Northcliffe himself conceded, 'the desire not to read the *Mirror* had become contagious'. He fumed: 'Women can't write and don't want to read.' The lady journalists were gradually sacked – a task which was handed to a hard-bitten Scotsman, Hamilton Fyfe, who remembered how 'they begged to be allowed to stay. They left little presents on my desk. They waylaid me tearfully in corridors. It was a horrid experience – like drowning kittens.' The *Mirror* was saved by Northcliffe's resources and by the introduction of the photograph into newspapers through the invention of the half-tone block. The resulting illustrated journalism proved a success and by the approach of the First World War its sale rivalled that of the *Daily Mail*.

Northcliffe's unpredictable and often generous attitude to his workforce was, in part, responsible for nurturing some of the attitudes that were later to form the Fleet Street 'labour problem'. Although firmly anti-socialist, he believed in paying his skilled workforce handsomely, and his relative financial strength in Fleet Street enabled him to play the role of market leader in wages. In 1919, for instance, he overcame the unfounded suspicions of his staff about pay-cuts and persuaded them to accept a shorter working week of five days. The paper of the journalists' union (*The Journalist*) described him fondly as 'a warm supporter of the principles on which this union was founded and many of the policies it is pursuing'. A little later Northcliffe asserted: 'In my opinion a worker who does not join a union is a fool. The only wish I express is that no one will be forced to join a union who does not want to.' On being told in 1918 that the unskilled print workers' union, NATSOPA, was threatening a strike against the NPA, Northcliffe told a colleague with relish, 'The printers are realising that the invention of the rotary press and wood pulp paper have enormously increased the power and the profit of the newspaper owners. As soon as the newspaper owners were hit by the war, they doubled and, in some cases, trebled the price of their product. I have not yet

30

heard that they have doubled or trebled the wages of their workers, whose costs of living have in many cases doubled or trebled.'

Four years later Northcliffe finally walked out of the NPA, in protest at the other owners' attempts to join in the general bout of wage-cutting prevalent in British industry at the time. 'I am not likely to join combinations of rich men for grinding down poor men,' he said. His persistent attacks on the greed of his proprietorial colleagues, which he finally enshrined in a bizarre pamphlet entitled 'Newspapers and their Millionaires', caused grave embarrassment to his fellow owners.

In the pamphlet Northcliffe rounded on his new Fleet Street colleagues – 'shipping kings, cotton waste kings, coal kings, oil kings and the rest of them' – men that objected if their workforce could own 'motor cycles and side cars'. He stated that 'in the last thirty years the status of the British printer has greatly improved. He is one of the most highly skilled craftsmen we have. He is subject to a daily strain that few of my readers understand. I rejoice at this better state.' Northcliffe pointed out that British newspapers did not face international competition and were almost exclusively owned by very rich men. 'I am sure that if the millionaires will go and look at the production of their newspapers they will not want to reduce wages. The strain on the editorial and mechanical staffs is about as much as human beings can bear. I have done some of the work myself. I know.'

Northcliffe's only serious attack on his workforce in the pamphlet was his description of an attempt by the machine managers to influence the paper's coverage of a dispute on the railways. By letter Northcliffe had bluntly warned the men, 'I am entirely satisfied with the attitude of my journals and rather than be dictated to by any body of men I will stop publication of these papers.'

Like Beaverbrook, the Canadian-born owner of the *Daily Express*, Northcliffe's primary interest in his papers was not profit, but the dissemination of news and his own world view. However, with an income of £200,000 a year and a final personal fortune of over £5m., Northcliffe could afford to watch the contemporary rise of the unions with some equanimity.

Simultaneous with the rise of the Northcliffe press, trade unionism in print had spread from craft workers to general labourers. Between 1914 and 1920, the total membership of print unions rose from 75,000 to 190,000, including an increase from 6,000 to 20,000 for the new unskilled union NATSOPA. The bulk of the increase was in the general print and provincial newspapers – where conditions were much less favourable – but part of the increases were due to the spread of the closed shop within Fleet Street.

The success of Northcliffe's papers, the drive for mass sales and Northcliffe's encouragement of trade unions in an industry whose fragmented production process naturally fostered strong unions had combined together to create a revolution in newspaper economics by the thirties. That revolution created an economic framework that was to remain in place right up until today when Shah and others have begun to disturb the status quo. The Northcliffe revolution meant that although profits of the mass-circulation papers could reach new heights, the capital outlay in starting such papers, as well as the running costs of materials and labour, soared. Consequently, the prospect of anyone but corporations and millionaires starting new papers receded. In the new climate the small subsidised party political papers such as the *Westminster Gazette* withered. For the commercial papers that remained, most found themselves pushed towards one or other of two polar opposites. To flourish, a national paper had increasingly to attract through its editorial content either a definable section of the wealthy and consuming middle-classes, and thereby attract enough advertising or, failing that, a paper had to circulate amongst the mass of the working class. As Northcliffe himself pondered, the high wages paid in Fleet

Street and the increasing cost of paper meant that newspapers ran the danger of becoming entirely subordinate to advertisers. 'I see no way out of this impasse, other than by maintaining a great daily sale and thereby keeping the whip hand on the advertisers,' he concluded.

The lunatic lengths to which owners of the popular newspapers felt compelled to go to obtain that sale was revealed in the thirties when the four major popular papers, the *News Chronicle*, the *Daily Mail*, the *Daily Express* and the *Daily Herald* (the official paper of the TUC) became involved in a suicidal circulation war.

The blame probably lay primarily with Lord Southwood, chairman of Odhams Press which saved the *Herald* from extinction in 1929. The new owners set about methodically constructing a mass-circulation paper overnight. Over £2m. – more than the personal wealth of Lord Beaverbrook when he bought the *Express* – was poured into the *Herald* in order to secure for the paper the title of Britain's biggest daily sale. In the space of two years the sales figures increased eightfold to 2m., but the *Herald* bought its readers by offering free gifts and attractions such as sixteen volumes of Charles Dickens for eleven shillings. Other papers were forced to join in, offering Dickens and other literary classics at cheaper prices. Massive armies of canvassers were hired. Between 1924 and 1935 the staff of national newspapers nearly doubled, 40 per cent of the increase being attributed to newspaper-sellers. From door to door the new sales teams went offering mangles, pens, cameras, cutlery, tea kettles, even washing-machines, to those prepared to take out a subscription.

'There had been nothing like it,' ran an article in the *Evening Standard*, 'since the showers of manna fell in Sinai. The *Daily Express* led the way. Men looking over the mountains of Wales in search of Mr Lloyd George's long-promised sunrise saw instead armies of canvassers debouching into the valleys. They carried samples of boots and coats and pants. A whole Welsh family could be clothed from head to foot at the price of eight weeks' reading of the *Daily Express*.' In June 1933 the *Daily Express* could honestly proclaim that, with a figure of 2,054,348, it had achieved the largest net daily sale in the world. The *Daily Herald* was not far behind. The cost of this promotion had been crippling for all sides. In one year the four popular papers were estimated to have spent over £3m. However, it proved only a short-term investment for the *Herald*. Once the promise of free gifts fell off, so did the circulation. 'The *Herald* was a machine-made project almost completely without personality,' as one contemporary critic remarked.

The paper most severely wounded by the circulation war of the thirties had been the *News Chronicle*, the smallest of the four mass papers. During the war and immediately thereafter, in the era of paper-rationing, the *Chronicle* was cushioned from the economic forces that were to lead to its eventual downfall. With rationing, the advertising agencies had been forced to place their adverts in whatever paper they could whilst readers had been lured into buying more than one of the shrunken papers on offer. As paper-rationing was lifted in the mid-fifties, the *Chronicle* might have been expected to enjoy a unique journalistic advantage through being a Liberal paper in a period of institutionalised conflict between Labour and Conservative. Instead, sales slid in the late fifties by 15 per cent a year. Moreover, as papers such as the *Express* became free to expand in size, advertisers deserted the *Chronicle*, dismissing its readers as 'nondescript'.

The failures of the *Chronicle* and the *Daily Herald* both underlined the importance of advertising to newspaper profitability, but also raised the question as to why it was so expensive to run a newspaper. Given the paper's working-class readership, the *Daily Herald* had to be able to say that its readers had a massive collective purchasing power. Southwood had originally envisaged a sale of 1 million as sufficient to satisfy the advertisers, but he found he had badly underestimated.

Similarly despite a sale of 1,162,000 at its close in 1960, the *Chronicle* had lost £300,000 in its last eight months. Soon afterwards, Odhams – the owner of the *Daily Herald* – was bought by the Daily Mirror Group, which had been anxious to gain control of Odhams' magazine interests, and the merged grouping became the International Publishing Corporation (IPC). The merger reflected a trend towards ownership of newspapers by ever larger corporations. Widespread public anxieties over the concentration of press ownership led to the appointment of a Royal Commission in 1961–2, the second in fifteen years.

The Commission itself concluded: 'Within any class of competitive newspapers, the economics of large-scale operations provide a natural tendency for a paper which already has a large circulation to flourish and attract still more readers whilst a newspaper which has a small circulation is likely to be in difficulties. The problem is not so much why the *News Chronicle* could not survive with a circulation of one-and-a-half million, but how it could get anywhere near to surviving in competition against newspapers with a circulation of over four million.' The Commission concluded gloomily: 'The papers with a smaller circulation can survive only if they differentiate themselves in a way which will appeal to special types of readers and of advertisers, and so reduce the intensity of competition with their more powerful rivals.'

But the Commission did not simply wring its hands and blame the inevitable laws of newspaper economics. It went on to argue that a major reduction in costs was not only eminently achievable, but necessary if papers were to remain competitive with other media. The Commission stonily pointed out: 'The average earnings of manual workers in the national newspaper production industry are the highest of any paid to manual workers

35

in this country.' This bald statement was embellished by a special study of four Fleet Street houses that found average manning in production departments to be 1,297 per house when the actual job required only 849 workers. The greatest overmanning was in the machine room and in the publishing area, where the study found an excess staffing of 34 per cent and a consequential excess labour cost of 40 per cent. With all wages and salaries representing roughly a third of total costs, the potential for transforming the proprietors' balance sheets was regarded as immense.

The report marked the first public recognition of the Fleet Street labour relations problem, although the NPA had itself, in an internal inquiry in 1957 conducted by Bobby Childers, a *Daily Mail* manager, already acknowledged the scale of the decline in efficiency since the war. Childers' study showed two things: firstly, that the laws of the immediate postwar Labour Government, which placed a duty on employers to offer jobs to former employees out of the army, had meant a degree of overmanning at a time of thin newspapers due to paper-rationing; secondly, that managements had been unable to withstand a further wave of overmanning in the mid-fifties, brought about by the lifting of paper-rationing, which in turn unleashed a demand for advertising space that had been pent-up since the war.

Frank Rogers, production director at the *Daily Mirror* from 1960 and later managing director at IPC, agrees that the lifting of paper-rationing and the subsequent bonanza for some papers, including the *Mirror*, was a watershed in industrial relations. 'With the lifting of paper-rationing, the *Mirror* was only concerned to capture advertising; this meant increasing the size of the paper and this, in turn, meant negotiating with the unions. For whatever reason – perhaps the unions wanted greater membership at TUC Congress – the chapel negotiators wanted more men, mainly casuals, rather than more pay. At one stage we had negotiated for 800 people each in the machine and publishing rooms. If they had all turned up on one night they would have suffocated. It had become so bad that the larger the pagination, the higher the manning and the greater the loss.'

Ted Blackmore, the *Mirror* labour relations director, remembers the prevailing mood once paper-rationing was lifted: 'It was gradual attrition. Each time we wanted to change the number of pages, it would be two bob for this and three bob for that, but, by God, they mounted.' On one night Blackmore refused to accept a demand from the warehouse. The presses were late running and copies were lost until Blackmore eventually capitulated. 'The next day,' he recalls, 'they hauled me up in front of a committee of directors, asking why I had caused a delay in printing. It was a very silent and grave meeting. I thought I was for the chop. They said, "Young man, we are in the business of producing newspapers. Don't do that ever again." Later I saw the Chairman, Cecil King, and complained that it had been unfair and that I did not know what my brief was. He said, you have a clear brief – "always get the paper out, but do it at the cheapest cost."'

One management in its evidence to the Royal Commission in 1961 despondently admitted the degree to which they had lost control: 'These negotiations were not carried on as a scientific investigation into the optimum number of men to be employed but as a form of collective bargaining between the management and the chapels. Each side put forward the number of men whom they considered necessary and there was usually a wide divergence.' As a result of the negotiation, the final figure was agreed at some midway point between the two proposals.

But why, it is often asked, did managements cower – at least until recently – in the face of such pressure? Most simply because successful owners at the *Mirror* and the *Express* set the pace in wages and manning, and had no motive for a showdown with the unions. Their newspapers were highly profitable and remained so, for as long as they came out. Between 1948 and 1960, advertising in real revenue terms trebled, rising from £93m. to £343m. (1980 prices). Between 1937 and 1960 total national daily newspaper sales had risen from 9,980,000 to 15,835,000, an increase almost nine times greater than the growth in population and a peak from which circulations have slipped only slightly since.

But once the years of bumper profits began to fade in the mid-sixties, partly due to the arrival of television, management found it impossible to reverse the tide. As one NGA official puts it, 'Once you have learnt a trick or two and learnt that it pays off, it is only human nature to carry on.' It became increasingly clear that, faced with eleventh-hour pressure to make concessions, managements responsible for the welfare of a highly perishable product really had no sanctions of their own.

The process was best described by David Astor, the one-time owner of *The Observer*: 'If newspapers miss their trains, they cannot be put on ice, like food, and delivered the next day. If they are not delivered the advertisers must be repaid and all revenue is lost. So a short interruption of work whether for a union meeting or because of a torn roll of paper requiring machines to be reset is enough to cause trains to be missed and therefore the loss of all revenue. Moreover, it is the fact that lost newspaper production over a number of days, weeks or months cannot be made up by greater subsequent production – as for example car manufacturers are, to some extent, able to do – that explains the inability of newspapers to survive prolonged shutdowns.'

Nor did the proprietors, faced with a dispute, have the printing capacity to switch production from one point to another. Britain's national newspaper distribution system, based on the country's highly developed rail network, has ensured a centralised form of production that all proprietors have been locked into. Due to the small size of Britain, the density of population and the rail system, it is both technically possible and economically viable for a newspaper to be printed at one site in London before midnight and then to reach any far-flung British breakfast table the following morning. Unlike many other larger countries where companies own a variety of widely-scattered regional papers, the print works of Britain's national newspapers were built cheek by jowl in Fleet Street – a site roughly equidistant to the various mainline railway stations. The arrangement has immeasurably strengthened the union's hands: one chapel had only to stop one part of a newspaper's production process for the paper's entire national print-run to be stopped. (The only attempt to break out of the stranglehold occurred in the mid-sixties, when the Mirror Group considered printing in 8–14 regional centres using facsimile transmission from a Central London composing room. The £15m. proposal – a conscious if covert effort to escape the London print unions' clutches – was turned down by the IPC board on the grounds of risk and expense.)

But whether a paper is produced at one or many points, the nature of the production process inherently throws up ceaseless opportunities for disputes and fresh claims. Changes in pagination, print-run or layout all provide the negotiator with the chance to reopen some written or unwritten clause of the agreement. The rigid demarcations between different jobs and the solidarity between the complex matrix of chapels means that a tiny section of the workforce, responsible for a largely banal task, can prevent the whole newspaper appearing. No other chapel is likely to touch the job and if management grades take over, the product of their work will more likely than not be blacked further down the line.

The existence of 'scab labour' is virtually unknown since it is the unions themselves that act as a labour exchange and provide a management with its workforce. The craftworkers' pre-entry closed shop, a long-standing extension of the industry's apprenticeship system, survives intact despite the Government's laws aimed at the abolition of the closed shop. One of the many reasons for its survival is that managements need a casual labour system due to the nightly fluctuations in paper sizes and consequently in a paper's labour requirement. A worker capable of drawing pay from a variety of newspaper houses, thanks to his union's control of the labour supply, is happily equipped to withstand a shutdown at one paper simply by increasing his shifts at another. The year-long *Times* lock-out, in 1978–9, amply proved this to be so. As management sweated mightily over the mounting revenue losses, the London print branches through the call system – whereby management call for labour from the union branches – quietly moved much of the locked-out staff into full-time and casual vacancies elsewhere in Fleet Street.

If solidarity is food and drink to the chapels, it is anathema to management. Despite frequent attempts to reform it, the NPA has, over the years, patently failed to gain any authority over individual managements. Once a newspaper faced an intolerable demand, it would be highly unlikely to see the other papers rally to a friend in distress by offering him cash with which to withstand a shutdown, for example. Instead, the rival papers would crank up their presses until they groaned, in the hope that the fillip to sales would stick. If the chapels' motto has been 'Unity is strength', the NPA's has been, 'Your misfortune is my gain'.

Not surprisingly in these circumstances, the NPA failed on occasion to attract the most tough-minded staff. For instance, even an appeaser like Cecil King derided Fred Burnham, the NPA vice-chairman responsible for labour affairs through the fifties: 'Though a pleasant social figure, he was a major disaster in the industry. I remember once saying to him that his idea of negotiations was to lie on the floor and invite the union general secretaries to come and kick him, which they very willingly did.'

Sir Richard Marsh, chairman of the NPA, acknowledged the inherent difficulty: 'This idea that the proprietors must stick together and face out the unions comes up at the NPA Council about once every two years, but they simply cannot stand together and the reason is that there is no national newspaper industry in this country, in the same way, for instance, that there is a national motor car industry. Apart from putting words on newsprint, they are totally different products with different cost structures, markets and vulnerability to competition. A claim that makes absolute sense for one newspaper to hold out against will be one of supreme irrelevance to another. You cannot have a common front when one person is going bust in four days and the other can withstand a twelve-month stoppage. It's no good one proprietor having to tell his shareholders, 'Sorry, we were worried about how the unions were screwing Maxwell. We've gone bust backing him, but we had a good old go.'''

The result of such dilemmas is clear enough. The production unions have been stupendously successful at doing what, after all, was their founding purpose – improving the wages and conditions of their members. In 1985 the NPA acknowledged that the average weekly earnings of a Fleet Street production worker were £355, or £18,000 a year, for a working week that was unlikely to stretch much beyond twenty-five hours.

The skilled workers who earned on average closer to £500 a week, according to the NPA, are divided into two groups. First there are the small number of general engineers and electricians represented by the non-print unions – respectively the Amalgamated Union of Engineering Workers and the Electrical, Electronic, Telecommunications and Plumbing Union (EETPU). Second there are those represented by the NGA, led by the composing-room workers. On the hot metal papers they are: the Linotype machine keyboard operators who tap out the lines of lead type; the piece case workers who assemble headlines and the time hands who put the metal-cased pages together. On the papers that have transferred to photocomposition the keyboard operator types words onto paper and the piece case and time hand jobs have become 'scalpel and paste' make-up functions.

Hot metal pages are used to form a three-dimensional impression on a *papier mâché* mould which is then taken to the foundry and made into a printing plate, clipped onto the press, and with the correct level of inking leaves just the right mark on the web of paper that runs over the plate. With photocomposition the pasted-up page is photographed and a plate formed from the photograph. It is the job of a further group of NGA workers, the machine managers in the press room, to ensure that the presses run at the correct speeds and with the right inking. The proofs are checked by the final main group of NGA members, the readers.

The semi-skilled workers, many of whom work as assistants to NGA machine managers or readers, are almost all in the other main print union, the Society of Graphical and Allied Trades (SOGAT). Their average wage – including the SOGAT distribution workers – is just under £300 a week. SOGAT clerical workers are at the bottom of the high pay heap averaging £200 a week although some earn as little as £150.

Fleet Street production workers are by a long way the best-paid group of manual workers in Britain. They are also one of the most disputatious, with inter-union tension – especially where NGA and SOGAT staff work alongside each other – causing as many stoppages as union/management conflict.

But as Bill Booroff, the NGA London Region Secretary, put it: 'Print workers have injected into their veins before they start in Fleet Street the golden rule, "never take any notice of any warning by your management that the paper is going to the wall". Whatever reason and logic might suggest, who is to say that the rule's been proved wrong? There are more papers now than there were in

1975 and in the meantime, there's been a bonanza in terms of wages.'

The published pay figures from the NPA are a considerable under-estimation of real earnings. They also give no hint of the unique culture that has grown up among Fleet Street workers – especially the top-earning linotype machine keyboard operators – over the last thirty years.

It is one of the more enduring myths of the British class system that there is a special emotional bond between aristocrats and proletarians – born out of their mutual dislike of industrial capitalism and its hard-faced middle-class. The apparent nonchalance with which Fleet Street aristocrats have lined the pockets of a small section of London's skilled working-class might be cited as supporting evidence for the myth. But what, in fact, the employers' generosity has done is create a generation of worker-capitalists, the most energetic of whom run one – or even several – small businesses in addition to their paid Fleet Street employment.

This has been quite a recent development. Before the war, Fleet Street printers earned only a little above the average skilled wage and worked a full five-day week. They usually lived in Orpington or Bromley – because of the late-night train service. After the war many of them moved out to Billericay and other parts of the New Essex – again served by a good night train. When wage rates started to take off in the 1950s and 1960s, many of the best-paid lino-operators and piece-case workers acquired fast cars, took up golf and voted Tory. They continued, however, to think of themselves as working-class and, in many cases, to elect Socialists to screw the Fleet Street managements on their behalf.

Older Fleet Street print workers, while welcoming their recent enrichment, now bemoan the decline of good skilled craftsmanship and the comradeship of the old composing room with its sardonic wit and colourful characters. 'It's just a cash cow now, people come in, do their work and get out as quickly as possible,' said one

55-year-old lino man. He traces the rapid growth in outside interests to the decline of the standard working week. Increasingly, individuals were no longer contracted to arrive at work for a 40-plus hour week but instead the chapels were contracted to provide a service requiring a certain number of workers for a given number of hours each day. The result was a dramatic fall-off in the number of hours worked – now down, for some workers, to as little as 20 hours a week. To the long-established work-hopping tricks, and the esoteric Fleet Street slang which had grown up to describe them, were added the celebrated Mr Mickey Mouse and others – names scribbled on attendance registers to ensure that the wage-packets of nonexistent workers were collected and shared round.

Because the newspapers wanted only 'half-men' – from the late afternoon to late at night – the other half of many of the men started to put their spare time and money to work for them. And the money flooded in. After the war, the wage rate for a time-hand would have been about £8.50 a week in the general print in London – and probably only about £10.50 a week in Fleet Street. A time-hand in Fleet Street now earns about £450 a week and the differential with the general print has more than trebled.

But the really big scorers on Fleet Street are the lino-operators. On a hot-metal paper like the *Financial Times* a Lino earns about £800 a week before tax. On the *Sun*, the top payer in Fleet Street in 1985, there are said to have been celebrations recently on the advent of the first £1,000-a-week lino man. These figures are mainly derived from the London Scale of Prices which determines the rate per line of lead type. The system is essentially self-managed with the lino 'Foc' as the foreman. Managements used to monitor the system quite closely but it led to so many arguments and stoppages that, to keep the papers coming out, they handed over control to the union officials.

On a hot-metal paper the linotype operators' wages have usually set a ceiling – although foundry staff sometimes run them close – and it is the linos, in particular, who have spread their entrepreneurial wings. There are some extreme examples. Denis Tame, the lino Foc at the *FT*, put his money into buying some dry-cleaning franchises many years ago and soon made enough to buy a 30-acre farm in Sussex to which he would occasionally invite the former *FT* chairman, Alan Hare, for some shooting. From dry-cleaning franchises, Tame has graduated to a Dutch barn restoration business.

Most Fleet Street workers' businesses are more mundane – taxi companies, tobacconists, betting shops – anything that can be fitted in easily around the inconvenient chore of having to pop in to work for 20 to 25 hours a week. Most of those who haven't moved into business have simply become big spenders or enhanced the quality of their lives by moving further and further out of London. One electrician lives near Dartmoor and stays with his mother-in-law in London three days a week.

Another of the peculiarities of Fleet Street's high pay culture is the lack of direct evidence of it at the workplace. The older print workers still turn up looking much as they used to thirty years ago – a Ford Sierra may have replaced the Morris Minor but it is still roll-up tobacco and boiler suit. Not surprising perhaps as – especially on the remaining hot-metal papers – they are still working in a dirty print factory.

More striking is the poor quality of the working conditions for these men in the £30,000-plus-a-year bracket. Many Fleet Street newspaper buildings are like dungeons 'downstairs', with grisly works canteens and toilet and washing facilities that would shame a struggling Midlands engineering company. It is as if some employers have deliberately sought to nourish the last vestiges of London's nineteenth-century working-class militancy by preserving the kind of conditions that created it in the first place.

In defence of the highly-paid and often overmanned Fleet Street chapels it is rightly pointed out that the hours, although short, are usually antisocial and the deadline-linked work can still be stressful. One senior official of the overmanning specialists, the SOGAT London Central distribution branch, said more basically: 'We should be complimented not criticised for creating jobs at a time of mass unemployment.'

It should also be remembered that Fleet Street has been a high pay, short hours gravy-train for many other grades of staff; or at least for many individuals among the journalists, advertising staff and management as well as the print workers. And for an inappropriate link between effort and reward, it is hard to beat the £8m. that Lord Matthews pocketed last October when Fleet Holdings sold out to United Newspapers, even if he was, in part, responsible for transforming the Group's market value from £13m. in 1982 to £317m. in 1985.

4

Fleet Street: The Failure of Reform

'I asked why Arnold Goodman had accepted the chairmanship of the NPA, a bed of nails if ever there was one.'

Cecil King diary June 1970

4

Fleet Street: The Failure of Reform

Apart from the House of Lords, no British institution
has attracted so much attention from reformers and yet
proved so stubbornly resistant to their prescriptions as
the national newspaper industry. The history of Fleet
Street is cluttered with Royal Commissions, Joint In-
quiries, fresh starts, Programmes for Action and, most
common of all, return-to-work agreements brandished
by excited proprietors supposedly signalling 'the arrival
of a new era in Fleet Street'. The proprietors' repeated
inability to impose technological reforms on Fleet Street
from within was later to leave the field clear for an
outsider to try his hand.

A short history of reforming zeal in Fleet Street should
probably extend as far back as 1959, the year in which
the NPA set up a Labour Executive which consisted of
carefully selected senior Fleet Street managers responsible for generating 'fresh strategic thinking' on industrial relations. The Labour Executive's role was to take
the initiative away from the unions and prevent the
unions' negotiators continuing to make costly and ad
hoc additions to the 1947 agreement which had set the
framework for the industry since the war. However, the
Labour Executive was no sooner in place, duly establishing its strategic bridgeheads, than the proprietors

reverted to the past practice of making concessions in their house-level negotiations, thereby destroying the Executive's authority.

Undaunted by the setback, in 1964 a Joint Board for the National Newspaper Industry was established under the independent chairmanship of Lord Devlin, following a recommendation from the Royal Commission two years earlier. The Board was to act as a joint negotiating body with authority to revise and agree manning levels, abolish casual staffing and oversee agreements reached at house level. As part of the process, all house agreements were to be lodged with the NPA, on the basis that if a central managerial body for once actually knew what was going on, as the various Fleet Street chapels so evidently did, the NPA and the Joint Board might be able to exercise some control.

The Joint Board's ambitions knew few bounds. It commissioned a fresh survey of industrial relations from the Economist Intelligence Unit, and established three committees covering capital structure, production and managerial efficiency, and social benefits. However, this Board of union general secretaries and newspaper managing directors failed in its self-appointed task of 'taking the question of labour supply and demand out of the field of collective bargaining'. It withered in the face of chapel resistance to the proposals, only to be briefly revived in 1970, again unsuccessfully, as the National Newspaper Steering Group.

Following the Steering Group's swift demise, the industry was left to pin its hopes on the growing number of 'comprehensive agreements' that had been reached with the chapels in the late sixties. The purpose of the agreements was to minimise overtime, the number of casuals required and the degree of extra payments over and above the basic rate. A chapel would be paid this comprehensive rate in return for a supposedly comprehensive but often ill-defined service, which the chapel would be subcontracted to provide largely independent of management interference. Any savings made would be shared out on an agreed basis between the two sides. Management sought through the arrangement higher productivity, the unions a way round the Labour Government's incomes policies. In many ways the proposals loyally followed the thrust of the influential Donovan Royal Commission on Trade Unions, which had recommended a recognition of the de facto shift away from formal industry-level bargaining to informal shop-floor negotiation.

Although some managements won temporary productivity gains through comprehensive agreements, the majority probably suffered more significant setbacks. The agreements which established manning levels were often unclear and, moreover, had not been preceded by even a vaguely serious form of job evaluation. More importantly, the agreements often surrendered control to the chapel for the provision of the service, undermining the status of the line management. How the comprehensive service was to be provided by the chapel in terms of the number of men present per shift, their individual earnings or working hours, was now almost formally none of management's business. A form of workers' control had been established.

By the mid-seventies Fleet Street management faced a fresh cyclical downturn and a new threat of closures partly caused by the oil crisis recession. For the third time in ten years, management attempted to revive the reforming ideals behind the Joint Industry Board. Their strategy this time was to develop a closer liaison with national union officials, in the hope that their influence could bring about a formalisation of wage-bargaining that would deter the incessant wage push from the shop-floor. With the help of Bill Keys, the chairman of the TUC Printing Industries Committee, and an enthusiastic supporter of the need for reform, a Joint Standing Committee was established in late 1975. The Committee's task was to devise a threefold policy framework, firstly to encourage staff to volunteer to leave the industry with improved redundancy entitlements before their normal retirement age, secondly to enable those over retirement age to leave the industry with an improved pension, and thirdly to decasualise the industry.

In its resulting Programme for Action, submitted to Fleet Street workers in November 1976, the Standing Committee proposed improved pension and redundancy entitlements, partly financed by the industry itself and partly by the EEC. In addition, it suggested a new disputes procedure and an obligation for employers to submit manpower and technology planning proposals to the Joint Standing Committee each year. In each newspaper house Joint House Committees would be established, consisting of seven management representatives and two delegates from each union. The Committee would not be responsible for individual negotiations at chapel levels, but would be kept closely informed, as well as having a role in the smooth introduction of new technology. By the standards of the mid-seventies, the proposals represented a modest form of industrial democracy, largely out of keeping with the management of the eighties' insistence on the 'right to manage'.

Officers from all the unions solemnly put their names to the Programme and warned: 'Rejection will result in titles failing. The inevitable consequences will be compulsory redundancy for workers with little or no advance warning. No government aid will be available to workers or unions. New forms of printed communication utilising new technology, if necessary printed abroad, could compete more and more successfully with a diminishing range of British newspapers.' In the current bleak climate for print trade unionism, the proposals may seem relatively generous, offering as they did the opportunity for joint negotiation over new technology and an organised stately retreat. But in 1976-7 – the second year of shopfloor pressure against the Labour Government's social contract – the plans were seen in a different light.

52

Thatcherism was still only a gleam in the eye of Sir Keith Joseph's Centre for Policy Studies, and union power was at its zenith.

Moreover, management had foolishly agreed to leave the selling of the package to the union general secretaries. Without a doubt, a contributory element to the shop-floor's final rejection was an innate suspicion within the chapels of anything their soft general secretaries had cooked up in collusion with management to take away their power. Also, by the time of the ballots on the Programme, the immediate financial crisis of 1975 had waned. The threat of closure at *The Observer* and the *Guardian* had passed. The *Daily Express* had been sold by Beaverbrook Newspapers to Trafalgar House, and this implied that the supply of proprietors who were willing to throw away their millions after Fleet Street fame, if not fortune, remained undiminished.

Early in 1977, the NGA's London and Manchester membership rejected the Programme for Action by 3,778 votes to 889, whilst the NATSOPA membership voted down the proposals by a narrower margin of 4,598 to 4,296. The ignominious collapse of the most sustained attempt yet to construct a national framework for the reform of Fleet Street inevitably left individual newspaper houses to fend for themselves as they attempted to make a series of uncoordinated forays to bring in the new technology being used in America and to a lesser extent by the British provincial press.

At the time of the Programme for Action, the printing methods of Britain's national newspapers had been left largely unaltered since the 1890s when the linotype machine replaced hand composition. The linotype had first been used on the *New York Tribune* in 1886 and had quickly demonstrated that it could set copy about six times faster than the hand compositor. The first linotype machine was used in a British newspaper house in 1889 at the *Newcastle Chronicle* and within six years the machines had spread throughout Fleet Street.

The linotype worked by a compositor sitting in front of the machine reading journalists' copy and pressing a keyboard to release a brass matrix (a hollow mould of a letter in the alphabet) from a magazine. The matrices then travel down a conveyor chute, where they form a line of type (lin'o'type) in an assembly box. After ensuring that the type is spaced and justified so that there is a straight right-hand edge to the column of type, the compositor presses a lever and the line of matrices move up to a caster attached to the machine where molten or hot metal is poured into the matrices to cast a line of type or slug. After a proof has been pulled and read the galley is sent back to the compositor to be corrected, with individual lines containing errors extracted, reset and reinserted into the body of type. Once used to make the plate for the press, the metal is melted down for use another time.

Since the linotype caster makes fresh type for each job, the need for a hand compositor to distribute the type back into alphabetical order after use is eliminated. Although the linotype's capital cost is high, its running costs are low. But by the early 1980's the machines were no longer being made anywhere in the world, another factor making eventual modernisation inevitable.

In the late sixties, photocomposition or cold type began to displace hot metal in America and the British provincial press. However, it remained blocked in Fleet Street right up to the mid-seventies: In 1985, for example, three Fleet Street papers were still entirely hot-metal set and five more used a hybrid hot and cold system. With photocomposition, the images of the pages are composed photographically, instead of physically in metal type. The compositor retypes journalists' copy on a typewriter-style keyboard attached to a visual display unit which itself is linked to a computer photosetter. The text is hyphenated and justified automatically. The strips of bromide produced by the photosetter are then cut and pasted by a compositor on to a page-size board in order to make up the page.

The logical development of photosetting is direct-entry or, as it is also known, single keystroking. Here the text reaches the central computer typesetter direct from visual display units worked by reporters, sub-editors and advertising staff, as well as those compositors retained for the purpose of setting copy from outside contributors. The removal of the reading and second-keying function can save a newspaper around forty minutes on its deadline. More importantly to the employer, the technology eradicates the need for the highly-paid keyboard operator.

However, direct-input is not simply labour-saving. It can also help to improve editorial quality. The VDUs or electronic screens show the precise length of a story, helping to reduce the need for hurried late cutting that might excise a vital piece of information which is often the basis of the story. The screens are split so that a reporter can have agency copy, his first-edition story or a library story on one side of the screen and his own story-in-the-making on the other. Copy from one side of the screen can be moved en bloc to the other. Reporters in district offices can send their copy to the head office newsdesk within seconds. A sub-editor and district reporter can then, if necessary, spend time discussing the story as it sits on their respective screens.

Each journalist has his own private basket of material to which no one else has access but once a reporter electronically sends his copy to the newsdesk for evaluation and subbing, an elaborate hierarchy built into the computer software comes into play, restricting access to stories to various levels of editorial management. The sub-editor works by altering copy on the screen, ensuring that it will fit the space allocated on the page. The computer will also tell whether the proposed headline will fit. For any headline that does not, the number of characters or even tenths of a character by which the headline 'busts' will be displayed. The sub's typesetting commands tell the photosetter which fount, size and column-width to use in setting the story.

The capabilities of the computer are almost infinite. For instance, at one of the most developed British electronic newspaper libraries, installed at the Wolverhampton *Express and Star*, stories can be filed away by the computer and indexed by the system on virtually every word in the text. Through this system a journalist could, for instance, call up on his screen all the recent stories containing the words 'fire' or 'Wolverhampton'.

The system also offers editorial management new ways of assessing the productivity of individual reporters. The computer can tell the editor, for instance, exactly how many stories a reporter has written, their length, and when they appeared. It can even reveal how many times a particularly unappealing phrase such as 'cheated death' or 'shock move' has been used and by which reporters.

Staff in the advertising departments also work with electronic screens. As soon as a potential advertiser rings in, staff can check on their screen the advertiser's previous orders and credit worthiness. Prompt questions come on the screen for the sales staff to use to encourage the advertiser to take a longer ad. Cost and discounts are worked out by the computer, which can then store a booked ad for over a year in advance of its use in the paper. The sales staff type the ad into the computer's memory, to be disgorged at the appropriate time for the staff laying out a page of adverts.

In the most advanced electronic newspapers, copy edited by subs and the text of adverts is not sent to the photosetter for output as hard copy in order to be physically pasted up on to a page. Instead, the pages are designed on screen, including the placement of stories, headlines, graphics and photograph captions. Once the electronic page make-up has been completed, the whole will be output to a photosetter to produce a full-page negative ready for the plate room.

Most of these inventions – photocomposition, direct-input, electronic page make-up – were available in various forms of sophistication by the mid-seventies. The attempts in the second half of the seventies, following the collapse of the Programme for Action, to force through the new technology made a particularly inglorious chapter in the history of Fleet Street management. The largely uncoordinated forays into new technology were led by the *Daily Mirror*, the *Financial Times* and *The Times*.

First out of the traps, and flat on to its corporate face, was Reed International, which in 1970 had taken over IPC, including the Mirror Group (MGN). In June 1975, as the Programme for Action was being drawn up, MGN produced its 'Blueprint for Survival'. In essence all four English titles – the *Daily Mirror*, the *Sunday Mirror*, the *Sunday People* and the *Sporting Life* – were to abandon hot metal and be set by photocomposition. The Manchester editorial, typesetting and process departments were to be run down and fully made-up pages were to be sent by facsimile transmission from a Central London composing room for printing in Manchester. Pages were to be laid out using fully electronic page make-up on screens, instead of the scalpel, paper and paste traditionally used in photocomposition. The proposals, by the standards of Fleet Street, were technologically radical, but no attempt was being made to follow the full-blooded American example in the use of direct-input. The NGA would still set all the type. MGN was confident about its plans since it had already introduced photocomposition at its greenfield site in Scotland whilst it had, since the mid-sixties, used facsimile transmission from Manchester to Belfast for its Northern Ireland editions. As a result, the chances of making real labour savings through the use of largely proven new technology seemed bright.

The London composing room was to be cut from 270

to 170 men, and the byzantine, cripplingly expensive London Scale of Prices was to be bought out. In order to increase flexible working by the compositors between the Group's paper titles, the number of composing-room chapels was to be reduced from twelve to one.

Overall, the plans appeared well-thought-out and well-timed. But the NGA was determined to extract every penny it could from the negotiations which it knew would set the tone for future transfers from hot metal to photocomposition. In total, the negotiations involved the labour relations director, Ted Blackmore, in eighteen months of talks and about eighty meetings, some of which lasted as long as twenty hours. By the end, the compositors had extracted a rate of £174 for a four-day week of 34 hours, six weeks' holiday and a guarantee that wages would rise by a further £50 a week in the next three years. On top of this, the compositors working on the London Scale of Prices were to have the Scale bought out at a cost of about £6,000 per head.

'Our difficulties were compounded,' Blackmore recalls, 'because we had been sold a pup. The page make-up system did not work and partly due to the slowness with which the NGA compositors adapted to the new setting techniques, the number of pages set by photocomposition never reached anything like the level originally envisaged. We had to renegotiate with the NGA to get them back on to the use of hot metal and at the same time we had to hire extra staff whilst the training of the comps in the use of photocomposition continued.' The cost of the extra labour was nearly £2m. a year. The chaos was deepened when a series of differential disputes ensued, mainly in the machine room, one of which led to the closure of the magazine *Reveille*. Due to the technical difficulties in London, the closure of the Manchester editorial and typesetting operation, with the loss of 500 staff, never happened. In short, the Mirror Group had a disaster on its hands.

Only a month after the *Mirror* announced its blueprint,

in July 1975, the *Financial Times* revealed its own highly ambitious plans for a fully computerised paper using photocomposition. Although the *FT* had not suffered advertising or circulation loss on the scale of the *Mirror*, its plans were actually more wide-ranging than those of the *Mirror*. Not only would the *FT* have photo-composition, but its journalists and advertising staff would directly input their material into a computer type-setter, thus bypassing the compositor altogether. There were to be no half-measures. If it was all possible in America, there was no reason why it could not be done in Britain. The compositors' numbers were to be cut by two-thirds, to sixty-two. It was not literally the 'deci-mation' which the NGA general secretary Joe Wade angrily described it to be at the time; it was something worse.

The *FT* attempted to soften the blow to the union bureaucracies by offering to pay them the subscriptions of members they no longer had. A joint technology section would be established for all workers using the new technology. Each union with members in the section would receive subscriptions, as though all the workers in the section were members of their union, but in reality, each worker would continue paying only the one subscription to his original union. Thus, courtesy of company funds, an embryonic single union would be established. The *FT* also made strenuous efforts to pla-cate those who would be asked to leave the company. It would help find them jobs, and also top up the wages if they did not match their previous pay. But faced with the rebuff of the Programme for Action and the scenes of mounting chaos in the *Mirror* building, the *FT* quietly shelved its plans.

The *FT* management had made a political calculation that its proposals were too challenging for Fleet Street's industrial relations. Management at Times Newspapers passed a different judgement, and lived to regret it. The year-long lock-out at *The Times* from the autumn of 1978 was a high watermark for the NGA. The International Thomson Organisation (ITO) – owner of Times Newspapers – found its massive financial resources, based on North Sea oilfields and provincial newspapers, worthless in the face of a union whose assets were less than a tenth of ITO's annual profit. The NGA spent £500,000 in strike pay to its 300 members at the papers: the ITO's eventual loss due to the dispute was £40m.

Following a series of petty disputes, mainly over pay, the company announced in April 1978 that it wanted direct-input, photocomposition and new manning levels throughout the company, involving cuts of over 40 per cent, a new disputes procedure and new wage-levels. If no agreement was reached by October 1978, the papers would be suspended and the staff dismissed. Before the lock-out occurred, in a concession that has often been subsequently ignored, the NGA offered to accept photocomposition and major job losses so long as direct-input was abandoned. Inevitably, the union saw the dispute in apocalyptic terms. The rest of Fleet Street, Joe Wade said, were waiting like vultures to see the union break its back at *The Times*. He warned: 'In industrial life as elsewhere there are some battles you win and some you lose – and if you lose a battle, it does not necessarily mean that you have lost the war. But the outcome of the war over new technology will now be determined by the battle at *The Times* – of that I am sure.'

The set-piece rhetoric was matched on the other side. Marmaduke Hussey, Times Newspapers' managing director, pronounced: 'We in Fleet Street have allowed situations to develop which we should never have done and which we are trying to deal with now. The right to manage is one of the issues at stake. It is a Fleet Street problem.' But the management's inept and confused handling of the problem, and in particular the speed with which they were trying to make changes, disenchanted political opinion on all sides.

The climate of opinion hindered management from

considering more radical solutions to the dispute. No strike-breaking operation was attempted at *The Times* headquarters near Fleet Street nor through the few non-union printing houses elsewhere in Britain. Instead, management assumed that the NGA's closed shop blocked off all the options in Britain. An attempt to print a limited edition in Frankfurt, for importation into Britain, was abandoned at the first sign of resistance in Germany. A group of pickets – perhaps a hundred strong – mounted by the NGA's German sister union, IG Druck und Papier, were placed outside the Frankfurt print works. By the standards that were to become common-place in Warrington, South Yorkshire and Nottingham-shire during 1983 and 1984, a determined police force might have been expected to ensure production of the paper. The Turkish firm that had been contracted to print the paper was willing to press ahead with the print-run despite the threat of violence, but the *Times* management on the spot called the operation off, fearing for life and limb. Faced with the same choice today, it is doubtful whether any Fleet Street management, let alone one led by Rupert Murdoch, would continue to be so circumspect.

In the view of Sir William Rees-Mogg, the editor of *The Times* in this period and a key strategist in the confrontation, 'We were five years too early. For the plan to be effective we needed laws preventing secondary boycotts. Also the *Times* strategy was designed for Roy Thomson, not his son Ken. Ken's caution was fatal.' Ken Thomson, who had taken control of ITO following his father's death, had never felt the same personal commit-ment to the papers. The uncertain lines of authority were reflected in the management's muddle over their ultimate aims in the dispute. The *Times* dispute was said to be the management's Armageddon; if so, they seemed to have precious little understanding of exactly what spoils they were seeking in the battle. Bill Freeman of the London Machine branch of SOGAT recalls: 'Thomson

made the major error of thinking that his fellow proprietors would stand by him. We were able to exploit
the greed of his competitors by putting the bulk of
our suspended people to work as casuals and levying
ourselves to support the remainder. A by-product was
that our chapels were able to extract higher payments
and bonuses from the competitors for the extra work.
Those payments soon became permanent. The net result
was to raise wage levels in the industry by some 20 per
cent in that year and when *The Times* and *Sunday Times*
reopened, in some cases Lord Thomson had to pay
double the previous wages to get his workers back.'

The *Times* shut-down was the last in a series of proprietorial failures which stretched back to the fifties. If
change was inevitable in the newspaper industry, its
implementation was going to demand something more
sophisticated than *The Times*' rhinoceros-like charge –
something like a redrafting of the rules of combat.

For that, newspaper employers needed outside help.
They also needed to learn a few tricks from their wily
opponents. The print unions have, through the meticulous observance of the closed shop, expected and received automatic loyalty from their members; as the
Times dispute proved, they have also had the financial
resources to sustain long periods of strike action with
the help of Fleet Street or nationwide levies. Most important of all, throughout the postwar years the unions
have enjoyed legal immunity from damages claims for
almost all kinds of industrial action.

For employers to improve their return on capital and
press ahead with the industry's modernisation, they
required the same discipline but, again most important,
they needed changes in the law. At the beginning of the
1980s the Thatcher Government began to answer the
prayers of Sir William Rees-Mogg and the senior executives of other Fleet Street papers.

The 1980 and 1982 Employment Acts, although restricting the freedom of movement of all unions, were

drafted with the print unions particularly in mind. The two employers' bodies, the British Printing Industries Federation, for the general print, and the NPA, for Fleet Street, lobbied hard for a legal weakening of the closed shop and for the outlawing of 'secondary action' when ministers began consultations on the new framework for industrial relations in 1979.

The combined effect of the two Acts was to remove legal immunity from almost all forms of industrial action that were not aimed at the worker's immediate employer or related to conditions of employment. The print unions, who had become masters of 'secondary action' in enforcing and retaining the closed shop, were effectively shackled.

Section 16 of the Employment Act 1980, introduced by Jim Prior, withdrew immunity from civil action for those taking part in secondary picketing away from a worker's own place of work – such as that at Warrington. The next section of the same Act withdrew immunities from most other forms of secondary action, whilst Section 18 withdrew immunities from those who organised industrial action to enforce union membership on workers employed by a different employer or at different premises. The section was aimed at 'coercive recruitment' where the design union, SLADE, tried to pressurise workers in art studios, instant print shops and advertising agencies, who were starting to take over the print union's traditional work, into joining the union which in 1982 became part of the NGA.

The Employment Act 1982, the work of Prior's more aggressive replacement, Norman Tebbit, made it even more difficult to impose a closed shop by rendering void requirements in contracts that work was to be done by union members only, a commonplace in the printing industry. It also became a breach of statute to keep firms off tender lists on the grounds that they were non-union. The basis of the NGA's ability to enforce the closed shop was most directly cut away by Section 14 of the 1982 Act which removed immunity from 'blacking' action against goods produced by non-unionists.

Finally, and most important, for the first time since 1906 union funds were exposed to the threat of damages claims if official support was given to action which was no longer immune. A complex semaphore has subsequently grown up by which a union head office can indicate support for strikes not covered by immunity without exposing its funds. In 1983 the NGA was still more interested in challenging the basis of the Acts than in stooping to such sleight of hand.

Some provincial newspaper employers had already begun to probe weaknesses in the union's defences when they successfully printed through the 1980 NGA provincial strike. But for a more sustained recasting of the balance of power, most major employers realised the new laws were vital. Frank Barlow, chief executive of the FT, also points out that employers were looking for a change in police attitudes to ensure that the laws were properly enforced. During several disputes at provincial papers during the 1970s, unions successfully blockaded their narrow city-centre entrances and the police refused to act, fearing to appear 'political'.

By the end of 1983 there was no guarantee that the new laws, which had together been on the statute book for no more than a year, would work. They had not yet been seriously tested. The unions had been considerably weakened by mass unemployment but they remained a power in the land and the Thatcher U-turn on pit closures in 1981 was a reminder that the new legal framework might yet prove difficult to apply to powerful groups like printers or miners.

However the more subtle step-by-step approach of the Thatcher Government made unlikely the complete abandonment of the legal strategy, as had occurred in 1973 when Edward Heath effectively dropped the Industrial Relations Act after widespread trade union protest. Some people did speculate, however, that the new laws, whose application was left to individual aggrieved employers, might simply never be used.

Others, including the NGA leadership, believed the printing industry, with its institutionalisation of the closed shop and secondary action, was bound to be an arena of conflict, and that the spark was most likely to be ignited by a small employer without the corporatist caution of the big boardrooms. Indeed Norman Tebbit, then Employment Secretary, had mused out loud to journalists at a Christmas reception in 1982 that the showdown with the law would be triggered off by a small Asian newsagent against SOGAT '82.

He was not far out. The Messenger dispute – which began in July 1983 but did not achieve notoriety until it turned violent at the end of October – was a struggle between a half-Persian small businessman and the NGA print union. It was a dispute waiting to happen: the test case for the new laws, for the police and a test of the obstinate small employer's nerve.

5

The Nomad

'I don't really care what people think of me because I know I've got the blood.'

Eddie Shah

5

The Nomad

When Shah strode on to the national stage at the end of 1983 he became an instant hero of the self-made-man class. His instincts are certainly those of the bustling arriviste, impatient with the established ways and means, the iconoclastic enemy of organised labour *and* capital.

His early business career is in the classic pattern. He inherited no money, set up his first newspaper – along with two colleagues – with £3,000 raised from the sale of his first house, and subsequently struggled for several years before he started to make enough money to live well. But to be self-made usually implies to be of humble birth. On that point Shah fails, spectacularly, to fit the bill. He is the fourth cousin of the present Aga Khan and also the great-great-great-great-grandson of the first Aga Khan. Consequently, he is a member of one of the oldest, richest, and most tightly-knit 'royal' families in the world – tracing its lineage back to the prophet Mohammed.

The Aga Khan is head of the three-million-strong Nizari Ismaili Muslim sect. Ismailis are part of the Shiah Muslim community which is one of the two main divisions in Islam, the other being the Sunni Muslims. Nizari Ismailis are found on all continents, usually earning a living as businessmen or traders; but their heartland is

India, where they are known as Khojas, and the vast majority of followers are Asian. Since 1837, the Khoja Ismaili leaders have been a dynasty without a kingdom. In that year, Aga Khan Mehalatee, governor of the Persian province of Kerman, began a rebellion against the Shah (king) of Persia. He was defeated and fled to Afghanistan, in 1841, where he was adopted by the British to further the cause of empire, and later established himself in India.

The Aga Khan was, and is, worshipped as a near-divinity by his followers and enjoys a status equal to the prophet Mohammed himself. He is also supposed to be paid about one-eighth of each follower's annual income. That income, now estimated at £75m. a year, is today mainly spent on global social work. But it has, not surprisingly, led to intense controversy, and even bloodshed over the 'true' succession, in this rigorously inter-marrying family.

The third Aga Khan, the famous racehorse owner, adopted a western style and counted Beaverbrook among his friends; his son, Aly Khan, became the famous international playboy before he was killed in a car crash in 1960. Shah remembers as a young boy in the early 1950s accompanying the third Aga Khan to a ceremony in Karachi where the 'old man' was presented with his own weight in platinum by his followers.

Back in 1908 Shah's side of the family lost the title and the financial inheritance when the third Aga Khan left his Indian wife for an Italian woman. Haji Bibi, sister of the deserted woman, began a long court action to claim at least some of the money but failed. Shah's disinherited relatives, who reverted to being orthodox Shiahs, remained comfortably off in Bombay, and his grandfather was one of the first members of the family who decided to work for a living.

It is tempting to see Shah's own nomadic character as part of a cultural inheritance from this extraordinary line. His father has ensured that Shah knows his genealogy;

scribbled at the end of a family tree sent to his son many years ago are the words: 'After you have examined, read and digested our tree, if you can still make out the "head and tail" of it, you will appreciate why the Aga says you are always unique in as much as you have in your blood the combined blood of all the sons of the first Aga. Congrats! God Bless You.'

Shah certainly possesses a deep self-belief and sense of destiny – characteristics which may owe something to having been repeatedly reminded, as a child, of his royal origins. More than one person who faced the Messenger dispute with him has commented upon how he handled his fame like a man who had been waiting for it to arrive. He himself now says: 'I have always known somehow that I would have three children and run newspapers.' If the family rift had not occurred he would also be – within the Ismaili sect – a Said or holy man. Although he says he has been an agnostic for as long as he can remember, he does claim some sensitivity to matters of the spirit and says he has a telepathic link with his wife, Jennifer.

When the many critics of Shah's management style at the Messenger Group describe it as run like a religious sect, with a charismatic leader figure, faithful believers and doubters drummed out, they may be closer to the mark than they realise. The impact on his outlook of this exotic inheritance must remain conjecture. What is certain is his own thoroughly ambivalent attitude towards it. This is in part because his roots are such a distance from his adopted culture of the down-to-earth Manchester businessman.

During the Messenger dispute, for example, he would tell reporters that he was a cousin of the Aga Khan and then pledge them to secrecy – knowing the disclosure could harm his 'little man' image. Now, the more confident manipulator, he says: 'I like these things about me to come out gradually – to be rumours at first and then be proved true.'

As a rebellious adolescent Shah felt some discomfort and awe about his background. In recent years, as he has started to make his own mark in the world he has started to take more pride in his lineage. But he is still oddly ignorant of his relatives and their – admittedly complex – dynastic struggles, grandly claiming that he lives too much in the present to remember the past. The same apparent lack of interest applies to his own early life.

Shah was born in Cambridge on 20 January 1944, the first of four children to Hazel and Moochool Shah. He has three sisters, two living in England – a nurse and a lawyer – and the other married to an accountant in New Jersey. His great-grandfather on his father's side had been the first Persian/Indian to be an officer in the British Army – but it was his grandfather, Shahan Shah, who began the family's residential link with Britain. Shahan Shah married his cousin and came to London to qualify as a surgeon at St Bartholomew's Hospital. During the First World War he joined the British Expeditionary Force in France and was awarded the Military MBE. He later stood, unsuccessfully, as a Liberal parliamentary candidate, and subsequently returned to India to become dean of Grant Medical College in Bombay, the most prestigious medical college in the country.

His grandfather on his mother's side, John Isaac Strange, also cut a dash. He made his living owning and running most of the Cambridge boat-yards and later started his own mink-farm.

Shah's father, Moochool, was born in New Delhi in 1922 and, after school in Bombay, followed in his own father's footsteps by becoming a medical student at Bart's. In 1940, his student hostel was bombed and he was buried alive for nine hours. The college was evacuated to Queen's College, Cambridge, but his academic interest had gone. Instead, at the age of twenty-one, he met and married Hazel Strange. A year later their first child, a 'war baby', was born.

72

Moochool gave up medicine and became a journalist working for agencies in Pakistan, Paris and London. In 1950, he was a sub-editor for a year at the Reuters office in Fleet Street. He decided in his early thirties to switch careers again and, after a short spell as a shipping executive in Pakistan, in his spare time began reading for the Bar in London. Subsequently he has become a world authority on maritime law and was for many years the head of maritime legislation at the United Nations Conference on Trade and Development in Geneva. He is now in semi-retirement and holds a senior fellowship at the University of Dalhousie in Nova Scotia.

Shah did not get on well with his father when he was young. One friend says, half-seriously: 'The national paper is really for his father's benefit. After his adolescent rift he wants to prove that he can do something worthwhile, that he's no longer the eighteen-year-old drop-out.' His father seems to have been duly impressed. He says: 'I seem destined to be the son of a famous father and the father of a famous son.'

Shah's early years were highly peripatetic and involved long separations from his mother or father or both. Aged eighteen months, he went with his parents on the first postwar convoy back to India where he lived with his mother for a year. They then returned to Cambridge and spent a lot of time with his mother's parents. When he was five, the family went back to India where Shah was left with his other set of grandparents while his parents returned to London.

Shah admits that the separation did have a 'dramatic effect on my life', particularly as, on his return to England at the age of ten, his parents were looking after his first cousin's three children as well as two new daughters of their own. 'I moved into a house that was full of people who I really didn't know and that had a very bad effect on me and made me withdraw into myself; it wasn't until I was 22 or 23 that I started to rationalise what had happened.' The next twelve years were his 'wild' period.

After a short time at Hillside preparatory school near Reigate, where his parents were then living, Shah was sent away to Gordonstoun – the Scottish public school with the spartan reputation – which a couple of years later was to welcome Prince Charles. The school compounded his sense of being an outsider. 'That whole period was very difficult for me and I learnt how to be by myself a lot – it's only over the last ten years or so I've made friends.' Shah was now distanced from his family, falling behind academically and becoming a 'difficult' child. He actually failed his entrance exam to Gordonstoun but the headmaster presciently saw a spark of something and admitted him on the strength of an interview. He enjoyed most sports and did well on the playing field and the athletic track – he was even at one time on the reserve list to play for the Sussex Colts cricket team during the holidays. (Shah has always appreciated his food but retained quite an athletic frame until he started building up the Messenger Group ten years ago.)

Aside from sport, he seems to have disliked Gordonstoun. He was too wilful and self-possessed to be popular: 'I enjoyed being away from everybody. On Sundays I used to go out in a boat and just sit in the middle of this lake. I sound a terribly lonely kid but I wasn't lonely, I just didn't enjoy other people.'

His time at school does not seem to have taught him much. His ungrammatical writing and undisciplined speech bear witness to his rejection of a formal education, and he displays many of the magpie intellectual qualities of an autodidact. However, Shah is certainly not opposed to public schools in principle and is planning to send his eldest son, Martyn, to Shrewsbury. He also now sees the conventional hidden benefits that escaped him at the time: 'Where Gordonstoun did help is that it gave me a lot of independence to cope with things.' That may be stretching a point as he was only at the school for eighteen months (five terms) between January 1958 and July 1959, when he appears to have been thrown out or, at least, suspended 'for pinching sweets I think it was', he says.

He then attended in quick succession a grammar school in Reigate and a secondary modern school in Haywards Heath before getting some low-grade A-levels thanks to Davies's College, a private crammer in Brighton. During his time at the crammer he did a lot of writing, mainly poetry and short stories, and he even sweated through a short novel entitled *Cornice* when he was seventeen. 'It was about where east meets west. It was a make-up town somewhere around Turkey – it was really cosmopolitan – I suppose it reflected my view at that time.' One of his great regrets is not having made the grade as a writer.

He was not interested in college or his mother's preference, the army. 'Communication and media was always my thing. It's a communication of the idea that I love, which is probably why I'm good at what I do, which is creating something new, looking at things differently. But once it's up and running I'm not very good at keeping things going day-to-day.' Instead, he began a three-year stretch of odd-jobs in the theatre, starting as a scene-shifter on *Chips with Everything* at the Golders Green Hippodrome and finishing as an assistant stage manager in the West End.

His career in the theatre was brought to an abrupt end by an incident during Lionel Bart's *Maggie May* at the Apollo Theatre. Shah took it upon himself to move the complex set single-handed and pulled the wrong lever, causing Georgia Brown to walk down a staircase backwards singing her big number to the back wall.

It was 1965 and Shah was a restless 21-year-old. He drove a white transit van and people started calling him Eddie (Shah himself spells his name with a 'y' but is indifferent about what others choose to do). He had been named Selim Jehan by his father but was known at school as John (the anglicised Jehan). Strangely, he can't remember why he changed his name. His next job was as an assistant floor manager at the BBC Television Centre, White City. It was a menial job: he called the actors and actresses, made cups of tea and got bored quickly.

He was continuing to write and harboured serious ambitions of becoming a playwright. He suffered, however, from the same problem as a writer as he has with speech – a hyperactive mind: 'The hardest thing I found was that my mind was racing ahead on dialogue and I was limited by my slow typing speed.'

He says that for a while he flirted with the Left and even nearly joined the Communist Party. He was touched by the outer waves of the sixties' libertarian 'revolt' that must have been thrashing all around him in the world of theatre and television and developed a dilettantish interest in Eastern philosophy. Incongruously he also signed up as a member of Moral Rearmament, 'just for the folk-singing', he says. There is, however, a conservative, moralistic streak in Shah – he doesn't drink, works extremely hard but, more important, tends to see most large organisations – especially in London – as essentially flabby, decadent and corrupt. Fleet Street, in his view, is Old Corruption itself.

Shah next moved to Granada TV in Manchester where he was to stay for the next four years. He worked as a floor manager, starting on *Coronation Street*. Coincidentally, he shared a flat in London for a while with Geoff Hughes who was later to become a *Coronation Street* star.

He was not happy at Granada and eventually left under a cloud, recalling that he was put in a 'very embarrassing situation' by two colleagues. He was also simply bored after forty-three episodes of *Coronation Street*. 'At Granada, being a small company, everyone knew everyone else and I was out on a limb. I was out front with the lights on and I didn't get on.' Shah was – on his own admission – never an easy man to get on with; as he grew in age and confidence he became more awkward still. One man who remembers him at Granada recalls: 'The thing that really pissed everyone off about Eddie was that he had such big ideas about himself.' In Shah's view, he simply refused to play the office politics game.

One consolation was meeting his wife Jennifer in 1968 while she was acting in a Granada TV series, *The Caesars*. The story of how he 'won' her illustrates what a pushy young man he had become. When he met her again a few months after the series at the Hilton Hotel in London, he was working on the filming of the BAFTA awards and she was a guest there with a producer friend. 'She was sitting at a table with this guy and I just walked up and said see you at your place at 2 p.m. tomorrow.' Both men turned up at the appointed hour and Shah prevailed.

Shah's wife was born Jennifer White, forty-three years ago, in Cardiff. Her father was in the RAF and she went to the Arts Educational Trust School in London for young children with artistic promise. After a modelling course and some small roles in repertory, she became the first hostess on *Crackerjack* in the late fifties when it was presented by Eamonn Andrews. She won the Face of Britain contest in 1961 which considerably boosted her career and earned her a few glamour roles in films like *Casino Royale*, but she never broke through into serious acting. When Shah first met her she was earning about £10,000 a year from modelling – a lot of money in the late sixties – and she bought Shah his first (second-hand) Jaguar.

They married in 1970 at the Ross-on-Wye register office, with Jennifer's parents the only guests. They now have three children – two boys and a girl: Martyn 12, Tamsyn 7 and Alexander 5. Although she has not worked since their first child, Jennifer's talent for interior decoration helped to top-up the family coffers in the early Messenger days when they were constantly moving house.

She seems to play a very traditional, back-stage,

domestic role in his life – but close friends say her influence is considerable. Jennifer has a far neater mind than Shah's and can often see things as Shah concedes more clearly. Politically she is a more orthodox right-winger and is a paid-up member of the Conservative Party. As treasurer of her local Conservative Women's Luncheon Club, she might even count as a Tory activist. Shah also jokes that if the new paper is not an instant success, Jennifer will not allow him to fill it with pin-ups to boost sales. As one friend has observed: 'Shah has raised Jennifer on to a kind of pedestal.'

Jennifer was first found to have cervical cancer about ten years ago. After an operation it seemed to disappear, only to re-emerge in 1982 to cast a terrible shadow over both their lives for several months and play a part in the Messenger dispute. Her recurrence was wrongly diagnosed as backache for much of that year and when, in October 1982, doctors realised it was 'the old problem' they gave her only four to five months to live.

Since then she has made a rare recovery from this virulent form of cancer. Although still fragile-looking, she responded well to radiotherapy and later went on to chemotherapy. At the end of 1985 she was cleared again after her intensive annual check-up. Jennifer believes that Shah, as she calls him, kept her alive through the sheer force of his personality. During the darkest days he would lay down intricate goals for her to aim at – continually targeting her at some happy event in the future such as a child's birthday or Christmas.

Shah is very open about his wife's illness – so open, in fact, that some people accuse him of using it to 'win' people to his side. But he says he likes to talk about it to give hope to others in the same position and describes with real emotion his feelings on being told the news: 'I didn't realise at first what the doctor was talking about when he said it was the "old problem" – then, when it hit me, the world seemed to go into slow motion. I can still remember the position of all the objects in that room and wondering what they were doing there – wondering why anything existed at all.'

Like the Messenger dispute itself, Jennifer's illness has helped to mature Shah: 'Watching someone face that absolute despair has put life in perspective. It's made me unafraid of what might happen. I've learnt you've got to live a day at a time, you can't guarantee tomorrow.'

Back in mid-1972 Shah rang Jennifer, who was working in Italy, to tell her he had given up his job with Granada. 'I went to work selling space for Yellow Pages because I wanted to learn about advertising. And also because I'd spent all my life in a protected environment – certainly for the last six years in TV. All those writers who had been writing about everyday life but in real terms they knew nothing about it. I came out of this cocoon and was out where people were not quite starving, but you know it was quite hard. And I realised just how out of touch with people and reality I was and I decided to get a job somewhere I could learn about normal pressures of business.'

It was thus in his late twenties that Shah caught the business 'bug'. Over the previous ten years the budding playwright had assumed business was a deadening, uncreative force in the world. The failed writer now found he was a talented salesman, so he transferred the language of art into business. 'What so many people don't understand,' he now says, 'is that business is fantastically creative.'

The drifting son of a quasi-divine family had also found a comfortable home in the image and trappings of the self-made northern businessman. He now wears the uniform of his chosen clan as if he had been born into it. He lives in a £150,000, 1950s house set in four well-kept acres in the Manchester stockbroker belt of Mobberley; he drives a BMW and a Range Rover; his friends are local estate agents and solicitors and his children attend local private schools.

The outsider status that has been such a constant feature of his life to date has real ethnic roots, as we have seen, and partly because of that he does not fit easily into English social categories. The combination of Persian/Indian upper-class and Manchester middle-class has produced an unusual classlessness in his style and attitudes, more akin to a young American or Australian businessman. He remains proud of being a 'rich kid' who became street-wise.

Despite being born and educated in Britain, Shah remains to many British eyes and ears slightly foreign. He was certainly teased at school about it, and some friends believe he remains more conscious of his mixed-race than he lets on.

It became significant on two counts during the Messenger dispute. First, it was deliberately and cynically exploited by some NGA officials. After one big push outside the Warrington plant during the mass-picketing, there was a sudden lull punctured by a single anonymous voice, presumably directed at the workers inside the plant, shouting: 'Fancy working for a Paki then.' From that moment, says Colin Bourne, the northern organiser of the National Union of Journalists (NUJ), most of the union officials became far more careful about the emotions they were calling up. Yet the NGA's publicity literature, the communist *Morning Star* and the rival *Warrington Guardian*, insisted on calling Shah by his unused first names, Selim Jehan.

Second, Shah himself has the typically unBritish habit of taking British laws and traditions more seriously than the British themselves. During the heat of the dispute he often defended himself against physical or commercial attack from the NGA by maintaining that he was upholding 'what this country is meant to be all about', as if looking from outside at a 'textbook' Britain.

Like a man with no country who happens to have landed in Britain, he also speaks occasionally about leaving the country for good, as he did at the height of the Messenger dispute, for example. More than one colleague has commented that if his new project flops, his pride will not allow him to stay in Britain.

6

Eddie Goes Free

'The integral position of free newspapers in the regional press is now an established fact. They now enjoy a larger share of the advertising spend than paid-for weekly papers and the regional press is vibrant with competition.'

Ian Fletcher, chairman of the
Yellow Advertiser Group

6

Eddie Goes Free

Shah's business career had begun in humble fashion selling advertising space for the Yellow Pages directory. He soon landed a similar job with the *Manchester Times*, a free paper launched by the *Manchester Evening News* to kill off another free paper which was trying to lure away its advertisers.

At that time the free newspaper industry in Britain was just starting to take off, as it had already done in America and Europe. The frees' attack on the traditional, paid-for, provincial newspaper industry was quite spectacular in disturbing the peace of employers and unions. The new industry created not one Eddie Shah, but literally hundreds of self-made do-it-yourself newspapermen, contemptuous of the business and marketing conservatism of the provincial press conglomerates.

Many took their cue from Lionel Pickering, one of the founders of the British free newspaper industry. Pickering, the son of a British miner, had spent time in Australia working as a journalist. In his words, he had found the country 'berserk on frees and advertising'. Sydney alone, he estimated, had eighty-four free papers. Returning to England with £800 in savings in 1966, Pickering determined to launch a free paper of his own. With a £1,000 loan from his bank and £3,000 from his parents, he started the *Derby Trader*, assembling the eight-page paper himself and taking over thirteen days to deliver it around the streets of the town. Operating from the back room of his terraced house, he personally sold the adverts and laid out all the pages for the first four issues. The paper was not an instant success and failure was keenly felt. Pickering recalls going to bed in misery in the mid-afternoon, having suffered the humiliation of failing to sell a single ad.

Advertisers, however, gradually became less suspicious. The Trader Group now has ten titles dropping through more than 800,000 letter boxes in the East Midlands and over 120 printers are employed at the Group's press works. Turnover is £10m. a year and profit 10 per cent of sales.

Although the plant is unionised, as indeed most free newspapers are, Pickering's hostility to the unions is common amongst his peers. 'Whether the unions like it or not,' he argues, 'free newspaper men like me, who have come from nothing, have succeeded only by risking their own homes, marriages and everything, in those early stages to get their newspapers off the ground.

'Now the unions want to tell us how to run our business. It hurts to realise that your own people – the people whose wages you pay – are really the only ones who could bring you down now. They don't want any of the risks or responsibilities – just a shorter working week every year and an annual 15 per cent pay rise. No wonder the American free newspaper people won't touch unions with a bargepole.'

The mid-seventies were the growth years for the frees. In 1974 there were still only 184 free titles with a total distribution of 9m. Six years later the number of titles had doubled and profits escalated. What made them such an instant success?

The typesetting and printing of most frees was sub-contracted, thereby avoiding capital investment, high overheads and possible union difficulties. The NGA was not barred from the small typesetting companies which often specialised in this work but traditional NGA pay and productivity levels most certainly were. Part-time women workers were usually hired on secretarial pay rates. And the papers themselves sustained minimal editorial and administrative costs, commonly being run by just three or four people. Papers that live by advertising are a lot less expensive to run than papers that live by disclosure.

Advertisers enjoyed being courted for the first time in decades and were attracted by the lower rates and the blanket coverage the frees offered. The local supermarket or the provider of a general service, like emergency plumbing, was more interested in high penetration than in the ability of the paid-for paper to reach particular groups such as local professional people. The increase in the power of advertisers in relation to the local press had led, by 1985, to the extreme consequence in Sheffield of the local estate agents setting up their own paper, which has contributed to the closure of the *Sheffield Morning Telegraph*, one of the oldest newspapers in Britain.

In early 1986 the provincial free newspaper industry also opened its challenge to the national press when Reed International announced that it was aiming to establish a chain of free morning papers in the big provincial cities. Reed drew its inspiration from Chris Bullivant's *Daily News* in Birmingham, in which it has a half stake. In the mid-1970s, however, the frees were aiming at a generation of complacent provincial managers, many of whom had never known competition. Indeed, ever since the twenties a series of spoken and unspoken cartels had already been established, whereby one provincial newspaper owner had agreed not to stray into the circulation area of a rival.

In 1932, for instance, after a series of expensive circulation wars through the provincial towns of Britain, the brothers Gomer and William Berry (Lord Kemsley and

Lord Camrose respectively) reached a deal with Lord Rothermere not to encroach into each other's area. The effect of their battle had been to kill off a series of independent papers caught in the crossfire. The consequence of their pact was to ensure that few of the independents returned. Inevitably the strong papers, with the backing of the resources of a group, had the means to drive out the weak. Whereas in 1921 the five big chains owned roughly 10 per cent of the provincial evening and morning titles, the figure by the outbreak of the Second World War had risen to 40 per cent.

Concern about this 'tendency to monopoly' led to the establishment of a Royal Commission by the Labour Government in 1946 and even a book-length riposte from Lord Camrose, who also owned the *Daily Telegraph*, claiming that the Commission had been appointed due to 'suggestions of a nebulous character' by socialist MPs, such as Michael Foot, bent on state ownership of the press.

Nevertheless, in 1984 the five largest groups (Associated, Thomson Regional Newspapers, Westminster Press, United Newspapers and Iliffe Press) were responsible for three-fifths of the total circulation of the seventy-eight paid-for evening titles and half of the sales of the paid-for English and Welsh provincial morning papers.

The cartels developed by the newsgroups ensured that during the sixties and early seventies the provincial press for the most part was happily profitable. Circulations were steady. Local radio, television and free newspapers had not yet started to offer advertisers a rival medium. The regional newspapers' share of total advertising increased from 20.4 per cent in 1966 to 30.4 per cent in 1974. At the same time, revenue at fixed prices rose from £410m. to £663m. in 1975. Wage costs admittedly were relatively high, about 15 per cent higher than the average for manufacturing, but managements comforted themselves with the fact that overmanning and high wages had not reached the proportions of Fleet Street. Production (as opposed to editorial and administrative employees) represented 58 per cent of the workforce in Fleet Street, only 42 per cent in the provinces, according to a report by the conciliation service ACAS to the 1975 Royal Commission on the press. The same study showed that the provincial compositor's earnings were less than two-thirds of his Fleet Street counterpart.

However, even if many provincial papers were inefficient, managements in the provinces, up until the mid-seventies, could pass on their high costs with impunity through increased advertising rates and cover price. Owning a provincial newspaper may not have been a licence to print money, but it helped. Profits before tax as a percentage of revenue could reach over 15 per cent in boom years, and as a result the parent companies of many national newspapers were able to survive off the surpluses accumulated by their provincial sister papers. Associated Newspapers lost money on the *Daily Mail* but thrived on the profits of its Northcliffe Newspapers' regional chain. Thomson Regional absorbed the losses of *The Times* and the *Guardian* lived off the *Manchester Evening News*.

By the mid-seventies a series of forces were at work which began to spell decline and falling profitability. Some of the changes were beyond the control of any management: the depopulation of the inner cities, the reduction in public transport and the attractions of evening television regional news all contributed. But the editorial quality of the regional press itself had grown flatulent and tired.

'Few managements undertook readership surveys or methodically considered what advertisers wanted,' Chris Carter, then industrial relations executive at the Newspaper Society, admits. Frank Barlow, chief executive at the *Financial Times* and Westminster Press, also believes managements became excessively diverted by the challenge of taking the first undoubtedly necessary steps towards the conversion from the century-old hot-metal process to photocomposition.

Carter acknowledges that the transition was important, but its implementation flawed. 'We did not get the productivity advances out of the composing room that might have been possible, partly because the NGA craftsmen found it difficult to adapt effectively to the new QWERTY keyboard layouts after years of setting type on an entirely different machine. Whatever they say, there are few NGA craftsmen that can produce really good keyboard speeds. Craftsmen don't like it and if you come with the view that the change is a chore or degrading, your attitude is obviously not right.' Clearly the traditional paid-for industry was, like the national newspaper in the next decade, ripe for the taking.

Shah's small role in undermining the traditional industry arose from his time on the *Manchester Times*. 'It was while I was there that I suddenly thought, hang on, why aren't more people putting more editorial into it. If television with all its huge overheads can supply a service based on advertising, surely so can a newspaper. I suddenly thought it was logical. I looked at a few sums and I remember I went home and showed Jennifer the *Manchester Evening News* and said "that's a column inch and that's an advert with a rate of . . . and so on". And I said I want to sell the house and start a free paper and she said fine and that was it – the conversation was that quick.'

In describing these events Shah rarely mentions the role of two colleagues, Ron Windsor and Francis Grundy. Shah met Windsor on the *Manchester Times* and when it was closed from under them after nineteen weeks, they decided to exploit some of the lucrative newspaper advertising in the affluent parts of south Manchester.

Ron Windsor says: 'We actually got the idea from the

Manchester Times because it was in fact using a lot of editorial by the standards of free papers in those days. When it closed neither of us had jobs. I had brought Shah to the paper from Yellow Pages and he was an exceptionally good salesman but also very stubborn, it was quite a combination.'

Ian Templeton remembers Shah and Windsor coming to him with the idea of the freesheet and he put them in touch with a colleague, Francis Grundy, who put up £5,000 to buy some typesetting equipment. They moved to cramped premises above a betting shop in Ardwick. A few weeks later the first twelve-page issue of the *Sale & Altrincham Messenger* (*S.A.M.*) dropped on to thousands of doormats; the Citizen Kane of south Manchester had arrived.

But the first of Shah's many business rifts was not long in coming. Templeton says: 'They had a big fall-out. Windsor and Grundy complained to me that they couldn't control him and that he was doing all the wrong things. Shah insisted that they didn't understand the importance of building readership.'

The eventual parting was reasonably amicable. Templeton negotiated a deal whereby Shah took the Messenger title and Grundy took the typesetting. Windsor had a few days to decide where his loyalties lay and finally opted to join Grundy.

Although Windsor remembers Shah as awkward and 'terribly irresponsible', he is still fond of him and recalls one incident of 'classic' Shah: 'It was my turn to do the weekly run in the van to the new printers in Derby and not having done it before I assumed that one tank of petrol would be enough there and back. But just as I was leaving the motorway exit on the way back I ran out of petrol. And there was Eddie waiting for me with a can of petrol – exactly the same thing had happened to him the previous week.' The idea of warning Windsor to fill up in Derby was altogether too prosaic!

From above the betting shop in Ardwick, Shah, now

operating on his own, moved the *S.A.M.* to the sweeter-smelling ambience of a room above a flower shop in Sale. His main financial patron was Harry Green, now chief executive of the Warrington Co-op, who lent him £2,000.

A few weeks earlier, he had met Helen Graham at a party. He had asked her if she liked her job, and when she said no, he invited her to come and work with him. Soon after, she became the other half of *Messenger* – Shah's faithful and most trusted business partner to this day.

Graham is a divorcee with two grown-up daughters, one of whom currently works as a reporter on the *Warrington Messenger*. A talented, if unorthodox, business-woman, she is less than five feet tall but well-built. With auburn hair and glasses she looks younger than her forty four years but has the composure of the good school teacher she once was. When Shah offered her the job on the *Messenger* she was a bored biology teacher. Like Shah, she had no experience of newspapers or business but was able and willing to learn fast. The two of them have jointly developed an almost identical outlook on life and business, and even share many of the same catch-phrases.

'It was very exciting. It was a time of pitching in and doing a bit of everything. I still remember the thrill when we produced our first twelve-page paper, then sixteen-page, and so on,' says Graham.

The paper was now being typeset and printed in nearby Horncastle but Shah and Graham were doing most of the design and paste-up themselves with help from friends and part-time staff. The early *Messenger* inevitably had an air of feverish improvisation – to the eye of the traditional newspaper man it probably still has. As Graham puts it: '*Messenger* now reflects the fact that neither of us came from a printing background. We just did things in the most efficient way we could.' Not having been brought up to worship the time-honoured mysteries of newspaper production, they thought of it as just like any other product.

Shah and Graham worked hard on *S.A.M.* On press days they would sometimes have to stay up all night, enjoying the exhilarating ride along the learning curve. Shah took the figurehead role – the important glad-handing of estate agents, retailers, car dealers and any influential local businessmen who might advertise with him.

He also had a flair for newspaper design which he has not lost and dabbled on the editorial side, whose linchpin was Bob MacGowan, a devoted former *Daily Mail* sub-editor who rewrote press releases and fished around for local stories. Shah remains to this day editor-in-chief of Messenger Newspapers and has always had 'a firm idea of what the papers should have in them', according to Jan Lever, who became group editor in 1979.

She says: 'We have tried to reflect community values and we always remember that we are going into people's homes uninvited; so no sensationalism and none of those long-winded stories that journalists like to write for each other.' Shah enjoys the community role and is himself a generous contributor to local charities.

Graham, meanwhile, cut out a niche on the selling side. She was single-minded and effective and built up a team of 'her girls' whose telephone techniques quickly made the *S.A.M.* profitable. 'We always went for the big clients first, like Tesco and the North-west Gas Board,' she remembers. She also says that they specifically re-cruited staff with no previous experience in newspapers so that they would fit into the evolving *Messenger* ethos: hard work but team work.

The paper became established. Pagination increased, advertising flowed in. Shah hired a company secretary and a photographer. On the advice of Bryn Griffiths, then the NGA's northern organiser, typesetting and print-ing switched to Cumbrian Newspapers in Carlisle, about eighty miles up the motorway. There Shah struck up a lasting relationship with Roy Dickinson, then Cumbrian production director.

In late 1975, the *Sale Guardian* and the *Altrincham Guardian*, both traditional weekly broadsheets established at the end of the last century and both owned by Cheshire County Newspapers (CCN), were the first papers to feel Shah's hot breath on their necks. Douglas May, managing director of CCN, now admits: 'We didn't take as much notice of him as we should have done.' The two broadsheets subsequently merged, changed to a tabloid format and finally, in 1983, went free.

Shah gradually started to make money and, more important, sport ambitious new projects. 'But it was still not easy,' recalls Graham, 'all the money we made we ploughed straight back.' He was too impatient to build his business in a methodical, profit-maximising fashion. No sooner was *S.A.M.* established than he dreamed of Hyde and Ashton or Stretford and Urmston editions. The latter came to fruition in 1976. It was a relatively simple next step. Geographically next door, it meant that they already had many of the editorial and business contacts they needed.

By now they had an advertising sales staff of six, with the length of the two editions fluctuating between 36 and 48 pages. One of their sales staff, Frances O'Brien – now running her own consultancy business, but then a nineteen-year-old with little previous work experience – recalls the atmosphere: 'It was quite a happy ship, quite a family atmosphere. Eddie was very much the ruler of the roost – he was usually affable but he had that aura of a powerful man, always a little bit frightening. Helen was the day-to-day manager on the advertising side – but she jumped when he shouted and he did have a terrible temper.' Shah shouted a lot in those days but O'Brien remembers him often apologising for his outbursts afterwards. 'He was very street-wise and a bit flash, you know he was always driving fast sports cars.' (He has lost none of his flashiness. In July 1985, he arrived at the Portsmouth and Sunderland AGM in Portsmouth in the very latest Ford Granada model. While he flew from Manchester to Southampton, the [hired] car was driven all the way down from Birmingham to meet him at Southampton airport so that he could drive the final fifteen miles to Portsmouth.)

The pay was good at *Messenger* but, despite the team ethos, O'Brien recalls that 'no one ever knew what was going on at the top. Eddie and Helen were always having their secret chats, always scheming, there was certainly no great participation.' One subject of those chats would have been the next stage of expansion – to Stockport in early 1978. It turned out to be the first serious setback of Shah's business career. The paper flopped and he wisely withdrew after about four editions. 'The problem was we were still based in Sale and we just didn't have the presence that you need in Stockport, but we learnt by the mistake,' says Graham.

Soon afterwards O'Brien decided to leave to take a slightly better-paid job on the *Stockport Express & Advertiser*. Graham was disappointed – 'she used to think of me as one of her high-fliers,' says O'Brien – but was quite civil about her decision. 'Shah on the other hand screamed when Helen told him. I was called down and there was just this wall of anger – I was terrified and burst into tears. He kept shouting at me that it was rank disloyalty to join a rival. I had to leave that day – but they paid me for the next two weeks.'

Two months later, with Shah and the editorial team ensconced in a new headquarters in Stockport, the paper was relaunched there and this time made a better showing. By the end of the year there were Stockport East and West editions. The Messenger Group's four titles now claimed a weekly distribution of about 160,000, employed forty people, and at the end of 1978 brought in a revenue of £322,000 – up from £173,000 the previous year.

Since 1977 Shah had been thinking of starting his own

typesetting and possibly even printing operation. He also had plans to set up an insurance company, an advertising agency and another free paper for the centre of Manchester. First the Group's capital base was restructured and the company was registered under the name of Messenger Newspaper Group.

Before the reconstruction, 50 per cent of the share capital had been owned by Shah and the rest by Harry Green. Shah now retained 50 per cent and the rest was divided between Helen Graham (10 per cent), Harry Green (9 per cent), Cumbrian Newspapers (20 per cent) and Academy Court Holdings – the parent company of CCN – (11 per cent).

The reconstruction was significant because it brought on to the Messenger board as part-time directors two experienced newspaper managers who attempted to impose more discipline on Shah's energetic but sometimes wayward style. The first, Roy Dickinson, remains with him to this day. The second, Douglas May of CCN, fell out with Shah after four years on the board and is now one of his harshest critics. May's arrival on the board in 1979, as part of a defensive pact, was proof that Messenger was starting to hit its paid-for rivals.

The appearance of May and Dickinson coincided with the launching of *Our Town*, a colour free weekly for Manchester town centre. Printed at the Swale Press and part-financed by CCN, it folded after four weeks, costing May's group about £60,000 and Messenger about £30,000. Soon afterwards the company received a much-needed boost to its full-time management with the arrival of the brooding, 6' 2" figure of Mike Frankland. Trained as an accountant, Frankland was the financial brains of Messenger until early 1984 when he left after a policy disagreement with Shah.

By mid-1979 arrangements were well in hand for the introduction of Messenger's own typesetting unit at Stockport. The job had been getting too big for Cumbrian Newspapers and Shah had always intended to bring typesetting in-house. Now he had plans to use the hoped-for spare capacity to typeset some of Manchester City's supporters' club literature. A substantial typesetting operation such as Messenger's inevitably meant hiring NGA print union members and it never occurred to Shah to do other than look to the union to find his staff for him, as is the custom. There was no hint of the fall-out to come.

In 1979 Shah's turnover was up to £576,000 and in 1980 Messenger achieved just under £1m., with a pre-tax profit of £15,000. The poor return reflected the initial uphill fight of the Stockport papers. Ian Templeton says Stockport sustained some heavy losses and 'it took nearly three years to turn round'.

But before Stockport did begin to pay its way Shah was already planning expansion into Bury – moving for the first time out of his south-Manchester home base and up to the north-east of the city. The long-term plan was to encircle Manchester with Messenger frees. Bury did eventually come on stream early in 1982 – in the immediate build-up to the NGA conflict – but it never established itself and soon after the dispute he sold it for £300,000.

The Manchester ring did not materialise although another Messenger opened, at Warrington, in mid-1984. It faced some consumer and advertiser resistance following the dispute, in what is a staunchly Labour area, but is now better than breaking even.

Shah's tendency to gild the lily is illustrated by the claims he has made on several occasions to be running a business making close to £½m. profit on turnover of £5m. His actual turnover and pre-tax profit figures for 1981–5 were, according to Ian Templeton: 1981 – £1.4m. turnover and £56,000 profit; 1982 – £1.8m. and £115,000; 1983 – £2.1m. and £4,800; 1984 – £3m. and £260,000; and 1985 turnover was £3.3m. According to an interview Shah gave to the *Manchester Evening News* in April 1985, profit to the year-end 31 March was about £200,000.

On the other hand, the long dispute was a drain on his own management resources and at its height incurred an outlay of several thousand pounds in 'defensive' costs. But as Ian Templeton acknowledges, 'Messenger would have grown faster and been more profitable if more method had been applied.' Shah's talent for creating projects rather than administering them has qualified his purely balance-sheet achievement. In the late 1970s and early 1980s, several of the once sleepy provincial groups had also woken up to the competition represented by people like Shah.

In 1982, Shah set up a short-lived employment agency and he was also thinking seriously about housing developments in Spain, a newspaper in Stoke-on-Trent, a magazine chain and cable TV. Selling Messenger crossed his mind on more than one occasion. He thought even more seriously about buying the *Sporting Chronicle*, the daily racing paper, which was up for sale in 1982. Shah planned to turn it into a tabloid and give it away free in betting shops.

Another clever idea that *did* materialise, only to crash badly, involved the publication of special holiday novels. Shah commissioned authors to produce romantic fiction set in real resorts – such as Benidorm and Majorca – providing local information including maps, restaurant, bar and hotel guides, as well as a good read. He aimed to sell the books on special stands at Manchester, Birmingham and Gatwick airports – but they were mediocre in quality and poorly marketed. Shah was excited by the idea and used to say, 'It's a brilliant new publishing concept – I don't know why no one has ever thought of it before.' But the project was coming to fruition just as he began to develop another new concept at the start of 1984, and he didn't give it the attention it deserved.

The foregoing might leave the impression that Shah was 100 per cent owner of Messenger with no obligation to consult his directors or fellow shareholders. This is in fact one of the main complaints levelled against his management style by Douglas May. May is a refined, slightly pedantic man and despite the beating his group's two paid-for papers had taken at the hand of the *S.A.M.*, he probably adopted what to Shah seemed a rather haughty, patronising attitude when he joined the Messenger board. Shah saw in May everything he disliked about the world of traditional newspaper management, and the two men were always jousting.

May believes Shah was simply a 'bad businessman, he was undisciplined, volatile and with a completely butterfly mind. He had no grasp of finance and was terribly haphazard about keeping receipts and so on . . . In 1979 I raised the issue of budgets, which they had never really had before, and occasionally I would ask why, for example, editorial had gone 150 per cent over budget. Shah's response was usually to get in a huff and sometimes he would even walk out, he thought of himself as a national newspaper baron even then!' He could not, claims May, bear to be crossed and twice threatened to resign unless he got his own way.

May alleges that Shah consistently broke the Companies Act, usually through ignorance and poor organisation; he was frequently late filing accounts with Companies House, often taking decisions on his own which should have gone to the board for approval; and poor at keeping a record of the money he was taking out of the business for his own use.

May paints an amusing picture of the occasional board meetings. Shah, he says, would get fed up in the middle of a technical financial point and leave the table to practise his golf swing: 'Helen would just glow in admiration – but some of the rest of us got very frustrated.'

Shah undoubtedly could be exasperating. But his admirers see an almost visionary quality in him which they think might yet make him a great businessman. Ian Templeton, an apparently sceptical accountant, and by no means uncritical of Shah, says: 'You know the funny thing about Eddie is that he's almost always been right about things.'

His business record from 1974–84 was, however, mixed to say the least. To his credit, Shah's flair and hard work had built up from nothing a company of six free newspaper titles employing over a hundred people. Despite his lack of experience he had the courage and confidence to learn by his mistakes – of which there were plenty.

Although he likes to live in some style and pays himself very handsomely, Shah is not strongly driven by the desire to pile up profit for its own sake. Indeed his failure to amass very much profit at Messenger is largely because he was far more attracted to investing in, and building up, new projects.

His company bore that increasingly familiar stamp of youngish entrepreneurs – the mix of old-fashioned paternalism and 1960s liberalism: Shah was always tieless and instantly on first-name terms. Richard Branson's Virgin Records is a larger example of the same combination. 'It was let's all join in but on Eddie's terms,' as one observer of Messenger put it.

A streak of insecurity made him poor at accepting criticism and treating people as equals. As Steve Hart observes: 'He did seem to select people at Messenger whom he could mould.' The same insecurity was responsible for an entertaining weakness for tall stories about himself. As Simon Haworth, the NUJ Foc at Messenger, recalls: 'Eddie called me into his office one afternoon and started telling me how in his late teens he'd slipped off to America with his elder brother and they had both signed up for the Marines and gone to Vietnam. He said his brother was killed but he was awarded some medal for bravery – he even showed me a scar on his leg which he said was a bullet wound.' Shah now says it was all a joke but the point was clearly lost on Haworth who remembers being 'rather shaken'.

Paradoxically, it was his very 'weaknesses' at Messenger – his stubbornness, his impatience with conventional business methods and measures of achievement, and his tendency to fantasise – which are the foundation-stones of *Today*. The key to translating fantasy into reality was a little local difficulty with the NGA.

7

Craft Union in Crisis

'Understanding the NGA is a bit like interpreting
Soviet foreign policy.'

Lord Harris of Greenwich, October 1985

7

Craft Union in Crisis

A dispute involving only six print workers at a small free newspaper is an unlikely stage for a historic clash between labour and capital. To understand why the Messenger Group became the site of such a conflict we need to look briefly at the history of the NGA and the structure of the British print unions.

It is one of the peculiarities of the NGA that it organises effectively among very small groups of workers. As a rule in the industrialised world, the smaller a company the less likely it is to be unionised. Not so in the print. Many of the NGA's 100,000 working members are to be found in groups of less than a dozen in small typesetting companies or even twos and threes in design studios. That is because, more than any other British craft union, the NGA bases its organisation on sets of skills rather than a whole company or industry.

In the pre-industrial past, small groups of skilled printing craftsmen first began to organise into chapels (because of the early link between printing and the Church) to keep out the less skilled or those prepared to sell their skills for less than the norm. For more than two hundred years after Caxton the print industry, like all trades, remained heavily regulated by Parliament and the Guilds. But as regulation began to break down in the eighteenth century, the chapels felt their skills more exposed to the cold winds of the market. They realised that to maintain stability of work and income they would have to reach out to other chapels to establish the common pay and working conditions which had formerly been established by the Guilds. So were born the primitive forefathers of today's print unions.

The first industrial revolution largely bypassed the print industry. Printers remained isolated in small groups and, unlike the hundreds of workers gathered together in, say, a giant iron works or coal-mine, could not rely on their own collective strength to give them bargaining power. A vital rule of organisation was thus created, still enshrined in the modern NGA's Rule 43, which banned the acceptance of work from an 'unrecognised' (non-union) house or a unionised company in dispute with its workforce; secondary action was thus built into the union's rules. This was only reinforced by the even more fundamental rule of the closed shop restricting entry into the trade to existing union members or those working their way through a lowly-paid seven-year apprenticeship (often the sons of members).

The union has been helped in enforcing these rules by the increasingly fragmented nature of the printing process. Outside the field of newspapers, most companies specialise either in typesetting (or other forms of 'origination') or in printing. So if a typesetting company sacks its NGA compositors or starts paying them below union rates, it will have difficulty finding a printer to finish the work because the NGA also organises the skilled press operators. It has been a powerful chain of mutual support.

Shah was able to take on and beat the NGA because he controlled his own typesetting *and* printing *and* distribution. Hence his concern in the months before the Messenger dispute began and still to an extent at News UK, the parent company of *Today*, to control as much of his operation as physically possible.

But breaking one link in the NGA's chain was not enough to free Shah from the union's influence in the provinces; and despite the Employment Acts of 1980 and 1982, it would still have been difficult for him to expand very far, as the other main non-union companies like Paul Morgan, the southern England free newspaper entrepreneur, and T. Bailey Forman in Nottingham had discovered. The Nottingham company had been the exception that proved the rule, becoming in the mid-seventies the only provincial newspaper company to introduce direct-input, following two disputes, first with the NGA and later with the NUJ. In Shah's case the limits on his conventional expansion may, ironically, have been one of the factors which prompted him to plan the national paper.

The bigger local newspaper groups are in fact not as exposed to the NGA's powerful rules as commercial printers because they retain the whole production cycle in-house. But managements have until very recently been reluctant to try to produce newspapers when the NGA is on strike; if they attempt to do so, the union can trundle out a few further weapons such as blacking advertising copy from NGA-organised studios. In Fleet Street, managements have been even less willing to man the presses, knowing that if they did so, the product would be blacked by other unions in the building or other NGA chapels. Even if the paper was actually produced it would (until the new laws were established) probably face blacking by the distribution or rail unions.

The NGA's authority in relation to its members has flourished in some cases through a real bond of loyalty and in others out of a pragmatic knowledge that breaking the union rules would deprive the transgressor of his card and thus, usually, a relatively well-paid and prestigious manual job. The rules also created one of the most formal 'us and them' cultures in British industry, tempered only by the extent to which print and newspaper employers have come to accept the severe restrictions on their authority and the dual loyalties of their skilled workforce. This is particularly the case, as we have seen, in the uniquely powerful Fleet Street chapels.

Traditionally, once the print worker has acquired one of the skills represented by the NGA, he belongs first to the skill group and the union and second to his employer. The union is pervasive; like a paternalistic employer itself, it appears as the provider and protector not just through its control of entry and its status in the workplace but also through its role outside the workplace as a welfare system (now declining in importance) and an employment exchange. In Fleet Street, employers have for decades gone to the union branches for their manpower requirements.

This powerful and conservative union culture has reflected an immensely conservative industry. But the long sleep is now over. The union (and management) culture has been slowly undermined for the past ten years by the encroachment of new technology and more swiftly during the past three years by the political-legal reforms of the Thatcher Government. Just when the union needed all the strength it could muster to control the introduction of new technology on the best possible job and wage terms, it has found one of its main weapons, 'blacking', and other forms of secondary action, ruled out of play. The NGA is thus in the midst of the longest and most painful crisis in its history.

The new technology has given birth to a huge 'alternative' and non-union printing industry of instant print shops and in-plant print operations (in big companies), exploiting the print capabilities of the office equipment revolution and wiping out thousands of NGA-employing, small jobbing printers.

In the commercial printing sector – more vulnerable than newspapers to foreign competition – it has also caused a flood of work to go abroad to places like Hong

Kong and India where it can easily be handled by semi-skilled and poorly paid operatives.

The technology has eradicated many old typesetting skills and those that remain it has turned into essentially secretarial ones. The challenge presented by the computer technology to the NGA's control is immeasurably greater than that experienced in the 1890s when the linotype machine, patented by Ottmar Mergenthaler in 1886, displaced the centuries-old hand compositor. In June 1894, within five years of the first linotype machine being installed in Fleet Street, the proprietors of the London daily newspapers agreed that 'all skilled operators shall be members of the London Society of Compositors'. The unions had been able to retain control largely because there was a genuine skill involved in working the new machine and partly because their previous protection of the skilled status of their craft had been so total. Desultory efforts were made by the employers to set up training schools for potential scab linotype operators, but the unions snuffed these out and were triumphantly successful in retaining in membership all the skilled operators.

By contrast with the linotype machine, the typesetting skills involved in modern photocomposition are not complex, involving little more than glorified touch-typing. If anything, the skilled linotype or hot-metal operator is the least equipped person to pick up good 'cold' typesetting speeds. This is because the keyboard, similar in layout to the standard typewriter QWERTY board, is radically different to that of an old linotype keyboard and, as a result, the transferred linotype operator has to work to shake off his previous training and instinctive habits.

With the invention of direct-input technology, it was therefore possible – and infinitely preferable, from the employer's point of view, because cheaper – to have journalists or 'tele-ad staff' with typewriting skills setting their own copy. Other than for the sake of preserving archaic custom or avoiding strike action, there was simply no point in going through the rigmarole of having copy set, often more slowly, for a second time by a former linotype operator. So, unlike the printing revolution of the 1890s when the new setting skills were not widely available, it would have been comically absurd in the 1980s for the NGA to attempt to retain indefinite exclusive control of a skill that, after all, could be found at any secretarial employment agency.

The NGA has hung on to its control of the superfluous second 'keystroke' for as long as decently possible; but since 1982 it has reluctantly conceded direct-inputting in principle and more recently in practice. It is easy to see why it has tried to postpone the dread day of the full introduction of direct-input for this will cut the NGA's ten thousand provincial newspaper members down to three or four thousand in seven years.

Although newspapers – provincial and national – represent less than 15 per cent of the NGA's membership, the self-preservation instincts of the NGA bureaucracy make it reluctant to see such a large proportion of its members and subscriptions simply disappear. It also believes rightly that when the 'keystroke' is transferred to less well-organised workers, the general standard of pay and manning in the industry will be depressed.

The most rational solution, for unions and employers, is a single printing union. But it is precisely in the printing industry that the impact of technological change on union structure comes into most bruising collision with history.

The NGA argues to the other unions that, as it is having to bear the brunt of technological job loss, its members should be allowed to transfer into other newspaper departments, thus enabling it to retain its legendary bargaining power on behalf of all newspaper workers. In attempting to redraw the industry's union map to its own advantage, the NGA is having to quietly mutate from a disciplined, blue-collar union to a more flexible white-collar one, in order to hold the mobile and less union-inclined workforce of the future. The union is also, however, finding its past catching up with it as those unions representing clerical workers, journalists and electricians all see an opportunity, through grasping the new technology, to guillotine the labour aristocrats of print.

In addition, the technology has inevitably tampered with the print industry's most emotionally charged dividing line – that between craft and non-craft workers. In the past sixty years, with only a few exceptions, the myriad union mergers that have occurred have tended to confirm rather than blur these distinctions between craft and unskilled worker.

From the outset of printing, the craft worker has attempted to control the labour supply and hence limit the number of apprentices entering the general trade. Indeed, the first object of many of the rules of the early compositors' associations was to limit the number of apprentices and, in particular, the spread of juvenile and female labour. But, in the attempt to restrict the number of journeymen and thereby protect the value of skilled labour, the boundaries established by the trade associations were inevitably directed as much against other workers as against employers. Organisations such as the Manchester Graphical Society, formed in 1797, the Northern Typographical Union, formed in 1830, and the provincial Typographical Association, saw themselves as an élite. The London Society of Compositors – which organised readers and compositors in a fifteen-mile radius of Charing Cross but most numerously up the road in Fleet Street – saw itself as an élite within an élite. The Fleet Street NGA still considers itself somewhat apart from the national union, as the union's leaders have frequently discovered when they have tried – and failed – to assert their authority on those fiercely independent chapels.

The work of the early associations led them to look down upon the less literate and unskilled workers in print. An illustration of this patronising attitude can be found in the preface to a list of 'fair printing houses' published in 1891 by the Printing Machine Managers Trade Society: 'A young man, therefore in joining our Society, may be said to have joined a body of advanced scholars, whose greater experience enables them to be of much use to their less advanced companions.' Eager though the labour aristocrats were to help their 'less advanced' brethren, their public spiritedness knew strict bounds. The craft unionists made it an article of faith that certain operations should be performed only by craftsmen and by none other.

The NGA did not finally emerge from these regional bodies until 1964 when the Manchester-based Typographical Association merged with the London Typographical Society. Through the late sixties, a series of other small craft print unions such as the London-based Association of the Correctors of the Press attached themselves to the NGA until, in 1982, the final craft union outside the NGA, SLADE, representing graphic design and litho workers, also succumbed. Although in practice the system of apprenticeship and some of the tightest union demarcation rules were being relaxed, the establishment of the NGA preserved the vertical dividing-line between craft and non-craft workers.

Today's major semiskilled and unskilled union, the Society of Graphical and Allied Trades (SOGAT), comes from as complex and long a lineage as the NGA, having swallowed up no less than seven unions between 1945 and 1975. An over-ambitious merger with the semiskilled and clerical union NATSOPA, which had to be digested at a second sitting, finally came to fruition in 1982. The basis of SOGAT's membership had been in the areas of general print, paper-making and book-binding where wages never reached the exalted heights of Fleet Street. Until the merger with NATSOPA, SOGAT had been primarily responsible within Fleet Street for the distribution of newspapers through its powerful London Central branch. However, after the merger it also came to represent a host of 'lesser fry' such as clerical workers, readers' assistants, cleaners and commissionaires.

The traditional hostility between the NGA and SOGAT, combined with more recent animosity between the NGA and the NUJ, has been further complicated by the arrival of the Electrical, Electronic, Telecommunications and Plumbing Union (EETPU) as a force in the printing industry. In the past three years it has been difficult to disentangle the inter-union technology disputes from the union-employer disputes.

With the NGA's strength already sapped by the new laws, it desperately needed some unity; but the left-wing panacea of one industrial union for the print has remained only an aspiration and the absence of a single union has been a ball and chain around the attempts of all the unions to adjust to technological change. The eruption of the Messenger dispute into this tangled history at the end of 1983 could scarcely have been less welcome to the print unions.

8

The Messenger Dispute

'The Messenger dispute was my big break just like Rupert Murdoch's was buying the *News of the World*.'

Eddie Shah

8

The Messenger Dispute

The NGA members employed by Shah were, with one exception, not union activists. They had, however, mostly come from well-organised newspaper offices and had a reflex loyalty to their union. Their attitudes were, at least indirectly, moulded by the NGA's history.

Shah, on the other hand, had come from outside the industry and built up a small, highly motivated company with strong loyalty to the family product. He had never experienced any organised resistance to his will in the company, and it was only for a short and disastrous period between early 1980 and July 1983, when he directly employed NGA members, that he had to deal with an effective countervailing force.

When Shah says that he is not anti-union, only opposed to the restrictive practices of the NGA, he is no doubt speaking the truth. But it is proper to add that he would probably have clashed with any union, or indeed any person, bent on deflecting his strategies. His wrath could be aimed at managers almost as much as union officials.

At the end of 1979 he was poised to transfer the typesetting of the four Messenger titles – *S.A.M.*, Stretford Urmston, Stockport East and West – from Cumbrian

Newspapers to his new head office in Stockport, south Manchester.

But even before he started employing NGA members in Stockport his handling of industrial relations had not looked promising. In early 1979, for example, seven Messenger journalists – who were all members of the NUJ – decided to set up a chapel. Simon Haworth, who was elected FoC, remembers: 'It was perfectly innocent. One night after company hours we all met in a pub and elected a couple of officers. Eddie got to hear about it when he came back from holiday and we were all summoned to his office where he flew into a rage and said we'd gone behind his back and formed this secret organisation and so on.'

Most of the NUJ members liked Shah and enjoyed working on his papers. The pay and conditions were good for the provincial press at the time – Simon Haworth says that in 1979 he was earning about £8,000 and also had a company car. 'Eddie worked us hard but could be very generous – I had my wisdom teeth out on BUPA thanks to him. We were actually envied by members of the Stockport NUJ branch working on other papers.'

The NUJ chapel remained in existence but never negotiated on pay and only occasionally tried to intercede in cases of individual discipline. It certainly offered no challenge to Shah's will comparable to that posed by the NGA between 1980 and 1983.

Shah's first contacts with NGA officials were orthodox and friendly; he had not only agreed to the Stockport closed shop but had also joined the union himself. Both Roy Dickinson and Douglas May, the two outside directors, had advised Shah against hiring NGA labour directly. 'We both told him that we spent about 75 per cent of our time on union business one way and another and that it was best not to start if you could avoid it,' says Dickinson. But Shah's mind was made up. Despite his lack of experience, he no doubt believed that his own

118

charm and generosity as an employer would dissolve any ingrained 'us and them' attitude. After all, was he not 'man-of-the-people-Eddie' who liked to hand out cigars on his trips to Cumbrian Newspapers in Carlisle and bussed down groups of printers for his Christmas party each year?

With hindsight both Shah and the NGA officials appear to have been inadvisedly trusting of each other in those early meetings. Shah, knowing little about the 'going rates', agreed with scarcely a quibble to the union's claim for a 75-hour fortnight at £145 a week (although he eventually paid only £140). He realised he would have to pay a bit over the odds because he wanted experienced printers and he also wanted to be excluded from the two main industry agreements – with the Newspaper Society and the British Printing Industries Federation.

For its part the Stockport branch of the NGA – for so long submerged in the shadow of the much larger Manchester branch – was excited about a new, apparently friendly, employer who was holding out the promise of a new printing press in the branch's area to follow the typesetting company. The officials turned a blind eye to the fact that the terms of employment included 14- and 16-hour days in the middle of the week. The agreement was also unusually vague in its failure to distinguish between basic pay and bonuses for antisocial hours – which was to prove a bone of contention.

Despite the initial friendliness, Shah was soon to develop a considerable loathing for Tony Burke, the 32-year-old Stockport NGA president, seeing in him all the swaggering arrogance of the 'mafiosa' trade unionism that he hated so much. He also believed that Burke was hostile to Messenger because his job – when he was not on union business – was with the *Stockport Express & Advertiser*, a Messenger rival.

The agreement for the Stockport-based typesetting company was, however, signed uncontroversially on 10 January 1980. On the management side Shah hired

119

George Doyle, who had been composing-room foreman at Cumbrian Newspapers and Steve Hart who had worked as an NGA compositor in Carlisle before going on to work as a keyboard demonstrator for Whittakers. (After the dispute Hart left Messenger and now works at Hastech, the print equipment company. At the end of 1985 he was setting up a 'direct-input' system at the *Liverpool Post and Echo* in a confrontational atmosphere similar to that at Messenger in 1982.)

Shah left the day-to-day management to Doyle and Hart and remained in his old Altrincham office. The first few months of the new operation were quite peaceful as the typesetting work was gradually transferred from Carlisle. The first production staff were: Steve Penny and Kevin Sherrin on keyboard (the former subsequently went into management and is still working at Messenger, the latter became one of the striking 'six'); Paul Wilkowski on paste-up, who also joined the management but left in 1982; and Alan Royston on camera and paste-up, who was the NGA Foc when the strike began in 1983. Three more staff – Phil Daniels, Neil McAllister and John Noble – soon joined from the *Cumbrian News*. Phil Daniels remembers the atmosphere: 'It was chaos, like a madhouse. People were doing a bit of everything: keyboards, process camera, paste-up. They didn't seem to have any idea.'

Steve Hart puts a different view: 'Yes, it was highly flexible, not a nine to five operation at all. There were a lot of talented people making their way.' The first casualty of this flexible culture was the nominal managing director, George Doyle. He had come down from Carlisle but, like the three printers, had not moved house. According to Hart: 'Shah just felt he wasn't committed enough. A newspaper traditionalist, he probably couldn't adjust to the different pace and style. He returned to Carlisle after about a month.'

Originally the Stockport NGA chapel worked a four-day week of two 12-hour days and two 8-hour days, but soon attempts were being made to force production into the first three days and nights of the week so that Wilkowski, Daniels, McAllister and Noble could return to Carlisle on Thursdays. This meant working a tough 16-hour day on Tuesdays. Shah recalls: 'On a Tuesday night it was like Dante's inferno in there. It really was hard work to get the papers out on time. But I worked in drama where you finish the show – papers are no different.'

The chapel members could barely complain about the long hours if these had been arranged for their own convenience. However, towards the end of the first year serious grievances were beginning to emerge, initially about alleged broken promises and secret deals. Alan Royston says: 'Shah demanded total commitment – it felt like we were working all day and night. I thought of getting out after a few weeks, but they were always saying it was going to improve, it would be like working for yourselves or for a national paper – everyone was made different promises. Shah was such a charmer, he would put his arms round you and say "What's the trouble?" It was quite effective.'

Daniels and most of the others were promised promotion into management or profit-sharing – which never came. Daniels was also promised a car which he did eventually receive but which was then taken back by the company.

The second problem concerned Shah's apparent bending of the union rules. According to Royston, a stronger union man than most of the others, Shah seemed to think he had been granted carte blanche from the NGA branch to make his own rules. Royston says that the statutory 8-hour minimum break between shifts was ignored, non-union tele-ad staff were brought in to read proofs and a large amount of advertising work was being used which did not carry the NGA sticker (to indicate that it is from a recognised house).

Shah was becoming equally – if not more – exasperated. Before the end of the year, harsh words had been exchanged on several occasions. He possibly began to wish he had taken the advice of his two directors and so avoided a direct relationship with the 'bloody union'. It was not just the shock of a challenge to his authority that irked him; it was also the refusal of some of the NGA members to join in the Messenger camaraderie. They saw themselves as workers paid to do a job and didn't want to sing the company song.

Steve Hart says: 'Some of the people, probably through no fault of their own, did not want to join the Messenger family. To Shah you are either a Messenger person or you are not – there was a unity there from the van drivers to the journalists. But some of the NGA people felt uncomfortable about that, it wasn't really part of the industry's tradition, and it used to upset Shah. For example, every time we hit a new weekly revenue point – £20,000, £30,000, £40,000 – there would be little parties but a guy like Royston who saw himself as a real "working-class hero" never came along.'

Helen Graham, who was chairman of Shah's Stockport typesetting company, says: 'We were very open but it became clear that they weren't like the rest of us. The NGA rulebook was always coming out – there was just automatic distrust of management. We thought it would improve but it just got worse.'

Simon Haworth, the journalists' Foc, tells the same story: 'When the NGA people came in it was all: we can't do this, we can't do that, just a completely different set of attitudes. You could feel the tension very soon.'

The arguments did not yet develop into open conflict. The Stockport NGA officials, when they heard of the unrest at Messenger, were keen to dampen it down with the promise of a new press still being dangled before them. They were probably encouraged by the 10 per cent pay rise Shah implemented in April 1981, putting NGA staff on £170.50 a week.

After the initial skirmishes of 1980 Shah was not seen

around the Stockport office for about nine months. When he next appeared, in the autumn of 1981, he was putting the finishing touches to an ambitious expansion plan for 1982. It included his own printing press (he was still at that time printing in Carlisle) and a new paper and second typesetting operation in Bury.

Had he already decided to take on the NGA? Shah does not deny that for many months before the dispute erupted he had been planning his 'escape route'. But was the planning of non-union typesetting in Bury with a printing press nearby a defensive measure to strengthen his bargaining position with the union – or was it a consciously offensive strategy simply to throw off the Stockport NGA?

When the scheming began – on Steve Hart's admission as early as autumn 1981 – it was probably a defensive move but by mid-1982 as relations with the NGA deteriorated and Shah's confidence grew, the line between offensive and defensive tactics became blurred. (A similar blurring marked Rupert Murdoch's strategy in Fleet Street at the end of 1985).

When, at the end of 1981, Steve Hart told the NGA members that Shah proposed to buy some new computerised typesetting equipment for Stockport, the chapel's immediate response was that pay increases would be necessary. Hart also asked if they would – at least initially – produce the new Bury paper in overtime for a trial six-week period. The answer was noncommittal.

On 26 November Shah wrote at length to Arthur Scott, the Stockport NGA branch secretary, saying there would be no expansion as planned at Stockport because of the chapel's intransigence. The order for a new press for Stockport was also cancelled. He ran through a list of grievances, concluding: 'As we would rather expend our energies in expanding our business, thus ensuring job security for those already employed by us, as well as future employees, we feel that this cannot be achieved any further with the Stockport Chapel which is led by those few disruptive elements.'

Christmas 1981 produced one of the most famous 'tales' about Shah's relationship with the union. A few hours before Shah's lavish annual Christmas party, he says he was approached by one of the NGA staff and asked if they could be paid overtime for attending the party. Shah remembers this as a 'moment of truth', when he suddenly saw how ludicrous the union's stance had become. Alan Royston smiles knowingly when he hears the story again and says: 'I just don't know where he gets these events from.'

At the start of 1982 the pace quickened. Shah called a meeting of all the seventy Messenger staff – minus the eleven journalists and the NGA – to tell them he had bought a printing press, ironically from the Co-operative Press in Manchester where much of the trade union movement's printing had been done. He was installing it at the Winwick Quay estate in Warrington rather than in Stockport, a fact to be kept from the NGA.

At the same time Shah and Frankland began clearing office space in Silver Street, Bury, in preparation for the launch of the *Bury Messenger*. Two months later, tentative discussions began with the NGA West Pennine branch, which covers Bury, about another typesetting agreement. Meanwhile, at Stockport, several months of intermittent negotiations over a new NGA house agreement were coming to a head.

These three separate issues were to coalesce over the next year to produce the famous dispute. They were: the NGA's exclusion from the proposed typesetting company in Bury and the printing operation in Warrington and the search for the new house agreement in Stockport. By the end of the fraught year Shah had secured his 'escape route'.

The main issue in the house agreement was an attempt to reschedule working hours. A tentative agreement was reached with the chapel but approval had to be given by the Stockport branch. On 29 March 1982 Tony Burke came into the Stockport office and told Hart, as Shah was no longer speaking to him, that the provisional agreement was not acceptable. But Hart also had a surprise for Burke. He informed him that the company already had a provisional closed-shop agreement with the West Pennine NGA branch for typesetting the *Bury Messenger* at £145 a week – £25 a week below the Stockport rate.

Hart wanted regular transfer of work between Stockport and Bury, which Burke would not accept: 'Obviously we said if there was a plague of locusts and the whole building fell down there would have to be transfer but what we wanted was a formal limit on it.' After Burke's firm stand on transfer, Hart cancelled the closed-shop agreement with the NGA West Pennine branch, much to the irritation of Owen Coop, the branch secretary. Meanwhile, there had been little progress on the Stockport house agreement as Hart insisted on the right to transfer to Bury as a condition of a new hours agreement. Shah now laid down an ultimatum: agree by September or Stockport will be closed.

Since May 1982, a brand-new – and highly advanced – computerised setting system had been installed at Bury. Hart began to train three women typists – hired on three-month rolling contracts – to operate it. 'We were flabbergasted by how good they were,' he remembers. 'We began to see the possibility of working with non-NGA inputters but in an NGA context – getting the best of both worlds.'

The system was a simple, standard word processor with a phototypesetter attached. It was produced by a small Derby company, Commercial Graphics, whose managing director was a man called Ian Burns. Burns had been in touch with Shah since the beginning of the year and had convinced him that his 'Page-Planner' system represented a breakthrough in newspaper production. Shah was not difficult to win round and even became an agent for the system. Burns' system ultimately proved problematic but it had increased Shah's awareness of the immense possibilities of the new technology and the two men discussed at great length its political implications for the industry.

Burns, who was friendly with John Ibbotson, soon to become the NGA deputy general secretary, also acted as an important go-between for Shah with the NGA hierarchy in Bedford. In retrospect, it looks as if he was buying Shah more valuable time to win his independence.

On 3 September 1982, at a crucial meeting at the Cresta Court Hotel in Altrincham, a new house agreement was finally signed. By now John Ibbotson had become involved and – perhaps having some inkling of Shah's intentions – he managed to persuade Tony Burke and Phil Daniels (who was then Foc) to accept a deal that gave the management most of what they wanted.

Shah was not present at the negotiations – but was in constant touch with Helen Graham by telephone. He now sees that meeting as the real turning-point: 'We were saying by then "We've got to take them on, we've got to take them on" – but we weren't quite ready at that point. We couldn't have produced without them and yet we still got agreement to virtually everything we wanted. I must say I was against pushing them too hard but Helen – who is a much better negotiator than me – realised they were giving.'

Ironically it was the NGA's concessions which pushed Messenger over the brink into open combat. 'We realised the emperor had no clothes. We had been the vulnerable ones but now we realised we could do it – they weren't invincible,' says Shah.

Non-union typesetting had already begun in Bury in August and the NGA had been slow in responding to it. But on 19 November Owen Coop, John Ibbotson and Frank Walsh, the NGA northern regional official, gathered again at the Cresta Court Hotel to hear an extraordinary plan from Shah. Frank Walsh remembers: 'What he was saying was quite revolutionary – he said he wanted a new type of agreement for Bury in which people could have the option of whether to join the union or not. He also wanted all keyboarding to be done by non-NGA staff.'

Shah's name was first heard around the national council chamber at the NGA's Bedford headquarters on 15 December. He sounded like another candidate for the union-busting league, along with T. Bailey Forman. Only the Messenger issue was potentially more serious. The 1980 and 1982 Employment Acts were now in force and Shah had already hinted to the chapel that he might have recourse to them. Mike Grierson – Shah's solicitor – confirms they had been discussing this as early as 1981 and had indeed decided to split the Messenger into different companies to increase the NGA's vulnerability to unlawful secondary action. They certainly did not stumble across the new laws as Shah sometimes implied during the height of the conflict.

The NGA had under-estimated Shah. He cannot bear being patronised and had always felt that the union officials – used to negotiating with national newspaper employers – had treated him with some disdain.

The resentment he felt towards the union was now compounded by what he saw as its insensitivity towards his wife Jennifer's illness. December 9th brought another 'moment of truth'. It was the day Jennifer nearly died; her temperature was rising and falling alarmingly and Shah says union officials were constantly trying to get hold of him by telephone at Christie Hospital in Manchester.

The NGA defends itself by saying that, while sympathising with Shah's position, it also felt he was using the illness as an excuse for avoiding meetings. On more than one occasion, Shah was alleged to be out playing golf when he cancelled a meeting, saying he had to go to the hospital.

But the union was already on the defensive. They could, and perhaps should, have quietly retreated, drawn a ring-fence around the *Messenger* as they had done with a few other small non-union operators, and carried on with business as usual elsewhere. But too many people in the industry would have interpreted such a retreat as a sign of weakness.

The other option open to the NGA at the end of 1982 and start of 1983 – that of pulling out the Stockport members – did not look promising either. Alan Royston, when summoned to the NGA headquarters before Christmas, said that to take action now was probably too late.

Shah had by December 1982 also started non-union printing at Warrington. It was not easy in those early weeks, as he recalls: 'We were standing there in this plant in Warrington, our eyes were running, trying to get this bloody press working and it got worse and worse, and I was thinking "Where am I going to print it?"' But apart from a brief return to Carlisle, they managed.

The union was forced to grasp at straws. Shah had allowed Owen Coop to speak to the Bury staff about joining the union – but they had been hired in the expectation of a union dispute so none were likely to be sympathetic.

The NGA's vulnerability to the emerging new ground rules of the newspaper industry was again exposed. The union, used to the automatic discipline of the closed shop, was unaccustomed to having to sell itself. Coop made a hash of the presentation and was then faced with a barrage of what he believed to be specially rigged hostile questions.

One of the aggressive questioners was John Hart – Steve Hart's younger brother – who now works as an electronic page-layout specialist at *Today*. His individual history graphically illustrates the NGA's problem. He had always wanted to follow his father and elder brother into the printing industry but, in the late 1970s, there were only a tiny number of apprenticeships available at *Cumbrian News*. If John Hart had been offered one, he would no doubt have become a perfectly contented NGA member – perhaps even a local official. To get work in the industry, however, he had been forced into the anti-NGA fold.

Nobody joined the union after Coop's presentation and it is surprising that the NGA did not pull out its members in Stockport at once. Instead they continued to handle work destined for the non-union staff in the typesetting unit in Bury and the printing works in Warrington.

Shah was actively encouraging his NGA staff to take strike action. On 11 June they were even required to paste-up advertisements for their own jobs on the *Messenger*. Tony Dubbins and John Ibbotson now decided that action must be taken to press, belatedly, for a closed shop in Bury and Warrington and they gave Shah a deadline – settle by 22 June or face industrial action. Finally, on 4 July, American Independence Day, the NGA pulled out its eight members in Stockport.

When national attention later focused on Messenger, Shah liked to repeat that the dispute had just 'evolved'. In a sense it had evolved over the previous two-and-a-half years but Shah, in the latter stages, also had a very clear strategy guiding his actions. The object of that strategy was to establish the right to manage. The immediate cause of the strike was, it is true, a row over the closed shop, but that was just one element of a more fundamental argument about control. Shah could only claim the right to unqualified management control by breaking the NGA's hold and that necessitated hiring his own staff and refusing the closed shop.

Phil Daniels was on holiday in France when the strike began. Sitting on the beach one afternoon he recalls: 'I said to this couple, I said, when I get back I am going to be on strike, and the fellow I work for is going to be the first one to use these new acts that have been introduced by Tebbit and Thatcher.'

Shah was well aware that pulling their members out at Stockport was only the first, and probably the least effective, instrument in the NGA's dispute locker. Far more damaging were the 'blacking' instructions that went out to studios supplying the Messenger titles with advertising material and, indeed, the pressure put on the advertisers themselves not to use the Messenger: 'An act which would be appreciated by members of the Association working on other newspapers and who may be handling your work,' as the NGA circular expressed it. A few advertisers – including the Co-op – did pull out.

At the first sign of such pressure Shah was ready to use the new laws on secondary action. In early June he actually wrote to Dubbins and warned him that he intended to do so. Later that month he further strengthened his position with ballots of the non-NGA staff at Bury and Warrington which overwhelmingly rejected the closed shop.

The 'Stockport Six' began picketing the Stockport office at Victoria House, Stockport: Daniels, Royston, Sherrin, Noble, McAllister and Stan Hart. The other two NGA members, Dave Owens and Brian Dean, briefly joined the strike but after a few weeks crossed the picket line and went back to work. None of the six had ever been on strike for more than a few days before and at first they stood looking rather awkward, as if unsure of what they were trying to achieve. The feeling between the pickets and the rest of the workforce was initially an odd mixture of joviality and bitterness.

The NGA wrote to Dickinson of Cumbrian Newspapers and May of CCN, asking them to withdraw themselves and their company's investments from Messenger. Dickinson replied that he had tried to dissuade Shah from confrontation but to no avail. May's response was that the CCN stake had already been sold and he was on the point of leaving the board anyway.

The union's next step was to pressurise Reed International into selling the 49 per cent stake it had taken (through its subsidiary St Régis Newspapers) in the *Bury Messenger*. It used old-fashioned secondary action at the *Daily Mirror* (then owned by Reed) and the company sold its stake to Shah for £1.

Shah then took the first legal plunge and obtained a Manchester High Court writ alleging that Reed had been induced by the NGA to repudiate a contract to invest £33,000 in the *Bury Messenger*. This was potentially secondary action under the 1980 Employment Act and Shah sought damages of £13,000 from the union under Section 15 of the 1982 Employment Act. It is an action that never came to court but Mike Grierson now admits they would probably not have won.

Two years later, Shah hinted that the hundreds of hours of intense negotiation over the next twenty weeks were a charade and that he never really had any intention of letting the NGA back into Messenger. At the time things did not seem so clear-cut. Indeed, in the second week of the dispute Shah asked Dubbins and Ibbotson for a meeting. It was a surprisingly friendly, rather philosophical, discussion about the closed shop at the end of which the NGA made the considerable concession, in its terms, of suggesting a closed shop at Bury and Warrington in which only half the relevant staff would be in the union, thus allowing Shah to accommodate those genuinely anti-union employees.

The NUJ Stockport chapel now found itself briefly in the eye of the storm. In a bewildering succession of about-turns between early August and October, it acted as a punch-bag between the two sides. In the process, the NUJ had to bear the first serious round of legal action from Shah who attempted to break the NUJ head-office pressure on the chapel to support the NGA. Initially the eleven *Messenger* journalists had agreed to observe the inter-union niceties, whatever their personal feelings about the print union: they went to work but did not hand their material to the non-union printing staff. When this proved ineffectual, Tony Dubbins wrote to Ken Ashton, then NUJ general secretary, and warned him that relations between the two unions would be broken off unless more effective action was taken. The journalists then started doing no work at all.

In early September, coincidentally as the TUC met in Blackpool for Len Murray's 'new realism' congress, Shah was granted an interim injunction restraining the NUJ from inducing its members unlawfully to break their contracts of employment at Messenger. He now told the journalists that unless they disobeyed the union instructions and returned to normal working, he would seek sequestration of the union's funds.

In a flurry of meetings over the next few days and weeks, the chapel would narrowly decide to return to work, only to be persuaded by a national official – often later the same day – to come out again. (Curiously, one of the leading supporters of a return to work – according to NUJ northern organiser Colin Bourne – was a man named Steve Hammond, a member of a small breakaway sect of the Workers Revolutionary Party. Before joining the *Messenger* he had actually been working on the WRP paper *Newsline* for some years. When, at his interview, he was asked where he had worked previously and had replied 'for a revolutionary working-class paper', Helen Graham's reply was alleged to be, 'Oh well, can you start on Monday?')

The NUJ was found to be in contempt on 16 September 1983 but saved from a major showdown with the law by the chapel's decision to return to work on 19 September. Finally, at the beginning of October, seven out of the eleven journalists were persuaded by the leadership of the NGA to stop working again and they all lost their jobs.

Inside the *Messenger*, meanwhile, a new pattern of life

had grown up and the paper kept coming out despite the dispute. The improvisation was even more hectic than usual and the quality did undoubtedly suffer from the absence of experienced NGA staff. A few more young staff were taken on to fill the gaps and the union claimed they were paid nearly £70 a week less than its own members. That was probably true in the case of the unskilled seventeen-year-olds – but £100 a week was still a good wage for someone of that age and the more experienced staff continued to earn as much as, if not more than, the NGA employees.

By mid-October a fair amount of common ground appeared to have been reached between the two sides. Shah said he had, in principle, no objection to the closed shop for all future staff as long as staff members, whom he had told would not have to join the union, could continue to work. But the union officials recall that Shah, without their experience of negotiating, had a tendency to wander off the point during talks and to make suggestions which he would later withdraw. 'He was always moving the goal posts,' said Tony Dubbins. The NGA officials came to believe he had already taken the leap into the non-union universe and the talks were for public relations purposes. They were probably right.

The main stumbling-block remained re-employment of the 'six' and it was to press that point that the dispute now entered its final physical stage. It was prefaced by a 600-strong rally on 27 October in Manchester's New Century Hall, at which the union staked out its moral ground on the victimisation of six lonely workers and its opposition to a law which did not allow the traditional support of one group of workers for another.

The 'six' were certainly no longer alone on the picket line. Through September and October the line had gradually swelled with visiting delegations from other branches, unemployed members, and the ubiquitous ultra-left paper-sellers. On 1 November the first mass

133

picket was staged at Stockport, involving about two hundred people.

On 9 November the pickets were presented with their only opportunity for outmanoeuvring the police. A crowd of about three hundred gathered at Stockport very early that Wednesday morning and boarded coaches that the police expected to go to Bury. In fact they went to Warrington for the pickets' first visit to the Winwick Quay estate where, that afternoon, the presses would start the weekly print-run. There were eventually about five hundred people facing a single policeman. (Much of the local force was busy policing a peace demonstration at Burtonwood airfield five miles away.)

It was a calm and orderly gathering during the day, with many senior print union officials making speeches. But in the early evening a bizarre, spontaneous ritual began which must have been terrifying for the nine members of Shah's staff inside the plant. It started with a few people smashing windows and pulling off pieces of plastic piping. A group of printers then began kicking at the metal shell of the factory unit and soon struck up a regular thumping rhythm. Others responded and picked up whatever they could find to beat in time against the aluminium walls. It was like a large open-air 'banging out' – the customary ceremony when a printer retires.

Eddie Shah, the man for whom this din was intended, was twenty-five miles away in Bury. In many respects his career was just beginning. On 9 November 1983 very few people had heard of him – six weeks later very few people had not. The mass picketing, the court cases, the meetings at ACAS, and the NGA's eventual retreat from the Messenger dispute, provided Shah with the perfect launching pad for his next remarkable step.

9

A Secret Year

'I think the City is actually as bad as the unions in the way this country is run. They're only interested in their percentage.'

Eddie Shah

9

A Secret Year

The national newspaper industry's short and chequered history has been dominated by exceptionally rich eccentrics who in turn have found themselves increasingly dominated by the even more eccentric laws of national newspaper economics.

It would have seemed faintly ridiculous to hear, in early 1984, that Eddie Shah, who had been running the twentieth-largest free newspaper group in the country, was seriously proposing to promote himself to this élite club and at the same time invent a new set of economic laws.

The club has seen some hectic musical chairs over the past seventy years. But the continuities are more remarkable than the changes and small businessmen like Shah have never even got on to the waiting-list for membership. Indeed, membership fees have risen so high in the past twenty years that many long-standing members have reluctantly resigned.

Consequently, many of Fleet Street's proudest, independent, family-owned titles have been forced to find shelter in the dubious embrace of large multinational conglomerates seeking a little prestige. It has been an unwelcome step that has compromised editorial independence and provided a financial crutch rather than an invigorating reform of the business.

Following the recent change of ownership at the *Daily Telegraph*, only the *Guardian* and *Daily Mail* retain any strong links with their corporate roots; and the *Mail*'s parent company had the foresight to spread its interests out of newspapers a long time ago. The rest are either relatively small parts of diversified communications empires such as Robert Maxwell's British Printing and Communications Corporation, and Rupert Murdoch's News International; or, like *The Observer* since it was acquired by Tiny Rowland, they are even smaller parts of wider conglomerates.

Some things have changed less. Although public corporations have, generally, superseded family-run firms they are corporations upon which one man has a dominant stamp, as the above shows. These 'new press barons', like the old ones, have usually aspired to control of papers as a route to respectability and influence as much as business success.

Shah had different ideas. He saw launching a new paper as an intoxicating commercial opportunity. A chance, too, to scatter the members of the Fleet Street club by breaking in through the back door. As he said recently: 'In a world that has changed immeasurably in almost every way in the last fifty years, the printing of newspapers in Britain stands out as one of the very last bastions of low technology. It is astonishing that nobody has taken the bull by the horns before now: every other country in the world changed their production processes long ago. It is in every way a classic marketing opportunity.'

It may have been an idea whose time had come but in February 1984 – just as the miners' strike was gathering momentum – Shah peered over the edge of a gaping credibility gap. At a time when the impact of the Government's trade union laws had not yet properly sunk in, the idea of a non-union, greenfield site, national paper was still met with the stock response that the unions would crush it. And if it *was* feasible, then surely someone bigger than Shah would have tried it by now? Shah's reputation as the victor of Warrington was a strength and a selling-point – but it was also a weakness. He was a dangerous fellow.

He quickly needed to find a reliable nucleus of consultants to help fill the large gaps in his knowledge and experience, raise several million pounds for what was bound to appear a highly risky venture, start thinking of buying a whole new generation of newspaper equipment, find premises, and even think of hiring staff. The scale of the task at the start of the 'secret year' made the 'great game', as Shah came to call it, even more exhilarating. But it became a journey which was to demand an extreme concentration of effort. He never dreamed it would take as long, and so hopeless did the prospect seem on at least two occasions that he seriously considered going to America to raise the money or giving up completely.

The year was also an education in high finance for Shah which left him with a strongly critical view of the investment institutions in the City and an extra stone in weight thanks to the endless lunches and the good living in London's top hotels.

'At the beginning we literally thought "who's got so much money they wouldn't mind having a little flutter on a good idea like ours?" We read the papers, racked our brains and flicked the pages of *Who's Who*,' says Shah.

Aside from the eventual backers, the list of individuals contacted does indeed read like a top business *Who's Who*, and includes: Lord Weinstock, managing director of GEC, the UK's largest industrial company; Sir Michael Edwardes, the former boss of BL and now chairman of Chloride; Gerald Grosvenor, the Duke of Westminster and reputedly the richest man in Britain; and Sir Hector

Laing, chairman of United Biscuits. Shah even thought of writing to his relative, the Aga Khan.

Initially Shah's contacts and confidants in the money-raising quest were rather less elevated figures such as Ian Templeton, his accountant. Templeton is a suave 44-year-old, a founding partner in the Manchester firm of Elliott, Templeton & Sankey. The son of a Manchester GP, he was educated at Campbell College, an Ulster public school, and Manchester University. He is an accountant attracted to broad-brush projects like Shah's, who likes to delegate the detail.

Templeton says that surprisingly few people had contacted Shah during the dispute. This was partly because he was not a member of any of the local employers' organisations and not on the Manchester media circuit. Some local employers were in fact positively hostile to Shah. But one national paper manager in Manchester whom Shah had consulted in the past said more sadly during the dispute: 'I'm sorry, Eddie, I can't help you now you're way off the fairway and into the long grass.'

Several of those who did make contact during the fraught weeks of late 1983 were to play important roles in the ensuing year; in particular, Andrew Neil, Lord Harris of Greenwich, the SDP peer and former Labour minister, and Norris McWhirter, editor of the *Guinness Book of Records* and chairman of the right-wing Freedom Association which had been battling against the closed shop for ten years.

One less welcome call came from Robert Maxwell several months before he bought the Mirror Group. He was worried about the Messenger dispute's destabilising effect on the whole print industry, of which he owns a large chunk. He phoned Shah at ACAS and told him, somewhat hypocritically in the light of more recent events, that he should not behave in such a way in a democratic country. Shah became irritable and the conversation concluded with him slamming down the phone. A few minutes later Maxwell was back on the line. A voice boomed out: 'By the way, Mr Shah, I've got balls too.' Later, through a third party, he offered to buy Messenger for £3.5m.

Andrew Neil's warning – and the NGA's hope – that the Establishment would lean on Shah had been unusually personified by Maxwell. Harris, on the other hand, the former adviser to Hugh Gaitskell and Roy Jenkins, had become in Shah's words 'the only real member of the establishment to back us right from the start'.

Harris visited him in Bury on 17 November. 'I just wanted to make sure he was not a right-wing nut or a punch-up artist and he struck me as an entirely decent, liberal-minded chap fighting an important cause,' says Harris, who bears a striking resemblance in speech and mannerism to his old boss Roy Jenkins. A few days later he led a debate on the dispute in the House of Lords.

He was one of the first members of the Shah entourage to receive the full telephone treatment – several calls a day, often at strange times, from cars, hotels, offices, or home. Harris, 55, a lordly Mr Fixit, who is now chairman of a job creation consultancy, was back in his element. He joined the Messenger board in January 1984 and was soon to find an important role smoothing Shah's passage into parts of the London establishment. His friendship with Michael Mockridge, a senior partner in the law practice Coward Chance, also ensured Shah the support of highly respected City lawyers.

If Harris, the Gaitskellite Social Democrat who ran Labour's publicity department from 1962–4 and joined the SDP sixteen years later, can be seen as the mildly left-wing conscience of *Today*, Norris McWhirter provides a blast from the libertarian Right. McWhirter, 60, was to play a more background role, however. The former broadcaster and Olympic athlete, whose twin brother Ross was shot dead outside his London home by the Provisional IRA in 1975, knows a little about newspapers as his father, William McWhirter, edited three nationals – the *Daily Mail*, *Sunday Pictorial* and

Sunday Dispatch. Educated at Marlborough and Oxford, McWhirter is an admirer of Margaret Thatcher and well-known in right-wing business circles, another connection that Shah was to benefit from.

Towards the end of February 1984, a few days after his meeting with Andrew Neil at the Savoy, and after long discussions with his wife and Helen Graham, Shah had decided to throw his weight into the project. He says: 'I knew it was possible half an hour after that meeting at the Savoy and it was then that I really decided to do it. I'm part Eastern you see and that gives me great faith! If something is meant to be then it will be.'

A few days later he told John Harris of the plan; Harris responded: 'I knew immediately that a greenfield site project was an excellent idea and very well timed.' Templeton said: 'Anything is possible if you're sufficiently behind it.' One of the financial modellers from Templeton's firm, Steve Ellwood, was put on to the figures with Mike Frankland, Shah's finance director at Messenger. At the same time Shah worked on a business plan.

On 4 March they had their first meeting. Templeton told Shah: 'We're just going to sell you. Without you, people will not look twice at it – they'll just laugh at the figures.' Shah officially announced the plan to a Messenger board meeting on 16 March. One of the few people on the board who would not have known by then was Roy Dickinson, 57, now managing director of Cumbrian Newspapers in Carlisle.

Shah had already decided he wanted Dickinson as his production director, the post he had filled at Carlisle when Shah started printing the *Messenger* there in 1975. Shah says: 'Roy has taught me all I know about newspapers.' He is a friendly, highly-strung man who is overshadowed by Shah but claims he knows how to 'handle' him. After that board meeting he talked to his wife and decided to join Shah if he could raise the money.

It was Dickinson who first suggested using a franchise system for distributing the new paper and as a way of avoiding its probable blacking by the existing union-dominated wholesale distribution system. Shah at that point had not thought very seriously about distribution; his initial circulation aim, however, was in the region of 500,000. Colour was not yet a priority but regionalised printing was.

At the end of March Shah flew to the US and back to raise £50,000 for the cancer appeal at Christie Hospital where his wife had been treated. Soon after his return in early April, he had one of his first meetings with an equipment supplier. Tony Stalker, the UK general manager of Hastech, the American-controlled direct-input systems producer, visited Shah at home. He just happened to drop into the Messenger office in early 1984 to see his old friend Steve Hart when Shah spotted the Hastech sticker on his case and asked him to send him some estimates. Stalker found Shah 'a mercurial man to deal with'. He left him waiting for almost a year before placing an order with Hastech for equipment worth £1.5m.

Towards the end of March, Peter Sanderson, deputy manager of Lloyds Bank's regional headquarters in Manchester, received one of the most bizarre requests of his career when a well-known Warrington customer bounced into the bank and asked him how to raise the money to start a new national paper. Shah had no idea how to go about such a fund-raising exercise. Sanderson referred him to the Lloyds merchant bank – Lloyds Bank International (LBI) – merchant banks being the traditional coordinators of money-raising on this scale.

The first serious finance meeting came in April when Shah met Richard Fortin, a director, and Derek Ablett, a senior assistant director, at LBI. 'They were rather pompous,' Shah remembers, 'it was all "well we can see the advantages, but, but, but".' They were of more use in Templeton's recollection, suggesting a full 'long form'

143

report on Messenger and the national paper scheme by a firm of accountants who had no existing newspaper commitments. 'Of course we had to wait several weeks before they actually came back with the name of Thomson McLintock,' says Shah.

Ian Templeton also wanted to bounce the idea off a few stockbrokers he knew so that afternoon they had a brief and positive meeting with Bob Lederman of Capel Cure Myers and a less positive meeting at Hoare Govett at which, however, the idea of setting up a separate company for the new paper was suggested for the first time. The two fund-raising options appeared to be either to float the Messenger Group on the stock exchange and raise cash through selling shares in it or simply find a merchant bank which would find investors to put cash up front.

If there was a point in Shah's mind after which there was no turning back, it was in early June when he visited the USA for the American Newspaper Publishers Association conference in Atlanta and saw in action some of the sophisticated systems he was soon to buy. He spoke to *USA Today* about their satellite printing and began to realise the enormous importance of colour.

But there was no hint of the still top-secret project when he made his first public appearance since the dispute at the conference of the Institute of Directors in London on 21 June. He spoke in the language of a disappointed Thatcherite radical who had breached the enemy lines only to see them close again behind him – this was the time of the miners' mass pickets – and he also had a swipe at the Government's refusal to use its own laws against the NUM. He received a warm enough reception from the IoD (which had also provided useful support and advice during the dispute) but his bitterness was no doubt enhanced by the failure of a few merchant bankers and stockbrokers to pour millions of pounds into his project. However, the fund-raising was soon to be placed on firmer ground with the completion of

The Shah family in 1956 at their home near Haywards Heath. *From left to right*, Shah's father Moochool; his mother Hazel with the youngest child Mary; Shah himself aged twelve and dressed in his prep school uniform; Fatima and Toomani.

Shah with his eldest son Martyn and wife Jennifer in front of the plane in which he crossed the Atlantic to raise money for Cancer Research. (*Manchester Evening News*)

Tony Dubbins, NGA General Secretary. (*Financial Times*)

NGA officials hurriedly removing Apple computer equipment from the union's Bedford head office, after the High Court had ordered the first major sequestration of a union's assets. (*Press Association*)

August 1983, before the storm: lawful and peaceful picketing of the Stockport Messenger office by the original 'Stockport Eight': *from left to right*, Neil McAllister, John Noble, Dave Owens, Kevin Sherrin, Alan Royston, Stan Hart, Phil Daniels and Brian Dean. Soon after this picture was taken Dave Owens and Brian Dean returned to work. (*John Smith, IFL*)

November 1983: pickets huddle together for warmth outside
Shah's Warrington print plant on the Winwick Quay estate.
(*John Smith, IFL*)
Police in hokey-cokey formation after the seizure of the NGA's
'battle-wagon' on the night of 29th-30th November 1983.
(*Financial Times*)

Police clear a path for the newspaper vans during a violent night
of unlawful mass picketing. (*Financial Times*)

'This should do the trick!' (*Peter Brookes/The Times*)

Andrew Neil, editor of the *Sunday Times*. (*Camera Press*)

Lord Forte, chairman of Trusthouse Forte. (*Financial Times*)

Left: Mr Norris McWhirter, editor of the Guinness Book of Records and chairman of the Freedom Association. (*Press Association*)

Below left: Lord Harris of Greenwich, one-time Personal Assistant to Hugh Gaitskell. (*Terry Kirk, Financial Times*)

Below right: Sir Richard Storey, chairman of the Portsmouth and Sunderland Newspaper Group. (*Press Association*)

An old picture of the 'hot-metal' linotype machines still used in the composing-rooms of some Fleet Street papers. In the foreground is the 'stone' where the lines of lead type are set into pages. (*Syndication International*)

A typical modern composing-room with the compositors retyping journalists' copy using photocomposition equipment. (*Hugh Routledge*)

The first-floor newsroom of the *Today* offices: journalists at work on their VDUs. Using 'direct-input' technology, journalists' copy goes straight to setting.

70, Vauxhall Bridge Road, the unprepossessing editorial offices of News UK. (*R. T. Bell*)

Six months before the launch of *Today*, Jonathan Holborow, editor of the daily *Today*, Brian McArthur, editor-in-chief, and Eddie Shah, in the still-to-be-furnished newsroom. (*R. T. Bell*)

New-tech Eddie at his Hewlett-Packard microcomputer.
(*Financial Times*)

The third Aga Khan receiving his followers in Karachi in 1951.
On the far right is Eddie Shah, aged seven. Third from the right
is Shahan Shah, Shah's grandfather. (*Press Association*)

Thomson McLintock's reports. Looking now at the summary of the report on the planned national, produced in October 1984, it is surprising to see how close the original figures are to the final product.

The report established £8.5m. as the equity capital target to be raised for the new company – with another £10m. for the presses and other equipment to be raised through conventional hire purchase and loan agreements.

It also makes clear that Shah had already decided not to distribute in Scotland, initially at least – and was in fact aiming for less than 70 per cent of England and Wales. The circulation estimate which had by then risen to just under 700,000 now appears extremely pessimistic and has indeed been revised upwards, but the profit calculation of £13m. out of an annual revenue of about £50m. was still remarkable for a new national newspaper.

The explanation can be found in Thomson McLintock's dry summary of the project: 'Advertising and editorial content of the newspapers will be prepared by the use of "state of the art", electronic integrated text, graphics and photographic handling systems and will be transmitted simultaneously to four regional print centres.

'The centres will be equipped to print the newspapers, making extensive use of full and spot colour and providing for regionalised editorial and advertising content as required. Distribution will be by road from the print centres to Newco's own network of wholesalers (the franchisees) who will be responsible for onward distribution to newsagents and other retailers. Initially, distribution will be available to at least 68 per cent of the population of England and Wales.

'The whole organisation will be staffed at levels and cost appropriate to the optimum use of the technology available and without regard to existing custom and practice within the newspaper industry. Total number of employees is projected at 487.'

It was estimated that the 124 production staff would be paid an average of £11,320 – only a little more than half the average production wage in Fleet Street; the 127 distribution staff delivering the papers either to franchisees or direct to newsagents averaged £9,600; the 107 editorial staff averaged £34,900 plus expenses – closer to the Fleet Street norm; and another 129 'other' staff, mainly advertising and administrative, averaged £14,200.

The cover price was then estimated at 15p, 3p below the paper's main mid-market rivals like the *Express* and *Mail*. But it was advertising, particularly colour advertising, that provided the paper's real price-cutting thrust. Advertising space in the paper was planned at 38 per cent – close to the mid-market average – but one-quarter would be in colour. The £11.58 'rate per thousand', in advertiser's jargon, costed a colour page at an estimated £8,000 compared with £36,000 in the *Daily Express*. The *Express*'s circulation is nearly three times Shah's then estimate but £3,500 for a black-and-white page compared with £15,300 was still likely to be attractive to advertisers.

Thomson McLintock's report on Messenger made for less exciting reading – indeed showed a company not in the best of health – and the men from LBI started to get cold feet. They were now advising that money could not be raised directly from investors but pushed the idea of a flotation of Messenger on the stock-market. LBI said they would produce a flotation document based upon the report on the new paper which Capel Cure would then take to the market.

Meanwhile David Sainsbury, the supermarket empire's SDP supporter, had responded with a firm 'no' to Harris's tentative fund-raising inquiry. But Harris had also been introducing Shah to a few more people who might be useful. Graham Dowson, the former chief executive of the Rank Organisation who left after a boardroom row in 1974, analysed Shah's figures and advised him to look to the venture capital markets. 'I thought here was someone who might finally have what it takes,' he remembers. Harris also introduced him to Walter Terry, the former political editor of the *Mail*, with whom he had one of his first serious discussions about editorial content and staffing. (Terry is now on the political staff of *Today*).

Shah has a low opinion of Fleet Street journalism and from the start had firm, if ill-defined, ideas about how the paper would, above everything else, be setting new editorial standards. Since his meeting with Andrew Neil he had been aiming for the middle-market but with an emphasis on news 'without the usual political slant and without recourse to titillation and gossip'.

In early August Shah disappeared to Miami for a much-needed holiday with his family. But the paper was clearly never very far from his thoughts. He spent so much of his time calling the UK that his telephone bill alone came to £800. He also bumped into another Englishman on the beach, Ken McIntosh, who was later to provide a link with Rupert Murdoch's senior executive in the UK, Bruce Matthews.

Back in England in mid-September, Shah met Norris McWhirter for the first time at his home in Wiltshire. In retrospect it probably qualifies as the single most important meeting of the 'secret year'. McWhirter had heard vaguely of Shah's plans but he now received a full rundown from him and also heard of his disillusion with the traditional money-raising channels. 'I asked him who are the men with nerve and he told me to try Lord Taylor and Lord Forte,' recalls Shah. McWhirter offered to write to both men – Frank Taylor, president of Taylor Woodrow, the construction group, he knew through the Freedom Association and Charles Forte, chairman of Trust House Forte (THF), the largest hotel and catering group in the world, was an old acquaintance.

On the morning of 8 October Shah visited the eighty-year-old Lord Taylor at 10 Park Street in Mayfair. The meeting was a tremendous boost to Shah's flagging confidence. He had already been talking to Templeton about raising the money in the US if there was no breakthrough by Christmas. Suddenly here was one of Britain's top industrialists shaking him warmly by the hand and showing immediate enthusiasm for the plan. Taylor, the Blackpool-born builder, is well-known for his staunch right-wing politics and his antipathy to unions. Shah's image naturally appealed to him. He said he would look closely at the figures and ask his board about the possibility of an investment.

Between visits to three more merchant banks – Baring Brothers, S. G. Warburg and Hambros – Shah made another much publicised appearance receiving the Aims of Industry 'Man of the Year' award from Mrs Thatcher. Playing down his own inevitable association with Thatcherism, Shah remembers making another speech that was somewhat critical of the Government.

Directly after the Aims of Industry presentation, Shah went along to see Roger Brooke of the venture capital group, Candover Investments, who – as a former director of Pearson Longman owners of the *Financial Times* – had more sympathy than most with the project. Shah found him very helpful and, like Taylor, he had no objection to his name being used as a potential investor to help attract others. (Candover eventually came in with only £100,000 but in the early publicity in the financial press the name was given top billing.)

Shah was keen to attract investment from at least one other newspaper group – both to use its experience and because support from within the industry would be reassuring to outside investors. It obviously could not be a rival national paper. But the two technological pacemakers in the provincial press, the Wolverhampton *Express and Star* and the Portsmouth and Sunderland newspaper group (PSN), both medium-sized, old family businesses, were interested in joining Shah.

In early October Shah rang Sir Richard Storey, chairman of PSN, told him of the plan and asked if he was interested. 'I was hugely intrigued,' recalls Storey. Just a few months before he had himself sketched out a plan in the magazine *Admap* for a satellite-printed national paper – prompted by discussions at the annual newspaper advertising conference in Berlin.

Storey, 49, whose great-grandfather founded the company in 1873, had sent several messages of support to Shah during the dispute through Mike Frankland whom PSN had earlier tried to poach. His company may be an old family firm – but conservatively run it is not. The *Portsmouth News* was one of the first British papers to introduce computerised photocomposition to replace the old hot-metal machinery in 1969 and ever since Storey has been a radical figure in the industry. He had threatened on several occasions to bypass the print unions if they did not cooperate in technical change.

When Storey heard of Shah's plan he may, perhaps, have felt a twinge of jealousy that someone else had finally picked up the Fleet Street gauntlet. 'I have often wondered why nobody had tried it before – why didn't Jocelyn Stevens have a go after he left the *Express*, for example? I suppose the point is that it's much easier to be a creative entrepreneur if – like Shah – you have virtually nothing, no existing corporate responsibilities,' says Storey.

A few weeks later Shah made what was, by all accounts, an impressive presentation of the now well-rehearsed Thomson McLintock document to the senior management at PSN. The company was still in the middle of fraught direct-input negotiations with the NGA, so it took great care to keep the meeting secret.

Storey says: 'We gave a tentative yes but we wanted to know more about the proposed content of the paper and the other backers. We were worried that it could look like some fascist mob out to smash the unions. Because of our own NGA negotiations some members of the board thought it was madness. I thought it was hazardous but worth it.'

Shah had also begun talking to Mark Kersen, managing director at the Wolverhampton *Express and Star*. Kersen's paper was soon to become the first since the pioneering *Nottingham Evening Post* in the mid-1970s to introduce direct-input by journalists despite opposition from the NGA.

At the end of October Alan Graham, son of the Monaco-based chairman of the *Express and Star*, came to see Shah at his home in Mobberley, near Manchester, and offered to invest money in the new paper. Graham, however, like several other rich and established figures whom Shah met that year, seemed to arouse his 'self-made-man's' sensitivity to the airs of the grandees. 'It just didn't work out,' says Shah, describing a typically emotional rejection of what was, after all, one of the first firm offers of financial support.

It serves to underline his deep confidence in the project even at this stage, and opened the way to Portsmouth and Sunderland. Before finally pledging cash Sir Richard wanted Shah to meet his three non-executive directors – Francis Cator of the merchant bankers, Schroder Wagg, Christopher Bedeslow, a QC, and David Waterstone, chief executive of the Welsh Development Agency and a man with wide experience of assessing new business ventures. They were all impressed, and the money – about £½m. – was virtually in the bag.

But it was only a start. On 25 October Shah lost faith in LBI. He left a meeting with Richard Fortin and said to Ian Templeton: 'OK, let's do it ourselves then.' The only thing left was to squabble about the money Shah owed them. He says they billed him for £20,000 and he paid them £700.

Shah had discussed with Templeton, Harris, Dowson and others the possibility of cutting out the middle man and going straight to companies which might invest in him. 'I just decided to go "on the road" with Ian,' says Shah. Templeton recalls: 'We just wanted to find someone who would say "Right, we like it, we will put up £1m. and set up a package bringing in other people."'

Coincidentally that was the next response they received, from Mike Stoddart of Electra, an investment trust. He first proposed raising all the money required, then dropped to £1.5m. Shah remembers Electra as friendly 'but prima donna-ish'. In typical 'told you so' style Shah was later to offer them a mere £100,000 stake. It was insignificant by their standards and Shah knew they would turn it down – as indeed they did.

Most people Shah saw in the City presumably supported the principle of his stand against the NGA – but he believes many were alarmed by his controversial image and frightened of the unions. He says: 'The Scots, though, were a lot better – if we were doing it all again we'd go to Edinburgh first.'

The City is, of course, handling other people's money and the caution with which they viewed Shah's risky project may yet be justified by events. Some of Shah's early presentations were rather confused as he jumped from one point to another and his business track record up to 1984 was not particularly impressive. Indeed, Ian Templeton now says: 'I kept trying to stop Messenger's history being dragged in because it clearly did not help.' Contrary to Templeton's strategy of playing down Messenger, Shah regularly raised the issue by offering to sell the company.

Like the army of 'bloody professionals' (the lawyers and accountants) whom he is always castigating for their incompetence, the City is brushed aside by Shah as another effete and self-interested branch of the Establishment.

It was perhaps rather surprising, therefore, at the end of 1984 to see Shah not only dining frequently at the Reform Club with Harris but actually joining it. Mild controversy appears to have surrounded even this little event, with SDP members providing the bulk of sponsoring signatures and, perhaps surprisingly, only one Tory. Naturally, Shah did not see joining clubland as capitulation to the Establishment. Family sentiment may also have been involved as his grandfather had been a member.

The search for support was now leading Shah and Templeton to look, in Templeton's words, 'for organisations that were quite tightly controlled – without lines of middle management to wade through'. British and Commonwealth (Bricom) fitted the bill perfectly. The enigmatic financial services and transport group – and the leading corporate supporter of the Tory Party – is effectively run by about four men. A meeting with Neil Forster, managing director at Bricom, had been arranged through Graham Elliott, another partner in Elliott, Templeton & Sankey who knew Forster through his directorship of British Midland Airways.

Forster was immediately impressed: 'We thought his presentation was well done and excellently researched.' He adds that although they knew it would be a risk project they were attracted because 'it was a just cause and about time that sanity prevailed in the industry'. Shah's star finally appeared to be in the ascendancy. The day after the meeting with Forster on 1 November Shah had his first formal meeting with Lord Forte at the Grosvenor House Hotel, one of the eight hundred THF hotels he owns worldwide. He had already met him briefly at the Aims of Industry reception, but he now spent forty-five minutes chatting to the intense, 77-year-old, Italian-born tycoon. Forte, probably seeing in Shah some of his own youthful spirit, reminisced about how he had built up his company from a single milk bar in Upper Regent Street in 1935.

Trust House Forte, like Taylor Woodrow and Bricom, is one of the largest corporate donors to the Tory Party – and is also non-union. Forte himself, an engaging combination of Italian patriarch and English country gentleman, has always sought the company of politicians. He is now a Conservative, but has not always been so. Coincidentally, he had first come across Harris when, in the late 1950s, he helped to fund the private office of Hugh Gaitskell the Labour leader.

Forte has often toyed with the idea of breaking into newspapers but his one venture into magazine publishing – with *Investors' Review* and *Time & Tide* – flopped. Curiously, however, on Forte's personal staff is an elderly man named Edward Martell – a leading member of the eccentric right-wing group, the Self-Help Organisation – who during the national newspaper strike of 1955 produced a small-circulation anti-union paper called the *New Leader*, printed by the Kent Messenger Group.

A few days later – through Forte – Shah met Martell and Sir William Rees-Mogg, 57, editor of *The Times* 1967–81, who is now chairman of Sidgwick & Jackson, a publishing subsidiary of THF, and an informal consultant to Forte. Beneath Rees-Mogg's donnish country gentleman's manner is a meticulous mind – which has spent much of the last twenty-five years thinking about the problems of national newspapers. Shah knew he was facing an important test.

Rees-Mogg was impressed. 'I thought he had a good grasp and a good technical knowledge and while he obviously has a lot of entrepreneurial energy he was not a dangerous enthusiast. The figures looked good. We had looked at similar ones during the *Times* dispute.'

Shah had passed the examination and gained a crucial adviser to whom other investors – such as Neil Forster – were directed for a detached, but positive, appraisal. He now felt he was in the home straight of the financial quest – but first came six tense weeks veering between optimism and deepest gloom. The yo-yo began on an up with Taylor, Bricom and THF all very interested. John Menzies, chairman of the newsagents and wholesalers group, who had been introduced by Graham Dowson, was also inquisitive. Shah felt confident enough to tell Lord Weinstock, managing director of GEC, to 'stop interrupting me' at a lunch arranged by Lord Harris.

Weinstock, although interested, decided it would be inappropriate for GEC money to be pledged. Through one of his sons, a private investment was discussed but Shah, sensing – rightly or wrongly – the same condescension he had perceived in the Graham family, declined the help offered.

A week later bad news sent Shah's spirits plummeting. He had just returned from a presentation to the Duke of Westminster at his home, Eaton Hall in Cheshire, when a call came through to the Warrington office from Lord Taylor who, almost apologetic, said it had been decided that Taylor Woodrow could not make an investment. The same afternoon Templeton received a polite rejection from Raymond Slater, owner of Norwest Holst, the construction group.

The depression was dispelled almost immediately by a meeting on 23 November at which two of the potential investors – Donald Main for THF and Neil Forster for Bricom – got together for the first time. Highly provisional pledges of £2m. each appear to have come out of the meeting. With a possible £4m. under his belt, Shah flew home to a Mobberley Conservative Association reception organised by his wife. The local farmers, solicitors and accountants were now quite possibly chatting with Britain's newest national newspaper proprietor.

Shah had by now registered News UK as a company. The name is a conscious reference to News International, the company of Rupert Murdoch – the press baron he is fondest of and most closely models himself on.

On 26 November, Shah met Sir Hector Laing, chairman of United Biscuits and supporter of right-wing causes (he had recently helped set up a fund for working miners). He said he could not help Shah himself but provided financial contacts in Scotland – particularly Charles Fraser a lawyer with more than thirty directorships and a leading light in the Edinburgh financial 'mafia'.

The host of noncommittal responses or rejections Shah was now receiving from, among others, Citicorp, Barclays Merchant Bank, Hambros and Charterhouse Japhet did not worry him too much. On the positive side, Portsmouth and Sunderland were now definite backers and Shah had a very productive meeting with Ian Rushbrook of Atlantic Assets (a subsidiary of Ivory & Sime) introduced by Fraser.

On 27 November Shah had another meeting with the IoD. His description of it confirmed his self-image of the cheeky parvenu teaching the big boys a lesson. 'I called on these guys John Hoskyns, head of the IoD, and Graham Mather, the research guy who I talked to during the dispute, because I wanted to pick their brains – I mean – they're the bloody experts. And the funny thing was they were looking at me to give them the answers – I couldn't tell them what to do – it was crazy.'

Early December found him still riding high although the interest shown by John Menzies was, according to Shah, quashed by the 'conservatives' on his board. No doubt they thought it inappropriate to invest in a company which was committed to setting up a newspaper distribution system in direct competition with their own.

Shah had meanwhile been in touch with a number of transport and distribution companies about possible distribution plans. He commissioned the Australian company TNT to do a full study but when he discovered its indirect links with Rupert Murdoch through shared ownership of Ansett Transport Industries, he pulled out. Ironically, a year later, Murdoch used the same plan for his own alternative distribution network from Wapping.

On 19 December – ten months after that first meeting in the Savoy – Shah met Andrew Neil again for lunch in the Stafford Hotel. There was a lot to tell him. Shah had earlier asked him if he would be his editor and, although attracted by the idea, Neil said he had not been at the

Sunday Times long enough – only about fourteen months at that point.

While they were eating, Michael Heseltine, then Defence Secretary, came and sat at the next table and said a brief hello to Neil. He either did not recognise Shah or deliberately chose not to greet him. Shah's irritation at being, he believed, once again 'snubbed' by the political establishment neatly pinpoints his schizophrenic attitude to power – at once refusing the traditional proprietor's mantle and yet seeking recognition.

The end of December brought a final tug on the yo-yo. The Duke of Westminster's private office informed Shah that he was not interested. But far more of a blow was that a board meeting of Ivory & Sime's Atlantic Assets on 23 December – on which Shah was pinning considerable hope – also rejected a deal partly because John Menzies was chairman and they feared a conflict of interest.

'I was distraught, I thought it had blown at the eleventh hour,' says Shah. But Mark Tyndall of Atlantic Assets suggested trying the other Ivory & Sime investment company – British Assets – which had no Menzies link. A meeting was immediately arranged which left Shah with renewed hope over the Christmas holiday.

In early January 1985 British Assets and the last two major investors were hooked up. Charles Fraser introduced him to Angus Grossart of the Scottish Investment Trust and on a tip-off from Norris McWhirter he had also started talking to the MacAlpine building family.

By the New Year, Shah began to think more seriously about phase two: ordering presses and equipment, looking for sites, editorial and advertising strategies. Through January and February he was shedding one group of advisers and acquiring another. People would inevitably drift in and out of his inner circle according to which part of the operation Shah was concentrating on. He is a good picker of brains and has the charm to persuade people that their opinions on the subject in question matter to him above anything else in the world.

It is a charm which can naturally leave some people with the subsequent feeling of having been used.

But very few people have complained of being so exploited. Out of the many dozens of 'top people' whom Shah contacted, only two decided they did not want to see him or couldn't find the time: Brian Walden, the former Labour MP, now broadcaster and writer of world-weary comment on the state of Britain, and Alan Bristow of Bristow Helicopters.

On 2 January he breakfasted at the Hyde Park Hotel with Ted Blackmore, the former labour relations director of the Mirror Group, who probably knows more about the national newspaper industry and the people who control it than any man alive. Blackmore at the *Mirror*, like Rees-Mogg at *The Times*, had been associated with one of the recent failed attempts to reform Fleet Street. Shah was learning from their mistakes.

Ironically, Blackmore had been contacted by Bryn Griffiths, the NGA president, at the height of the Messenger dispute, suggesting that as an old friend of compromise and reason he might have a word with Shah. Blackmore rang Shah and left his number. Fourteen months later he got a reply but on a very different subject.

Blackmore, a chatty man with a jolly, slightly military manner, has helped Shah on 'everything except the technology', including buying newsprint, possible union pitfalls, costs, cash flow. Once the plan was out in the open, in February 1985, he was also able to report back on Fleet Street management's reaction, which fascinated Shah.

Other men on the scene included Brian Nicholson, 55, who had resigned as joint managing director of *The Observer* in October and Charles Wintour, 68, a former editor of the London *Evening Standard* and now, as editor of the journalists' trade magazine *UK Press Gazette*, pursuing his hobby as the doyen of Fleet Street analysts.

Nicholson's contacts – especially in the advertising

world – are superb. He became advertising manager at the *Sunday Times* in 1957 and a director of the paper from 1962–5. He then spent ten years as a director of Beaverbrook Newspapers – including four years as managing director of the *Standard* where he got to know Wintour.

A chubby, jovial man, Nicholson had been brought into the Shah camp by Graham Dowson after a lunch at Brook's Club. He subsequently met Shah with Sir Richard Storey at the Grosvenor House Hotel on 31 January 1985 and was bowled over by his warmth and exuberance. As with several other apparently hard-headed newspaper men, Shah appeared as a magnificent liberator.

'I left that meeting feeling that everything I had hoped for could be about to happen,' Nicholson remembers. 'When I think of the crazily disproportionate time I have spent in union meetings over the past twenty years it makes me want to cry sometimes. And here was Eddie – with such vitality and drive – I never doubted for a moment it could work. And I wanted to do everything I could to help.'

He immediately wrote Shah a memo on his response to the Thomson McLintock report, supporting the projections and agreeing with Shah that the new paper would be given a tremendous boost by media coverage around the launch but that every penny of the £4m. promotional budget was still vital.

Nicholson was in an excellent position to help Shah, not only arranging informal meetings with members of Fleet Street's advertising and editorial élite, but also more formally through his job at the head-hunting firm Robin Marlar Associates. He immediately began looking for the senior editorial team for the paper.

Nicholson – who is now on the board of News UK along with Harris and Dickinson – is one of Shah's most wholehearted admirers. For some months the two were constantly on the phone to each other and one day they even had a breakfast, lunch and dinner meeting. 'I have an amazing involvement with him – I feel an absolute commitment to him. He's a very charismatic man,' says Nicholson. Shah likes to be believed in.

Wintour, by contrast, remains characteristically cooler and more objective in his appraisal – but he too has provided a great deal of useful advice, particularly on senior editorial appointments, and the *UK Press Gazette* has overflowed with pro-Shah stories under such headlines as 'Irrepressible Eddie'.

In the final weeks of the 'secret year', during the early part of 1985, Shah turned his attention to the financing of the four presses he initially planned to buy, easily the biggest single element in the start-up costs. They were looking for a straightforward loan-financing agreement – but it proved difficult to find.

For a few weeks in January and February, Shah and Templeton feared that they might be set for a second year of agony. 'We chased the market very hard but nobody was interested – we got at least a dozen refusals. The problem was there was no guarantee from the shareholders – it was quite a risky investment,' says Templeton.

The rescue came from an improbable source. After twelve months of trudging around the capitalist City of London receiving generally noncommittal responses, Shah now secured his swiftest and most positive pledge from the communist Hungarian International Bank.

The Hungarian International Bank – the London subsidiary of the Hungarian National Bank – had been suggested to them by Eric Tanzer of Pershke Price, the agents for German press manufacturers MAN Roland (whose presses Shah had already decided to buy).

'It was an extreme piece of good fortune that we found them because it seemed unlikely that anyone else would be interested,' says Templeton. Tim Newling, the very British managing director of the bank, also turned out to have links with Templeton's firm.

After only two meetings a provisional agreement was signed pledging the bank to raise – at the head of a consortium – about £6.5m. to pay for the four presses: money that would then be paid back in instalments over five years. Shah had already paid £1.5m. deposit.

The Hungarian Bank had previously established a reputation for beating the capitalists at their own game and is, for example, a quick-witted dealer in foreign exchange. It also pays handsomely: in 1983 its then managing director, Jack Wilson, received an annual salary of £216,742.

Tim Newling seemed genuinely puzzled at the interest in this bizarre financial alliance when the story leaked out in April 1985. 'This is just a conventional leasing operation,' he said. 'In our opinion it's a very good company and will produce an excellent paper.'

That did not stop Robert Maxwell, quietly, and Brenda Dean, the leader of SOGAT '82, noisily, trying to pressurise the Hungarians to withdraw. But it was too late: the bank's City credibility would have collapsed if it had pulled out of a deal already signed, and a valuable flow of hard currency for the Hungarian economy took precedence over the feelings of British print unions.

Newling was to be puzzled again when, at the end of November last year, the first press was delivered by MAN Roland to his City office, holding up the traffic for half an hour. There had been confusion over the delivery notes and the lorry was soon on its way to Shah's London print works at Poyle near Heathrow.

The Hungarian deal tied the final strings in Shah's financial package. The formal celebrations to mark the signing of the equity deal began a little earlier, on the afternoon of 19 February 1985, when twenty-five men enjoyed a quiet drink together in the austere, modern City offices of Coward Chance.

They raised their glasses to toast an agreement which had pledged ten organisations to raise £8.5m. to fund a new company – an ordinary enough deal by the standards of that neighbourhood. Preceding the drink there had been a straightforward, rather subdued meeting lasting no more than an hour. The main representatives of the ten organisations sat round a large table and signed cheques ranging from £2m. to £50,000, then handed them to David Childs, the Coward Chance solicitor chairing the meeting. All then signed the official documentation.

Most of the businessmen, lawyers and accountants present seemed oblivious to the potential significance of the occasion – and they didn't exchange pleasantries for long before hurrying on to other meetings or back to their offices. As they stood briefly sipping their white wine they might have reflected upon what an unusual corporate gathering this was. In one corner was George Proctor, senior legal officer of Trust House Forte, one of the largest and best-known companies in the UK, chatting to Norris McWhirter's lawyer: THF had signed over £2m.; McWhirter's company, Novel Press, had parted with £100,000. In another corner John Skeffington, the finance director of Bricom's £400m. annual turnover, was saying goodbye to Chris Barton, the finance director of £45m. turnover Portsmouth and Sunderland. Bricom had committed £2m. – PSN £½m.

The six other companies which signed along the dotted line that afternoon were: Ivory & Sime £2m.; Scottish Investment Trust £1m.; MacAlpine £½m.; Candover Investment Trust £100,000; Richmade (a company specially constructed by Ian Templeton for some of Shah's friends, including Lord Harris and Brian Nicholson, to invest in the project) £50,000; and finally, Shah himself and the *Messenger* were putting in £250,000, £50,000 of which was Shah's own money.

The investors were obviously attracted by the potential profit – but for some the financial decision was prompted by political commitment. Irrespective of Shah's eclectic politics and the expected centrist stance of the paper, a part of the 'corporate Right' has been drawn to the romance of a project which represents so boldly the old-fashioned free enterprise virtues. To them, Shah is to the national newspaper industry what Thatcher is to the wider body politic – an invigorating attempt to shake off years of corporatist compromise and decline.

Trust House Forte, Bricom and MacAlpine are all well-known for their strong support of the Conservative Party. Some of the other investors are not so easy to pigeonhole politically. Ivory & Sime, Scottish Investment Trust and Candover are less interested in politics than in acceptable risk and reward. The presence of blue-chip THF and Bricom persuaded them to look at the figures – they appeared exciting – so they joined in.

But this youthful and highly contemporary newspaper would not have been possible without the succour of three elderly Tory peers: Lord Taylor, Lord Forte and Lord Cayzer, the chairman of Bricom.

The one man who had not taken a glass of the wine now stood by the door saying goodbye to the investors. As he himself prepared to leave the office he looked weary and felt the first tremors of another cathartic breakdown similar to that he had experienced at the end of the Messenger dispute. Shah spent the next two days in his room at the Grosvenor House Hotel, alternately sleeping and sobbing uncontrollably.

10

The Ice Breaks: The Provinces

'The course of the last ten or fifteen years in the printing trades has been one long process of education from America. An employer must reckon it part of his duties nowadays to take a trip over the Atlantic as often as possible to enquire into new processes and look up new machinery.

G. B. Diblee, manager of the
Manchester Guardian *writing in*
the Economic Journal 1901

10

The Ice Breaks: The Provinces

In the autumn of 1984, as Eddie Shah hawked himself around the City in search of the money with which to challenge the national newspaper industry, a more public chain of events had begun to unravel in the provincial industry which, by the spring of 1985, had ended in three family-owned companies overcoming union resistance and producing papers for the first time using direct-input. The long-awaited thaw was under way.

Two of the three papers, the *Portsmouth News* and the Wolverhampton *Express and Star*, won direct-input as the culmination of a long-term strategy. The third, the Kent Messenger Group, almost stumbled into it. The three companies developed an informal network of mutual aid – and a common connection with Shah – through their bitter disputes, the outcome of which had a wide significance for the provincial press. But the three disputes also had reverberations beyond the confines of the provinces. For one thing, Shah would arguably have faced far stiffer resistance from the unions in the run-up to launch of *Today*, but for the breakthrough. National newspaper managements also watched the weakening of the union grip with mounting glee. The resulting spread of new technology, they argued, had broken down the traditional barriers between the printing of national and provincial titles. Already the *Guardian* has signed a contract for the printing of 120,000 copies nightly at the *Portsmouth News* centre for distribution in the south whilst Mirror Group Newspapers has been considering printing in Bradford as well as London. Management at Express Newspapers have also considered printing at the regional presses of United Newspapers. There remains plenty of spare capacity to print national morning papers in the provincial press particularly at those evening papers which finish with their presses in mid-afternoon. Provincial newspapers have always enjoyed more peaceful industrial relations than Fleet Street and new technology has faced fewer barriers, but in the early 1980's with profit margins being squeezed the employers planned a fresh initiative.

The Newspaper Society, the provincial newspaper employers' organisation, had been looking for a common approach with the unions over the introduction of new technology since the sixties when a succession of provincial newspaper managements started travelling to the United States to view the technological strides being made at papers such as the *Pasadena Star*. By the mid-seventies, when photocomposition was still only being introduced in Britain, 84 per cent of US daily papers were set in cold type. The number of hot-metal line casters used in the American press had fallen from 10,290 in 1970 to 194 in 1980. At the same time the number of VDUs had boomed from 23 in 1970 to 46,217 in 1982. The most dramatic surge had occurred between 1974 and 1980 when the number of papers using direct-entry rose from 10 per cent to 80 per cent. However, in Britain the continuing profitability of the provincial press up until the end of the seventies had meant management had been less motivated to risk confrontation with the NGA over direct-input.

Nevertheless the men at the top of the NGA had always faced a delicate balancing act. They realised that once they relinquished control of the technologically un-

166

necessary 'second keystroke' many jobs would disappear and, as important, the union's industrial muscle would be radically diminished. Managements, with or without the support of journalists, would find it far easier to bring out newspapers without their printers. The historic sanction 'if we don't get the extra two per cent you don't get a paper today' would have disappeared forever. At the same time the NGA leadership recognised that if they clung to a negative bargaining position too rigidly for too long, they could find themselves swept aside anyway. The potential danger of inflexibility had been amply displayed during the two industry-wide strikes mounted by the NUJ and the NGA in 1979 and 1980. During both strikes a surprisingly large number of managements found they were able to bring out newspapers, even without direct-input.

At the Wolverhampton *Express and Star* in 1979, for instance, 156 of the 160 NUJ members responded to their union's strike call. Mark Kersen, the paper's managing director, recalls: 'The senior editorial staff worked 12 to 15 hours a day and produced papers on time. We put on sales and carried all our advertising. It taught us a lesson. The very next year the NGA had a national stoppage over a £5-a-week pay claim which lasted 2½ weeks. Despite the strike, papers as far apart as Bradford, Portsmouth and Wolverhampton came out. Take those two years together, and they were a watershed for the industry. We were able to show that we could write, set, put together, make up, print and deliver papers without the help of the NGA or the NUJ. It was a very salient lesson. Those disputes showed that the old business of confronting the NGA, only for them to put their hobnailed boots on and trample all over us, were over.'

The NGA national leaders are often portrayed as Luddites and the chief villains in the piece, but in reality both Joe Wade, the NGA's previous general secretary, and the current incumbent, Tony Dubbins, had warned the union's highly conservative membership that simple prevarication over technology did not amount to a policy. In 1978, for instance, Dubbins, then the union assistant general secretary, bluntly told the union's national conference that technology was on the point of wiping out craft skills. 'It is possible within a relatively short period of training,' he said, 'to be able to learn the new techniques of IBM composition, paste-up, small litho printing and to produce origination and printing acceptable to customers without having to go through a craft apprenticeship.' Similarly, four years later, Wade told the national conference the unpalatable truth: 'I have to say to you that unless we are prepared to take on board the full implications of technology, unless we are prepared to be flexible in our attitudes, we shall be engulfed in a tidal wave of technology which we shall not be able to control. Experience of the rest of the industrialised world indicates that direct-input is becoming inevitable simply because there is no alternative to it.'

Despite the warnings, the NGA collectively was slow to develop a realistic policy towards technology that took account of the interests of the other unions in the industry. Dubbins had been elected general secretary in 1983 on a policy of changing the union's élitism and isolation from the rest of the labour movement. As a young left winger on the National Council and secretary of the Thames Valley and Chiltern branch, Dubbins had been at the head of the criticism of John Bonfield, the union's general secretary at the beginning of the seventies, when the union had resigned from the TUC after it had registered under the government's Industrial Relations Act. By the time he took over as general secretary, Dubbins, the forty-one-year-old son of a newsagent, had steered a path towards the centre of Labour movement politics. His dark good looks and ease in the TV studio belatedly gave the introverted print union a more polished public voice, despite his guarded manner in private.

Dubbins is highly ambitious and much has been expected from his leadership. However the extraordinarily difficult circumstances of the union that he has inherited makes disappointment likely. His actions over the last two years inevitably look more like tactical manoeuvring than the working through of a long-term strategy.

As a negotiator he is still respected by management and he has certainly been a powerful voice for reform inside the union, pointing out that – like Shah – he has only ever known the cold type new technology. But it is perhaps the tragedy of both Dubbins and the NGA that the opportunity for new leadership and strategic rethinking has already passed.

To some extent Dubbins' advocacy of change in the late 1970's was complemented by a gradual change in the union's membership as more and more members came through recruitment of un-unionised workers, rather than the traditional apprenticeship. But the transition was painfully slow: the traditional hauteur and self-esteem still predominated. SOGAT were labourers, NATSOPA, Natties, and the National Union of Journalists, a middle-class professional organisation better known as the National Union of Jellyfish. The pre-entry closed shop had immense advantages, but as Dubbins admits it also 'means that you have members coming in at sixteen and leaving at sixty-five which tended to make the attitudes of the members very insular. They saw a stable industry behind them and, ahead, a completely unchanged and continuous future.'

In the face of direct-input technology, the most sensible way for the NGA to survive was to seek a merger with unions organising in the advertising and editorial departments. However, talks had broken down with NATSOPA in early 1978 whilst the strong cultural and class differences between the NGA and the NUJ led to the collapse of amalgamation talks between the two unions in 1982. The failure of the 1982 merger talks could not have come at a worse time for the NGA. Total profitability of Britain's thirty major regionals had fallen from £74m. to £32m. between 1980 and 1982 with return on sale tumbling from 14.2 per cent to 4.5 per cent. Newspapers are always susceptible to the overall health of the economy and the fall could be partly attributed to the general recession, but there was also widespread fear amongst provincial newspaper management about a long-term decline which management felt could only be halted by quickly introducing labour-saving technology. In particular they pointed out that the free newspaper industry was threatening to strangle the paid-for papers. In 1970 the advertising breakdown for regional papers had been 62.9 per cent for dailies, 35.7 per cent for paid-for weeklies and 1.4 per cent for frees. By 1982, the figures were 55 per cent, 24.2 per cent and 23 per cent respectively. On the principle that if you cannot beat them, join them, the established newspaper chains did try to ward off the threat of the free papers by establishing their own frees, but overall unit costs still had to be cut.

As a result, at the end of 1982 the Newspaper Society announced Project Breakthrough. A two-year deadline was set by which to reach a national agreement with the unions to enable management to instal direct-input technology. If no deal was struck by the end of 1984, employers would feel free to instal without agreement. Many managements, notably Portsmouth and Sunderland Newspapers, regarded the exercise as another futile ritual dance with the unions. PSN chairman Sir Richard Storey pointed out impatiently that the Newspaper Society had been looking for some such deal since 1966, following an NS technical tour of the US which had discovered VDUs, only to rediscover them, Sir Richard acidly remarked, on a second trip in 1972. But Project Breakthrough was also a propaganda exercise designed to galvanise the industry's more soporific managers, in the era before the Messenger dispute, into talking and thinking about technology and the growing urgency of change. At the heart of the propaganda was the American newspapers' experience with new technology which had led to more, bigger and better papers in the Newspaper Society's view.

The NGA drew a sharply different conclusion. Technology, they argued, had not increased American newspapers' profitability. Instead it had been technology's ability to hasten the process of deunionisation through deskilling that had boosted profits. Initially, the NGA sister union, the International Typographical Union, had resisted the change but had rapidly found itself overpowered. For instance, in early 1971 the managers of the Richmond, Virginia, *News Leader* and *Times Despatch* computerised their newspapers using photocomposition equipment. The owners had prepared for the dispute by training secretaries and unskilled labour to work the keyboards. Once the ITU struck, the management replaced the 180 skilled ITU printers who earned $200 a week with unskilled labour earning only $125 a week. The paper, which did not drop an issue, saved $800,000 in the first year alone. The cost of the equipment had only been $900,000. Today the papers produce thirteen editions a week, just as they did in 1971, but the ITU never returned. From then on, the ITU suffered a series of further set-backs: at the *Omaha World Herald* in 1973, the *Washington Post* in 1975 and the *Sacramento Bee* in 1978. The casualty list is painfully long. The resulting collapse of ITU membership coincided exactly with the arrival of direct-input technology. After years of steady membership the number of employed ITU members fell from 88,000 in 1970 to 50,000 in 1982, a 43 per cent drop, all at a time when employment in the industry was on the increase. While highly-paid male compositors were made redundant or pensioned off, women moved into the industry employed often as part-time typists to input classified advertisement and outside contributors' copy. Between 1970 and 1983 male employment fell from 275,000 to 256,000. Female employment rose from 97,000 to 166,000. On the back of this shift, US productivity and profitability had flourished. The number of hours required to set a broadsheet page fell from 9 using hot metal to 1.5 or 2 using direct-input, according to a study for the Economist Intelligence Unit.

One of the lessons that Dubbins and the NGA leadership drew from the American experience was the need to persuade other unions in the industry that they could not afford the luxury of standing back and watching the compositors' union, the strongest union in the industry, being flayed alive. The result would only be that all the unions were weakened. As the end-of-1984 deadline set by Project Breakthrough neared with no sign of a national-level agreement, the NGA attempted to create a common front with the National Union of Journalists and SOGAT. In March 1984 it published a document, with little prior consultation, entitled *The Way Forward*. In the document the NGA suggested that the three unions should try to persuade the employers to split union membership in the origination area three ways. The intellectual basis of this proposal was that direct-input – which the union now formally accepted – did not make the role of the compositor redundant; it merely transferred the typesetting work from the composing room to the journalist's or telephone advertising department's visual display unit from where the copy was being sent direct into the computer typesetter. The NGA and its members should be allowed to follow the job and establish collective-bargaining rights in these areas. Under the proposal only members of one of the three unions would be entitled to input the copy directly into the computerised typesetting equipment. Equalisation of membership would be phased in and the origination areas currently without NGA membership would quickly benefit from the union's organising skills being brought to bear. The plan, however, was rejected as impractical by other unions who regarded much of the NGA's argument as specious special pleading from a union facing annihilation.

172

Nevertheless, in late 1984 as the deadline for the completion of the direct-input talks neared, the NGA did come close to securing bilateral alliances with both the NUJ and SOGAT. In talks with the NUJ, a complex dual-union membership system had been proposed whereby NGA members could transfer to work as sub-editors, retaining their NGA membership card, provided first they also joined the NUJ and second the NUJ was recognised as the union solely responsible for collective bargaining in editorial areas. In the talks with SOGAT, the NGA proposed equally dividing the membership in the classified advertising department. SOGAT had, for many years, possessed formal recognition rights in this area with the Newspaper Society, but had in practice been unable to achieve many closed-shop agreements. However, both sets of talks failed. The NGA wanted its own collective-bargaining rights in the editorial area, something the NUJ was not prepared to concede, whilst the SOGAT executive rejected their own national officials' proposals for equal representation in the classified advertising area. The breakdown inevitably led to a succession of inter-union disputes in the provincial press through 1984.

September 4, 1984, the day that Arthur Scargill delivered his rallying call to the TUC Congress in Brighton on behalf of Britain's striking miners, appeared to represent a high watermark for uncompromising resistance to industrial change. Yet ironically, later that same day, elsewhere in Brighton, Ben Stoneham, the Portsmouth and Sunderland Newspapers' Industrial Relations Executive, and Derek Penketh, the paper's general manager (south), were to meet Tony Dubbins and put the seal on a deal that appeared to usher in a new era of cooperation in technological progress by one of Britain's strongest unions. The deal effectively paved the way for the introduction of direct-input at the *Portsmouth News* – the newspaper group's technological showpiece.

Although the deal gave the NGA's go-ahead only to an

intermediate stage prior to full direct-input, the agreement clearly set the parameters for full direct-input itself. The terms of the deal appeared to be a real coup for the NGA – ones that the union aimed to repeat throughout the industry. The management had agreed that NGA compositors who had been displaced by direct-input could transfer to editorial as sub-editors and retain NGA membership. Initially, three NGA members could be transferred to train as subs, but more might follow later. Crucially, however, the NGA would retain bargaining and representation rights 'on any matter' on behalf of its editorial transferees. For the first time the NGA had established a negotiating presence in the editorial department.

Much of the rest of the industry was astonished by the Portsmouth management's decision to give the reviled NGA such an apparent lifeline. But Portsmouth management had their reasons. Firstly, Sir Richard Storey felt a responsibility to his existing employees. If direct-input meant that more sub-editors would be needed, then it was right and proper, he felt, for the displaced NGA men to be offered the chance of a new career within the company. In any case, the numbers transferring were to be limited by the suitability of the NGA members wishing to switch to the editorial area since the NGA had failed to persuade management to concede a permanent quota for NGA men in editorial. Management also felt that the NGA chapel in editorial would never develop the same discipline and loyalty found in a traditional NGA production chapel. For one thing, the NGA editorial member would not have to rely on his chapel father for overtime and the better-paid jobs in the same way as he did in the production chapel. Secondly, an NGA journalist or sub-editor would be able, with his skills, to leave the company and not, like the compositor, have to rely upon the NGA's good will to secure him another job in another company. Portsmouth and Sunderland anyway had special reasons to favour the NGA over the NUJ. Portsmouth was the site of the company's highly profitable contract printing business and the company's senior management was wary of any lengthy NGA stoppage. Finally, Derek Penketh, who had played a significant role in the settlement, had himself come from within the NGA's ranks and had always found the NUJ erratic, if not impossible, to strike a bargain with.

But overall, this important settlement represented an implicit endorsement, in the NGA's view, of its long-standing claim that the compositor had a right to follow his job and his union a right to join him.

All this was undoubtedly favourable to the NGA's wider strategy of retaining a role in the preparation and setting of copy. Both sides agreed to keep details of the Brighton deal secret until 11 October 1984 to allow the NGA's National Council and the Portsmouth chapel to hear and endorse the news.

The nature of the NGA's Brighton deal was relayed to the NUJ by management in mid-October. At local level the deal was accepted by the journalists, but the union's national executive took strong objection to the wider implications and persuaded the chapel to withdraw co-operation unless the union was given 'sole and exclusive bargaining rights' for editorial staff.

Management however honoured their agreement and, as a result, from 12 December 1984 started suspending NUJ members that refused to cooperate with stage two. To Stoneham's surprise the NUJ paid the chapel members over £12,000 a week in strike pay, helping to keep the chapel solid for seventeen weeks and costing the union around £300,000. Management later analysed the NUJ's response by arguing that their strike was more than just a defence of territorial rights – it was the expression of a fear that a powerful disciplined union would swallow journalists' professional ethos, compete for members in the editorial area on the basis of its superior negotiating record, swamp individualism and effectively annex the NUJ. As the NUJ's deputy general secretary Jake Ecclestone put it, the NUJ was not prepared to become another victim of NGA imperialism, ending up, like so many unions before, as just another set of initials on the NGA banner.

Ecclestone, the son of a left-wing Sheffield priest and leader of the *Times* journalists during the year-long lock-out, was a key figure in keeping the strike going at Portsmouth, having taken effective charge of the union following the sudden departure of the union's general secretary Ken Ashton. Ecclestone's stance towards the NGA won him the opprobrium of his left-wing colleagues in the union who accused him of being involved in a bureaucratic dogfight, but Ecclestone believed that the NGA had acted in an underhand way.

During a series of tortuous meetings at the conciliation service ACAS, the NUJ attempted to kill off altogether the bargaining rights granted to the NGA in editorial. The management was not prepared to make any changes in the principles, but it stressed earlier clarifications such as 'There will be one set of terms and conditions for all unionised journalists. There will be no different terms for members of different unions. The terms in any agreement with any other union will be identical and parallel with those agreed between the NUJ and the company.' In addition, NUJ fears of being swamped by NGA transferees were eased by a management reiteration of its commitment that transferees would be limited to those 'interested, suitable and available'. The NGA were not in a position to reassert their demand for full independent bargaining rights. In September, after the Brighton deal had been made, the Portsmouth NGA chapel had become embroiled in a ten-day dispute over a separate issue of productivity pay. The chapel had badly split and management had got the paper out using direct-input, vividly illustrating the degree to which technology had already overturned the old balance of power.

Reviewing the dispute after the ACAS settlement, Ecclestone argued that the strike had been a worthwhile exercise in damage limitation. The union's picket lines had been an effective display to other managements that they could not connive in a 'de facto' takeover of their union by the NGA. When in July 1985 the NGA came to finalise its terms for full direct-input at Portsmouth, the NUJ's stance and the NGA's earlier ineffectual dispute were shown to have weakened the latter's hand. Although the NGA men who transferred to other departments would have the right of NGA representation, their pay would be subject to those departments' existing terms and conditions.

The unions' rivalry at Portsmouth also directly led to a second, more serious, example of inter-union fratricide at the provincial press's other technologically-advanced paper, the Wolverhampton *Express and Star*, a company with which Portsmouth had kept in close touch. In conjunction with the Printing Industry Research Association, the *Express and Star*'s parent company, Midland Newspapers Association, had developed Press Computer Systems (PCS), a firm dedicated to developing the software needed for a fully electronic newspaper.

In November 1984, as it became clear that Project Breakthrough was not going to produce a national agreement, Mark Kersen, the determined and quick-witted managing director of the *Express and Star*, announced that he intended to use direct-input for the paper, both in advertising and editorial, within three months. Kersen hired the local cinema in which to explain the company's ambitious plans to the staff. Unhappily *Company of Wolves* and *Star Wars* were showing that week. Kersen promised the staff there would be no compulsory redundancies, although a voluntary severance scheme would be established to encourage early retirement. All 107 NGA compositors were personally interviewed by the managing director in order to discuss what other jobs they might take up in the company. Kersen claims, 'the guys had stuck with us through thick and thin. We were not going to kick them out now. It was not paternalistic crap. It was the way that the *Express and Star* had achieved what it has. It meant for a while, until retirements came through, we would have had more people than we strictly needed but we were prepared to carry the cost.'

The £200-a-week compositors' earnings would be temporarily protected if they were transferred. A transferee was given two options. He could either receive a lumpsum payment, equivalent to three times the difference between his former annual gross pay and the lower average earnings in the department to which he was moving. Alternatively, he could continue to be paid his old wage in a new department, but would receive each year only half the payrise awarded to that department, until the two rates finally harmonised. The NGA claims that some members would have lost £80 a week. Kersen hotly denies this.

NGA members who transferred to the classified advertising department would be allowed to retain NGA membership, but there would be no closed shop or NGA bargaining rights. Kersen claimed later that he could not give the NGA bargaining rights in classified advertising since the company already had a union recognition agreement with SOGAT for that department. When challenged by the NGA that in practice the department was non-unionised, Kersen replied: 'It's not my fault that SOGAT used to have members there, but does not now. It does not mean that the agreement falls to the ground.'

Kersen, a former journalist himself, personally rejected the idea of NGA members becoming fully-fledged sub-editors or reporters. He offered them instead the role of 'editorial production assistant'. These assistants could stay in the NGA, form a chapel and be individually represented by the NGA but, in Kersen's words, 'the NUJ would be the appropriate union for bargaining purposes'. In the view of the NGA with its proud traditions, the job of the editorial production assistant sounded a good deal grander than it was in practice. The tasks included receiving and directing agency copy to journalists, keying-in contributed copy, producing routine tabular work, processing sports results, fixtures and scores, administering the electronic library, keying-in stop press, assisting journalists and following their instructions when operating page make-up machinery, including the assembly and design of text and advertisements on electronic screens. Bob Tomlins, the NGA's provincial newspaper negotiator, called the job 'shit house attendant'.

Kersen commented, 'All the NGA's negotiators ever did was to seek ways to preserve the organisation, shape and structure of the NGA here in order to preserve their power, authority and control. That's all I had to deal with. I never had to deal with 107 individuals in the composing room. We were going in different directions from day one.'

On Friday, 22 February 1985, as Shah completed the money-raising for *Today* the NGA members at the *Express and Star* were given an ultimatum – cooperate with the introduction of direct-input in the department of classified advertising on management's terms next Monday, or face suspension. The chapel, never a strong one by the NGA's exacting standards, split.

The management quickly won an injunction banning secondary action by NGA members elsewhere in the country against the *Express and Star* and its two associated companies, the *Shropshire Star* and Precision Colour Printing (PCP). The NGA responded with a strike ballot which it won by 154 votes to 33. Days later, on 14 March, although 160 members were still suspended, the journalists agreed to work direct-input in return for a payrise of £15 a week.

The NUJ viewed the deal as a tit-for-tat response to Portsmouth. It marked the low point in relations between the two unions and the deal was immediately denounced, in the ludicrously inflated terms beloved by union leaders, as the biggest act of treachery since the

Ribbentrop–Molotov pact. For good measure, the NGA likened Jake Ecclestone's behaviour to the sell-out by Judas Iscariot, the only difference being Judas got more for his betrayal. The lack of inter-union solidarity and the legal shackles imposed on the NGA rendered the union powerless to defend its sacked members. Covert attempts were made to defy the injunctions, by publicly repudiating blacking action whilst privately sanctioning apparently spontaneous branch-level action against PCP. A High Court judge ruled that the union was defying the law 'through a nod and a wink'. The union was fined a total of £15,000 for two separate contempts. Following its own experience with sequestration in the Shah dispute, and the NUM's growing entanglement at the time with a court's appointed receiver, Michael Arnold, the union thought discretion the better part of valour and paid both fines.

The NGA did, however, manage to strike back against the Midlands newspaper, with very mixed results for its members. In 1984, the Kent Messenger Group, a chain of successful Maidstone-based papers built up by the Boorman family over nearly a century, had chosen, at a cost of £650,000 of PCS equipment, to computerise their classified advertising and accounts department. At that stage the Group simply did not have the money to computerise its editorial department. At the end of the year, NGA officials agreed that the instalment of the equipment could begin, but on 22 January 1985, as it became increasingly clear that the PCS sister company, the *Express and Star*, was set to start editorial and advertising direct-input without NGA agreement, the union withdrew cooperation from the Kent Messenger Group's plans.

On 22 March the NGA issued a secret general policy statement instructing all branches to ban integrated computer systems from any company where management had not accepted the NGA's claim to represent workers in departments using new technology. The impact of the policy was soon felt. On 15 April, the day after the local chapel was addressed by NGA speakers in dispute at Wolverhampton urging them to take action, the NGA issued the company with an ultimatum either to stop work on the PCS equipment or face a strike. Talks resulted in the unions insisting that all the equipment so far installed should be removed. The union was sure that they were on firm legal ground and they could not be sued in the civil courts by Boorman for secondary action. It also seemed unlikely that Boorman would dare sack the NGA since there was little possibility that he could produce his papers without their help. Unlike Kersen, the company had made no well-laid plans for a dispute, the NGA calculated.

But Edwin Boorman, a member of the Freedom Association and the Group's managing director, said he now saw it as a matter of inviolable principle that his staff should not be forced to join a union and so emphatically rejected the union's claim to represent all the workers in the classified advertisement department. The talks foundered and the NGA quickly occupied the Group's two printing plants, near Maidstone and at Canterbury. After a weekend of tense consultation with lawyers about his right to sack the entire NGA membership, Boorman took the plunge and sacked all 144 NGA members. 'One of the people I sacked, and I'm not proud of it, was just fourteen days short of fifty years' service with the company.'

Boorman explains, 'I was ambushed. I had been on holiday at the time. I had talked to my managers as I usually do before I left about any problems that might occur whilst I was away. The PCS equipment was not on the list.' Boorman's problems were compounded by the resignation of his number two, and the retreat of his chairman. 'It was a hair-raising period. People kept on asking me what I was going to do. I just kept saying, "I've got to find out,"' he recalls. The first company he asked to print the papers refused to do so. A makeshift composite paper was printed at a non-union firm in

Worthing, but this was no substitute for the loss of the 65,000 *Kent Messenger*, 35,000 *Kent Evening Post* or the 500,000 copies of the Group's free series of papers. The company lost £98,000 in the first week, £108,000 in the second week. 'It's a frightening experience. I worked out we were losing £70 a minute. I had a share in the company and my family 26 per cent.'

A week after sacking his staff, Boorman rang Alan Graham, owner of the *Express and Star*, the godfather of his eldest child and a long-standing friend with whom he had learnt the newspaper trade. When Boorman told Graham he was in deep trouble, his friend suggested printing the papers at Shah's Warrington print works. Shah's help tided Boorman over while he assembled a makeshift operation at Maidstone. By May the department of classified advertising was operating direct-input. Women from other departments were being paid £4 an hour for typesetting and paste-up work.

Boorman held further talks with Tony Dubbins, but the NGA wanted the sacked men reinstated before substantive negotiations could begin. Boorman refused and claimed, 'I came away realising that they were not looking for an agreement but a means to neutralise PCS. They realised that the *Express and Star* was too powerful, but that the Graham family had invested a great deal in PCS. They wanted to show that this equipment could not be effectively installed in any newspaper, until the Wolverhampton dispute was resolved.'

The speed with which the Kent Messenger Group recovered from the loss of its NGA staff staggered the industry. Boorman claims: 'Propaganda is about repeating something often enough that people start to believe it, and if you say often enough this is a highly skilled job involving a five-year apprenticeship, tremendous skills and knowledge, you start to believe it. The reality is that we have seen through the propaganda.'

On reflection Boorman claims there are three key ingredients in breaking a strike – 'well prepared legal ground, a communications system from which the staff are given information they know they can trust, and finally preventing people becoming over-enthusiastic and working for too long.' Mr Boorman believes he has saved £1.7m. in annual wages by being driven to sack the NGA and says he will be 'disappointed if they are replaced by people who will cost more than £500,000'.

Mr Boorman insisted in November that the NGA would not return. 'You know the American Civil War was supposed to be about slavery, but in fact it was about the North hating the South. Our dispute was the same. It was supposed to be about technology. In effect it was about the NGA and how their attitude meant they prospered at the expense of everyone else in the company.'

The NGA chapel at Kent remained astonishingly loyal to their union, picketing the plant day and night for months on end. Ray Allen, the Kent Graphical Society secretary, insists that the men were prepared to taper their demands to achieve their reinstatement, but found Boorman stubbornly opposed to even considering their return to work. Six months after the sackings the NGA organised a national demonstration in Maidstone in support of their sacked men. Some NGA men travelled from as far as Scotland to show their support in the bright October sunshine. But as the march of eight hundred or so people wended its way through the town with banners and placards, the overwhelming impression gathered was of a town quite oblivious to their cause as the locals busied themselves with their Saturday shopping. Edwin Boorman had his own cutting answer to the march. For the first time since the dispute he was able to produce a 100-page edition of the weekly *Kent Messenger*. In that same week in October, another newspaper employer two hundred and fifty miles to the north-west was preparing his own, more far-reaching, answer to the unions.

11

Preparing for Today

'My principle is – take a trick while you can and go with the game.'

Lord Beaverbrook on himself

11

Preparing for Today

Driving along the A50 towards the centre of Warrington there is far more evidence of the town's shabby, recession-hit present than of its proud industrial past. But closer to the centre a large, recently refurbished Georgian building rises incongruously out of the drab 1950s blocks of offices and shops. Built to house an academy of science in 1757, it looks oddly unreal following its face-lift, like a model for a film-set.

There is also a distinctly Hollywood touch to the man and the project inside the academy for, in mid-1984, this became the administrative headquarters of Eddie Shah's new seven-day colour national paper, *Today*: the entrepreneurial fairytale of the 1980s.

In his top-floor office overlooking the River Mersey and the main road through Warrington, Shah sits playing with his desk-top computer. It is 11 October 1985 and the eighteen-month planning and fund-raising period for the new paper, begun in March 1984, is over. The hectic five-month pre-launch phase is about to begin – the target early March, 1986.

The scale of Shah's ambition has grown dramatically since he confronted the NGA two years earlier on the other side of the town, but he is still much the same ebullient trust-buster. He turns to the computer, taps a couple of keys and up pop the figures which Shah believes will make *Today* far more competitive than any other national paper on the market.

On a circulation estimate of 900,000 with a cover price of 18p for the 44-page weekday paper and 30p for the 80-page Sunday, his cover price income is £64m. a year. Shah calculates that if he allows for an 11 to 13 per cent cover-price cut to distribution franchisees and a generous 33 per cent to newsagents he will still receive cover price revenue of £33m. With advertising revenue estimated at £29m., after subtracting the agency commission of 15 per cent, that produces total revenue of £62m.

With *Today*'s annual running costs of about £40m., that could mean a first-year profit of £22m.; a quite unheard-of return by Fleet Street standards for a paper of this circulation level, and especially for a new paper. Shah taps another button and the median advertising estimates are instantly replaced by his 'worst case' estimates – still producing a profit of £15m.

By comparison, Fleet Street's chronic lack of profitability is graphically illustrated by the net profit for all papers in the four years 1981–5 of £27m on sales of over £5bn. The Mirror Group, reflecting this average in 1985, made a profit of £1m. on sales of £260m. Some titles, it is true, do make money – for example, the *Sun* made £23m. and the *Financial Times* £8.5m. in 1984 – but their return is still poor compared with many other industries.

If Shah can reach his profit targets over the next three years the company will be valued at over £100m., and with his own performance-related share in the company lying somewhere between 10 and 35 per cent, he is set to become an exceedingly rich man.

'But you must remember,' he says, 'these are very pessimistic projections on circulation and advertising. Even with virtually no advertising we could break even at about 600,000.' Circulation forecasts in fact shifted about considerably in the months preceding the launch: from 900,000 the figure rose for a time to 1.5m., then fell to 1.25m., and finally settled at just over 1m. The longer-term aim is still about 2m. by 1989. Initial print-run capacity will be 1.4m., rising to 1.7m. in early summer when the fifth press comes on stream.

Because of the high cost of newsprint – the main newspaper raw material – Fleet Street's circulation virility symbol is not always the best indicator of economic health. The popular papers, whose revenue comes roughly 70 per cent from cover price and 30 per cent from advertising, *are* more dependent on success in the bloody circulation war; however, for some quality papers which have the inverse revenue of 70 per cent from advertising and 30 per cent from cover price, the optimum economic circulation may not be the highest. With Shah's revenue tilted slightly more to cover price than advertising, circulation *will* matter; but assuming reasonable advertising income, his radically different cost base should allow him to break even on a circulation of 300,000 – about one-sixth of the sale of a typical mid-market title like the *Daily Express*. This fact alone could have enormous significance for the future structure of the British press.

Shah's costs can be looked at in two ways: start-up costs and running costs. To take start-up first, Shah's approximate £20m. launch cost has been loosely compared with the £113m. that Maxwell recently paid to acquire the Mirror Group or the nominal £317m. that David Stevens' United Newspapers paid to Fleet Holdings (the Express Group). Even if one allows for the fact that the Express Group takeover was partly paid for in United shares and not cash, it is still an unhelpful comparison. Maxwell and Stevens were buying existing businesses with large properties, a valuable Reuters shareholding and, in both cases, two profitable subsidiaries – the Mirror's Scottish papers and Morgan Grampian's magazines.

But £20m. is still a relatively small sum compared with recent conventional Fleet Street launches. The *Mail on*

Sunday, launched in 1982, is estimated to have cost Associated Newspapers over £50m. including the losses made during the first two years of publication, and that was a one-day-a-week paper sharing many of its overheads with the *Daily Mail*. The *Daily Star*, launched by Fleet Holdings in 1978 to soak up spare printing capacity in Manchester, cost in excess of £25m. including the initial heavy losses. Both papers are now barely breaking even.

Shah's estimated annual running costs are an equally significant break with the past. Newsprint (paper) and other raw materials will be his major cost at about £20m. a year, representing 50 per cent of *Today*'s running costs, That is about 15% above the Fleet Street average and will make Shah slightly more vulnerable to the fluctuations in the price of newsprint. (Old technology has one small and rare advantage in raw material costs: the lead used in the hot-metal typesetting process can be recycled, unlike the expensive film materials of modern processes.)

Direct distribution costs – on top of the cover-price cut to newsagents and franchisees – will, at £7m., form about 15 per cent of *Today*'s running costs. This is in part an additional expense which will be incurred, initially, because Shah is handling part of his own distribution, unlike Fleet Street papers which are distributed by the national wholesale companies.

Shah's key saving is in production labour costs. These form an average 25 per cent of Fleet Street costs whereas, for Shah, total production labour costs will be £2m. or 5 per cent of outgoings. His editorial costs, too, will be way below the Fleet Street average and, at £4.5m., represent only about 11 per cent of costs. 'Other' salaries, mainly of administrative and advertising staff, add up to £2m. a year. High early depreciation costs, publicity expenses and general overheads account for the final 14 per cent.

The estimated annual running cost of £40m. is less

than half the figure for the *Daily Mail* or *Daily Express* and even allowing for their higher circulations (and thus higher raw-material costs and higher revenues) Shah's paper should maintain a comparable cost base about one-third lower than its nearest Fleet Street rival: the difference between breaking even, as most national papers now struggle to do, and pocketing huge profits, as Shah hopes to do.

'State of the art' production technology may be the key to this projected revolution in newspaper economics, but almost as important is the simple fact that the new paper has based neither its editorial offices nor its printing centres in Fleet Street. There are considerable savings in rent, rates and overheads from operating in low-cost, grant-aided premises in industrial parks.

Nevertheless, *Today*'s main claim on history is as the UK's first satellite-printed full-colour seven-day-a-week national daily and one of the world's first entirely electronic newspapers. In choosing a production system now found only in a few US papers and magazines, Shah is leapfrogging at least two stages in the evolution of British newspapers. This system allows the paper to be created in the London editorial office without a single traditional print worker.

A journalist in the newsroom will write a story on his Hastech Magician VDU terminal (or outside the office on a portable computer plugged into a phone line) and when it is finished it will be sent at the press of a button to the main Hastech computer where the Press Association and Reuters wire services will also be stored.

The sub-editor, a journalist who checks, cuts and rewrites stories as well as writing headlines, will call up the story on his VDU screen and, after subbing it, will fit it into the electronic slot that has been reserved on a special page layout terminal; black-and-white pictures are also now scanned electronically on to the page. Almost incidentally the page is then typeset by a Lasercomp – a process that has been wiping out thousands of well-paid printing jobs all over the world.

The black-and-white page is then 'digitised' and sent up to the Mercury dish on the roof from where the information is sent to Mercury's main booster dish in docklands and then via Landline to the regional dish closest to each of the three printing plants. From these dishes the information travels to the Poyle plant, near Heathrow, where there are two presses; to the Trafford Park plant in Manchester, where there is one; and to Aston, Birmingham where there is another one. A fourth plant, to house the fifth press, is to be based in Rotherham, South Yorkshire, and will be ready four months after launch with a further plant planned for Bristol.

This process, which takes only about three minutes, is a quite conventional form of facsimile transmission long used in various forms by several national papers between their London and Manchester offices. What happens at the plants themselves is less conventional. A Datrax machine decodes the information and writes a laser message on to a film which is then exposed on to an aluminium printing plate clipped to the press.

For a colour page the process is slightly different. It is assembled in the same way but then output as four colour separations in London to be 'written' by a Datrax machine and then dispatched via the dishes and landlines to the Datrax reader at the other end.

The MAN Roland web offset presses, each manned by groups of only eight men on ten-hour shifts, will then start churning out the paper at a rate of about 40,000 copies an hour with an expected run of over 360,000 in nine hours, giving capacity for the four presses of 1.4m. Finally the papers are automatically bundled, stacked, and loaded on to waiting lorries – by contrast one of the most labour-intensive parts of the Fleet Street operation.

In six to nine months' time Shah is proposing to marry his Hastech and Crosfield equipment so the colour can be integrated with the black-and-white at an earlier stage. That would be a world first; otherwise all parts of the operation have been tried and tested elsewhere and there is no technical reason why, allowing for inevitable teething troubles, it should not work. Crosfield's colour transmission has already been proven at *Time* and *Newsweek* in the US. Hastech's page-make-up-on-screen system, although out-of-date by comparison with the latest models, has been used successfully at a few small US papers.

Today's system is not quite 'straight to plate', as it is sometimes described. Along with the most advanced US papers such as the *Wall Street Journal*, *Today* has found that certain refinements are still required in the area of plate technology before text and pictures can be beamed straight on to a plate. But Shah has eliminated two time-consuming and costly processes in the 'origination' of a newspaper: the resetting of journalists' copy by printers (as still happens on most British papers) and much of the scalpel-and-paste page make-up process (as still happens in most of the rest of the world even where direct-input is established).

In those few British papers which have recently acquired direct-input, the gradual intrusion of electronics into the hand-assembly make-up process is becoming the new arena of political conflict, except where the unions have been banished. Even by technological trendsetters such as the *Portsmouth News*, production of the paper is still seen as a combination of discrete crafts, each represented by a different union.

Today, with its radical labour flexibility, is introducing a single, linear, electronic, screen-based production process uncluttered by craft history. New skills *are* required, especially in page make-up on screen and electronic design, but should work with the technological possibilities and not against them.

'One of the hardest things for people to realise is the economics of a *real* newspaper once it's escaped from the lunacy of printing with low technology at one cramped site in Central London,' Shah says. He puffs at one of his ubiquitous Villiger cigars and taps again.

The screen displays a new set of figures showing the projected timing of the press run at his Poyle plant and the scheduled drop-off times to the distribution franchisees in the West Country at towns such as Taunton, Exeter, Torbay.

'Say we're twenty minutes late off the presses because of an important story,' he taps once more, 'and look we've got all the adjusted figures for the drop-offs, it's as easy as that, the computer can just do things that would normally take rows of clerks several hours.'

When he's enthused with an idea, as he often is, he starts gabbling so fast that he bites off the ends of his words and sentences and peppers his dialogue with his favourite reflex phrase 'Are you with me?', as if frightened that the listener has been left behind, as indeed he often has.

It is in moments like these that his considerable charm casts its spell; his eyes twinkle and in his self-absorption he seems to take on the innocent countenance of a young boy. It is hard to believe that Shah could be poised to become the most important figure in British newspapers since Northcliffe.

John Stephenson, his chief accountant recruited from Barratt Homes, breaks the high-tech reverie with some cheque-signing chores for Shah. 'All I seem to do these days is sign bloody cheques,' he blurts out in mock anger. Stephenson looks uncertain whether he should smile or frown.

At this time in mid-October 1985 there are still only about forty staff hired but the monthly wages bill is over £80,000. It makes Shah twitchy to be paying out such a large sum with nothing to show for it for several months to come. The first batch of employees include the expensive departmental heads: Roy Dickinson, 57, publishing director, the loyal old comrade from Cumbrian Newspapers; Fred Bridge, 40, circulation manager, from the *Daily Mirror* in Manchester; Mark Pritchett, 32, advertising director, from the *Mail on Sunday*; and Brian MacArthur, 46, editor-in-chief, former editor of the *Western Morning News* in Plymouth.

MacArthur is on £60,000, his immediate deputies – Jonathan Holborow, 42, weekday editor, from the *Mail on Sunday*, and Tony Holden, 38, weekend editor – are both on £45,000. Shah was planning to pay himself £100,000 a year.

The senior editorial team are already busying themselves in their half-equipped offices in Pimlico, interviewing staff and worrying about how they are going to produce a seven-day paper on an annual editorial budget of £3.5m. (later increased to £4.5m.). They are discovering that Shah's cost-cutting enthusiasm does not only apply to the NGA.

The managing directors of the three printing-plants-cum-distribution centres, which have been constituted as separate companies, are in place too. These crucial links in the management chain are: Poyle – Alan Harris, the former chief engineer at Garrard & Lofthouse; Birmingham – Geoff Collins from Eastern Counties Newspapers; and Manchester – John Finn, who has spent the last three years as a troubleshooter for Rockwell, the print equipment company.

By the time of the launch, staff numbers had risen to about 600, of whom 130 are editorial, 125 production staff, 190 distribution (excluding the franchisees) and 130 'others' including about 25 advertising sales staff.

The comparison with Fleet Street at the end of 1985 is here at its most absurd. The Express Group, for example, with a daily and Sunday title selling a little under double *Today*'s projections, employs ten times more staff – about 6,800. The *Daily Telegraph*, a closer comparison in circulation terms at about 1.2m., employs 3,300 people in London and Manchester.

Shah has a few words with Stephenson while he signs

the cheques. He confirms that the balance in the bank is still £7.75m., only £¾m. down from the original £8.5m. investment capital, and that by the launch the figure should be about £1.9m. (Because he raised the money so well in advance of launch he was able to earn nearly £½m. in interest before March 1986.)

He is interrupted again – this time by Mark Pritchett, the advertising director. Pritchett had not been the first choice for the job – Shah had tried to lure away several of the top advertising men in Fleet Street – but he is well-liked in the business and has experience of the most recent national paper launch, at the *Mail on Sunday*.

Pritchett is very much in the Shah mould – a tearaway who caught the business bug. He attended Dulwich College public school where he spent much of his time playing in bands or hanging around the Beckenham Arts Lab founded by rock star David Bowie. He played guitar in several Bowie bands but after eight years as a professional musician Pritchett took a job selling newsprint and then went on to the *Sunday Express* advertising department.

He was ringing in to report the response to News UK's presentations to advertising agencies over the past three days. The presentations at the Limehouse Studios in London's docklands had been elegantly stage-managed, with just enough polish to impress the advertising people but not too much razzamatazz to over-inflate expectations.

The half-hour presentation was built around Shah, MacArthur and Pritchett, who together explained the idea of the new paper while standing on a slightly tilted floor that lit up with pictures of the rest of the senior staff and with charts, figures and diagrams. Shah confessed to being very nervous before each show; it was, after all, the paper's first major public appearance. But the script was well-written and the confidence of its final line, 'Walk away to applause', fully justified.

The bucks fizz and the boat trip to Limehouse made

a jolly half-day out for the advertisers but what most interested them were the prices on show: a black-and-white full page at £4,600 compared with a figure in the region of £15,000 in the *Daily Express*; and a colour page at £9,600 compared with over £35,000 in the *Express*.

Lead times – the number of days or weeks ahead of publication by which the paper has to receive the advertising copy – have also been radically chopped. Colour has come down from about two weeks to three days and for black-and-white, Pritchett quipped, 'we normally like to get the ad before the paper comes out.' He also boasted of the high-quality colour reproduction which may tempt more food advertisers to leave the colour supplement ghetto; the regional flexibility available; and the innovation of a duty manager on the advertising desk through to the early hours of the morning – as on the newsdesk.

Advertisers consider themselves one of the principal victims of Fleet Street's high costs and low technology. They have had to pay dearly for advertisements which are often badly reproduced or do not appear at all because of disputes. Even before the presentations there was thus plenty of good will for Shah which had been nourished by some impressive colour mock-up pages sent round the agencies a few weeks earlier.

The agencies showed their appreciation by booking a remarkable £1.6m. worth of advertising at the end of that week. By early January 1986, about £6m. had been booked and £7m. was expected by launch. This represents over 25 per cent of the total advertising revenue for the first year of publication and compares very favourably with the 6 per cent (£2m.) taken by the *Mail on Sunday* before launch, which was itself considered highly creditable at the time. Shah's carefully-thought-through approach to advertisers paid such dividends that in the weeks before launch he was even wondering whether he really needed to take the usual expensive splashes in the advertisers' own trade press.

197

In October the first feedback was just coming in and Pritchett bubbles down the phone to Shah: 'The bookings are superb, they're just starting to flood in.' Shah listens, cracking his knuckles, and then says rather sharply that he still wants his departmental weekly report. Pritchett was clearly expecting to postpone this until after the provincial advertising presentations the next week but offers to write a short provisional report to be followed by a fuller one next week. Shah accepts the compromise.

A few moments later two of his leading lieutenants, Roy Dickinson and Fred Bridge, enter the room. Both men face a formidable challenge in the setting-up and running of a production and distribution system wholly untried in this country – with the additional difficulty that their employer is constantly overturning their plans.

They have come for an important meeting to discuss the distribution system. All national papers to date had been distributed to newsagents via the rail network and the main wholesalers such as W. H. Smith and John Menzies. The papers are delivered from Fleet Street to the mainline stations where special newspaper trains are waiting in the early hours of the morning. On the trains the papers are stacked and arranged into appropriate piles to be dropped at stations down the line, from where they are driven to the wholesale depots and then on to reach the newsagents between 5.00 and 6.30 a.m.

The present system is one of the most efficient parts of the existing newspaper industry and is almost entirely run by the wholesalers themselves who have the timing down to a fine art. Costs are also reasonably controlled. The Central London drivers benefit from the high Fleet Street wages, but the train-stackers and provincial drivers are on below-average rates for such anti-social hours.

Shah had originally sold the idea of a wholly independent distribution system to the investors on the assumption that the union-dominated Fleet Street system would not be available to him. The original plan was that about

200 franchisees would pay a £2,000 annual deposit to News UK and then take an 11 to 13 per cent cut of the cover price for each paper delivered, about 2p for the daily and 3p for the Sunday. Satellite printing will be sending *Today* along the nation's main arteries several thousand times faster than the fastest train, and from the three printing plants the paper was to have been distributed by drivers directly employed by Shah to points where they could be collected by the franchisees for delivery to an average 200 newsagents each (there are about 40,000 newsagents in England and Wales).

Fred Bridge had had no difficulty in finding small operators with their own vans ready to comply with the demanding schedules. It was estimated that each area should pay a franchise holder about £12,000 a year and the mutual incentive to increase sales was made easier by a phone link to a News UK computer to adjust orders.

However, when, in October, Shah came to look in more detail at distribution he realised that a franchise system was less practical for the rural areas: as fewer papers are sold, costs of distribution are higher, and the franchisees' cut would thus also have to be higher. After long negotiations with W. H. Smith, a provisional agreement was reached – full of unprecedented guaranteed delivery clauses – whereby W. H. Smith undertook distribution in mainly rural areas, which added up to about half of England and Wales. The other half would be covered by about eighty franchisees. But should the original distribution plan be changed at this late stage, at the risk of upsetting the investors? Was the original plan still viable?

It was a characteristically informal meeting. There was no agenda, little structure, no clear beginning, middle or end. Fred Bridge, less used to the Shah style, found it more confusing than Dickinson and was more deferential – but neither man disagreed with his planned aboutturn. In fact, notwithstanding Shah's democratic manner – he began his contributions with a tentative 'Can I just say something' – he had clearly made up his mind before the meeting. He was in effect checking with the two relevant executives that there were no technical obstacles to his preference for a mixed system.

They pored over multicoloured maps on the floor like marshals plotting a campaign – green for the franchise areas, red for W. H. Smith. Shah insisted that London be taken by News UK itself. 'I'd like us to do London ourselves – that's the hornet's nest,' he says.

He has been inspired by lurid stories from Ted Blackmore about the distribution 'mafia' in London who are alleged to systematically bleed the newspapers of hundreds of thousands of copies every night – selling them to newsagents on their own account – and stop at nothing to keep their empire intact. Even a major police inquiry in the late 1970s – which got as far as the Old Bailey – was unable to find enough people prepared to give evidence.

If there is any pressure on the London operation – which will be registered as a separate company, Dis/Co – Shah will sue. And if the pressure is more subtle, Shah jokes that he will burn one of his own vans and blame it on the union. Direct distribution of the paper in London necessitated taking on another hundred staff and finding a depot in East London.

At this point, Helen Graham came in from the *Warrington Messenger* office three doors up the road. She was averse to any part of the operation being dependent on others and stressed the potential profitability of a brand-new distribution system which could eventually carry a variety of papers and periodicals for others breaking out of 'the system'. But there was no serious resistance to the change of plan and when that was decided Shah called for celebratory Cornetto ice-creams all round. Cornettos are an essential lubricant of daily life in the Warrington office.

Shah's franchise system, moving in the opposite historical direction to the other parts of the paper, is a reinvention of the prewar system. Although exploiting the distribution possibilities opened up by Britian's motorway network, it has caused some consternation among newsagents who will have to wait for a second early-morning delivery following the drop-off of the other national papers which are all delivered together by the wholesaler. But through some hard personal lobbying of the National Federation of Retail Newsagents and some well-targeted publicity in the various retail trade magazines, Shah seems to have won them over. The eighty franchisees who were eventually signed up ranged from the original small operators (who dominate Sunday-newspaper distribution) to the major whole-salers like John Menzies, which took seven franchise areas despite having decided earlier not to invest in News UK.

Although this arrangement was sniffed at by last November's seminar of the Association of Circulation Executives as a remarkably crude distribution system with minimal marketing, there is no good reason why it should not be 95 per cent effective.

Shah got up from his desk and looked down to the front of the building at the lurid yellow-painted statue of Oliver Cromwell erected in the last century to mark the point at which the Royalist armies surrendered in the North. The freshly-scrubbed front of the once-derelict building gives the academy an unfortunate mock-Georgian look. The interior has had all the history banished by stripped pine panelling and navy-blue wall-to-wall carpets; it is also an extremely impractical building in which to run a busy office. But its grandeur appealed to Shah and it is an appropriate monument to his considerable enterprise.

Shah is forty-two but looks younger. He is unfit, has a slight stoop and a twitch, otherwise he looks, and is, in his prime. He is powered by a relentless energy which exhausts all those around him. Shah is constantly on the move, pacing up and down a room or partaking of his favoured form of thinking – a brisk walk round the block with someone to bounce his thoughts off.

He has always been a driven man but over the past two years the increased pace of his life has placed an enormous burden on him. Although he shows remarkably little physical evidence of that stress, he has needed to draw upon an enviable ability to quickly recharge his batteries; usually that involves returning to Mobberley at the weekend, playing table-tennis with his children, walking his dogs Emma and Picket (bought, as the name suggests, during the dispute), and watching American football on TV.

People meeting Shah for the first time are usually impressed by his affability and softly-spoken, matey manner. He certainly enjoys the popular touch and is determined that national fame will not make him aloof and pompous.

However, he can also appear an intensely private, almost reclusive, personality: this is partly to guard his family life, but even before the birth of the new paper he had few close friends and shunned the Manchester newspaper circuit.

Shah is by no means a complex character but the same paradox applies to his public exposure. He loves being at the centre of things and has, despite occasional protestations to the contrary, enjoyed becoming a media personality. Some advisers have even tried to restrain his enthusiasm, fearing over-exposure. Yet he also claims to find the publicity a terrible strain. His performances have indeed been mixed. If an audience is on his side, he can be charming and witty but he is often a poor public speaker and has even been advised to take lessons in public speaking.

His TV appearances have generally been good. During the Messenger dispute, the simplicity of his case and his vivid mind provided powerful material for press and TV. Explaining the more complex reasoning behind starting a new national paper initially proved more difficult.

Shah's first appearance as a potential national paper proprietor, in April 1985, was on Tyne Tees' *Face the Press* where, coincidentally, one of his three interrogators was Sue Cameron, then of the *Financial Times*, now Shah's political editor. Reading the transcript, most of Shah's replies appear incoherent. But to his credit he did stick to his promise not to adopt the airs of a political press baron by bluntly refusing to answer many of the less relevant questions put to him – on, for example, his view of the recent Budget. After that poor start, Shah has improved markedly, appearing on various 'softer' programmes where his inability to structure his sentences mattered less and the viewer was left with a more diffuse image of his amiable manner. Shah wants to remain an enigma but finds it difficult to do so when offers of free publicity for the new paper come so frequently. A less enigmatic public figure would be hard to imagine.

The Shah image, although consciously manipulated, is not therefore false. He really does fit most of the descriptions trotted out in the easy-reading magazine profiles: the cheeky chappie from the provinces; the down-to-earth, shirtsleeves boss with bags of courage and business flair; the little guy 'just trying to translate a dream into reality', as he says.

The image is, of course, a little too well-polished and leaves out much, notably his remarkably good connections. But, to a surprising extent, Shah *is* his image. Indeed, a criticism made by both friends and enemies is that he is too larger-than-life and too much like his two-dimensional image. In private he rarely stops striking his public poses and can thus easily become superficial and repetitive. One man who has recently done a lot of business with Shah sums up the anxiety of many around him: 'I think of Eddie as a giant myth who one day soon is just going to go pop.'

He can also be breathtakingly vain. When, in 1983, he

came second to Bruce Kent in the BBC radio Man of the Year poll, he attributed it to a CND plot. His ego is usually inadequately hidden behind some nobler motive: 'Of course I don't care about me but for the good of the paper . . .' He talks compulsively about himself and one of his most senior journalists on the new paper described him as 'easily the most selfish man I have ever met'.

Such characteristics usually repel but in Shah they often fail to. His arrogance is so open and direct as to be almost attractive. He loves, for example, to tell the apocryphal story of how Robert Maxwell met Tiny Rowland at a party and both bemoaned the fact that, having changed their names to win easier acceptability in Britain, they now found that the most popular man in the country was called Shah.

But Shah does have a darker side which helps explain the sharply-divided views about him. If he has retained a child-like openness, he has also not grown out of a childish petulance. He can be autocratic, devious and short-tempered. His explosions may have become less frequent but he can still wield his charm like a cutlass to get his way.

Another characteristic the chat shows do not project is Shah's need to control. He shuns groups unless they bear his own stamp. In the tribal, rather Darwinian, world that Shah inhabits he can be intensely loyal and generous if you are with him and paranoid and aggressive if you are not.

As befits a tribal chief, Shah is an immensely proud man and many of his achievements appear to have been driven by a desire to show a particular person that he should not be under-estimated. It has been suggested that he even based the News UK headquarters in Warrington to snub his old adversary Douglas May who has to pass it every day on the way to his own office.

He sees himself 'outgrowing' these petty opponents as he shoots through the firmament like an 'unguided missile' – a phrase he uses about himself to establish a further link with Rupert Murdoch, for whom it was coined. Shah's own transience and craving for control are summed up in another revealing metaphor: 'I rumbled what makes me tick the other night. My real love, you see, was always writing plays and that's what I'm still doing in my mind. Messenger was one play and now *Today* is another.'

Perched on part of the newly-designed stage-set in his Warrington office, Shah warms to the idea: 'Look, you see I'm the director and then you've got all the main actors like Brian MacArthur and so on. And when this play starts running on its own I'll go off again and write another one.'

That rootlessness is one of his many American qualities along with his love of gadgets, receptivity to new ideas and attraction to frontiersman ideals. He even describes his career with the unEnglish title of communicator. Shah also moves about the map with an American disregard for distances. Since 1977 he has flown a private jet and as he lives just a mile from the end of Manchester airport runway, he can be in London in an hour, and in Edinburgh in three-quarters of an hour. Golf partners are frequently surprised when he asks them to bring their passports to the game and whisks them off to play in France or Ireland.

Many of the books, pictures and mementoes around his office are related to flying and Shah likes to describe how he only took it up to conquer his deep fear of heights. The rest of the office trappings reflect his robust, sporting tastes. There is a framed photograph of an American footballer breaking through a pack of opponents, books on travel and sport, golf clubs in one corner, an antique typewriter and some old cameras in another. A copy of Jack Kerouac's beat generation evocation of the American Dream – *On the Road* – lies open on a book shelf.

'My father is a thinker, I'm a doer like my mother,' he says. His real business creativity is as the supplier of

205

sheer impetus. 'I don't think a lot – I just get on and do things – I have a good instinct for things.' Shah's impulsiveness is apparent just talking to him – as he hops from subject to subject leaving a trail of saloon-bar clichés leavened by the occasional insight.

Shah may be no intellectual but he has a shrewd practical intelligence, and has thoroughly researched his intended victim. The bookshelves show the evidence of extensive reading on Fleet Street, with one especially treasured volume of *Good Times, Bad Times* signed by the author Harold Evans, former editor of *The Times* and *Sunday Times*, and addressed to 'Eddie Shah "pioneer"'.

Shah has a talent for borrowing other people's ideas and adapting them to his own needs but he can also be arrestingly fresh in his approach to old problems. He likes to call it 'lateral thinking' and as Jeremy Deedes, his new managing editor and son of *Daily Telegraph* editor Bill Deedes, points out, it is the hallmark of *Today*. 'He is always saying is there another way of buying a product, of arranging pensions, or whatever, and there usually is,' says Deedes.

Shah may have outgrown the impatience of his Messenger days but at the end of 1985 he was already complaining of boredom with the whole national paper enterprise and promises to move on to other projects as soon as he can. He may not initially be moving very far. He wants to open several more satellite printing plants around the country, including Scotland, and already has plans for turning *Today* into a 24-hour paper with morning, afternoon and evening editions in London, Birmingham and Manchester.

His projects for the longer run are even more fantastic and include trying his hand at becoming a latter-day Lord Hanson. Hanson, chairman of the huge manufacturing conglomerate, Hanson Trust, started out running his father's small road-haulage business in Yorkshire and has subsequently made his name and fortune buying-up rundown, inefficient companies and making them pay.

Shah sprouted some of these notions after meeting Hanson at a recent Harrods dinner. He was impressed by, and attracted to, the simplicity of Hanson's original vision for shaking-up manufacturing lame ducks. That dinner, hosted by an old acquaintance, Professor Roland Smith, chairman of the House of Fraser, started to make Shah believe that, backed by the money he hopes to make on the new paper, the business possibilities are almost limitless. If *Today* is successful, the pull of newspapers may, however, prove too strong. Shah claims he was destined to run newspapers – not ball-bearing factories. And newspapers have special qualities.

12

Here Today . . .

'It's like going to the Moon in print.'
Brian MacArthur, editor-in-chief of Today

12

Here Today . . .

Ron Morgans, former associate picture editor of the *Daily Mirror* and the first picture editor of *Today*, described his new job shortly before the paper's launch as: 'Like climbing off a haycart and into a Ferrari.' Morgans has just constructed the first-ever national newspaper darkroom based around colour photography and equipped it with sophisticated new electronic equipment for cropping and 'touching up' photographs and for taking colour stills straight from TV.

In the weeks leading up to publication day, *Today's* editorial office in Pimlico, near Victoria, slowly filled with Morgans' new colleagues. The employees of the *Daily Shah* (Fleet Street's nickname for their distant cousin) belong to one of the most cynical professions in the world; but even the older, leathery-faced Fleet Street reporters among them could not resist some display of excitement. They felt themselves to be collective pioneers in a giant step forward for British newspapers.

The excitement was tinged with a sense of foreboding. Expectations had risen dangerously high; if the paper disappoints, the journalists can scarcely blame their tools. The responsibility is immense, although the more calculating point out that personally they can hardly fail. Most have joined for at least a small rise in salary; if the paper flops, their new skills will still be at a premium as the rest of the industry catches up.

As the VDUs began to be installed in November and December 1985, the bright, open-plan first-floor newsroom with its fourteen hexagonal desks began to take on the look of a typical modern office. In fact, with the rapid switch from typewriters to VDUs in provincial newsrooms, *Today* does not even look strikingly different from many modern British newspaper offices.

But it enjoys significant editorial advantages. First and most strikingly, one-third of the paper will be in full-colour with spot colour on many more pages. National papers can at present use extensive colour only for pre-planned special occasions – such as the FA Cup Final – because of the nature of their presses. Some senior Fleet Street figures, such as Bruce Matthews of *News International*, are not bothered by that and believe that colour can even be disadvantageous – especially if the quality is poor – making papers look garish and magazine-like. Evidence from abroad and from the small number of provincial evening papers that do use colour regularly is that it is only a marginal advantage.

Shah himself is a great colour enthusiast – comparing the imminent shift into colour in newspapers with that in TV fifteen years ago. It is not only the possibilities of colour news pictures that interest him but colour graphics too; one of his earliest design ideas for the new paper was the use of jockey colours next to the horses' names before big races 'so the punters watching on TV can see at a glance which is their horse'. The quality of colour reproduction in *Today* should be good, and expensive 'high grain' newsprint is being used to ensure that it will be. (It will also prevent the ink rubbing off on people's hands – something that Shah's market research showed was very unpopular.)

Today, as the only national to use full-colour, reasonably hopes to capture at least initially many of the nearly three million floating readers who make their choice

212

daily on the basis of the front pages on the news-stands. The paper's launch was even targeted for early March because of the colour opportunity provided by the Royal tour of Australia and New Zealand.

The second potential advantage lies in later deadlines and therefore later news. Cutting out time-consuming production processes and part of the distribution means the response to a late-night story should be far quicker. Brian MacArthur, editor-in-chief, estimates that a new story could move from the VDU to the street in as little as forty minutes.

In its first few months *Today*'s earliest and most important front-page deadline will be 9.00 p.m., about the same as the rest of Fleet Street. In fact, because of the limited printing capacity before the fifth press starts up in Rotherham, the north-east editions printed at the Manchester plant will not carry the late football results – a cause of some anxiety to the sports staff.

But edition changes through the night should be far easier and can go on being made until about 5.00 a.m. compared with the rest of Fleet Street's final deadline of about 2.00 a.m. Big late-night stories like last year's Birmingham riots should therefore get much later coverage in *Today* than elsewhere.

The advantages of colour and later news are combined in *Today*'s Sunday colour supplement (a pullout section of the paper rather than a separate magazine). Tony Holden, weekend editor, points out that most of the present colour supplements have to go to press five to eight weeks before publication date, hence they are packed with non-topical, 'timeless' features. Holden discovered the drawbacks for the journalist on one of his last freelance assignments for the *Sunday Express* magazine: he went to France to write a piece about Beaujolais Nouveau only to find 'they hadn't even picked the bloody grapes'. *Today*'s supplement deadline will be only a matter of hours before the paper itself.

Another potential – although unquantifiable – advantage *Today* has over the Fleet Street papers is its 'spirit'. Walking with Shah as he passes through the newsroom greeting everyone by their first names, one can witness the *Messenger* spirit transported to the metropolis. There is the same air of feverish improvisation, the same naïvety too. It remains a moot point just how far the benevolently despotic management style of a small free-paper group can be injected into *Today*.

The manning of the new paper is very tight – far too tight, is the consensus view. *Today*'s total editorial staff of 130 is less than one-quarter that of the *Mail* or *Express*. Shah expects a lot from his pioneers but promises that numbers will rise if his target of 1m.-plus circulation is reached, and points out that both the *Sun* in 1969 and the *Daily Star* in 1978 started with fewer reporters. Jonathan Holborow, the daily editor, nevertheless says gloomily: 'Eddie has not budgeted for flair.'

There are only about 30 general reporters and 28 sub-editors and designers but their numbers are supplemented by 18 specialists, 12 sports staff, 8 features staff, 24 in the photographic department and 10 editorial executives. About 60 per cent of the reporters are from provincial papers and one-quarter of the total staff are women, an unusually high proportion for a national paper and something which Shah himself pressed.

Shah, MacArthur and Jeremy Deedes, the managing editor, claim to have created an informal and egalitarian working environment. There is single status on most conditions of employment – except, of course, pay – and apart from the top executives the pay differentials are not that wide. All staff are also on a private health scheme, and covered by a no-compulsory-redundancy clause.

The chains of command are short and visible by contrast with the distant and secretive cliques that run most nationals. The editorial executives have their glass-fronted offices looking on to, or very close by, the newsroom. Shah and Deedes have also encouraged the senior journalists to think like managers as well as newspaper-men. They say they have set their faces against the 'get the story at any cost' school of editorial management – and hope that the staff, whose employee shareholding will be between 2 and 10 per cent of the company, will share the cost-consciousness.

As Deedes says: 'At present in Fleet Street most journalists are like freelances who just happen to have a regular desk and a telephone in a particular building, there is no identification. People fiddle their expenses as a matter of course because they think if I don't take it the management will just give it to the printers.'

How will the 'spirit' of *Today* translate into the starker facts of industrial relations? Because of Shah's repu-tation, the senior staff all reiterate that this is not an anti-union organisation. For production staff, Shah has concluded a radical single-union deal with the Elec-tricians Union (EETPU) including the main features of the new Japanese company-unionism sponsored by the EETPU: a no-strike deal; total flexibility of labour; and a works council to meet once a month.

Keeping faith with Shah's stance during the Messen-ger dispute, the first point in the News UK contract of employment is the choice to join or not to join a union of the employee's choice. It is a choice which has, however, been made almost superfluous for production staff by the single-union deal.

On the editorial floor the management hope that a union chapel will not be needed; they will certainly not encourage it. With or without a national agreement with the NUJ, it seems likely that a local chapel will be formed. Staff selection has not tried to screen out union activists at any level and indeed a few weeks before launch Shah began worrying that the NGA had quietly slipped a few active members into the company.

Pay rates for journalists on the new paper will average about £20,000 – a little less than the Fleet Street norm mainly because of the low age-profile: the average age

215

on the paper is not much above thirty. Despite Shah's populist instincts, most of the older staff belong to the public-school mafia which run so many British institutions and Fleet Street papers. Nevertheless, Shah's profoundly anti-Fleet Street sentiments are stamped all over *Today*. His jaundiced view of Fleet Street reporters with feet on desks, taking four-hour liquid lunches every day and writing two stories a week, is replaced with the vision of a small, cost-conscious and highly productive team.

In the weeks before launch, MacArthur remained well aware that no amount of 'spirit' or new technology will make *Today* a good, or even successful, paper. Yet the extensive research that the paper has generated over the past eighteen months has proved encouraging. Specially selected panels of people have been interrogated on their newspaper-reading habits and, perhaps predictably, have found a great deal lacking in the current choice. (Not satisfied with what people claim their preferences to be, the researchers also observed how, and what, people *actually* read through two-way mirrors.) The research claims to show that the market is not as tightly sewn up as is sometimes supposed. It is estimated that over 4m. people do not buy a paper at all and 1.6m. buy a newspaper less than one day in four.

MacArthur is also aware that magazines and newspapers born out of market research have usually been perfectly targeted failures. The paper is thus not aiming for a particular segment of the market but hopes its more diffuse appeal will pull in readers from the bottom end of the quality broadsheets (*Daily Telegraph*) and the top end of the down-market tabloids (*Mirror*) as well as luring them away from its more obvious rivals, the *Daily Express* and *Mail*. Shah and MacArthur have in fact taken as their model the visual media: *News at Nine* and, especially, *News at Ten*. MacArthur says: 'Those programmes have understood that striking presentation, with good colour graphics and pictures, plus intelligent coverage that avoids bias, appeals strongly to the very people that we are seeking as readers. We are aiming to capture the same immediacy and visual interest that draws to TV news several times the audience of any newspaper.'

Short of actually introducing *moving* colour pictures, *Today* cannot, however, compete with TV news on its own ground – indeed, one reason for newspapers vacating the middle ground over the past twenty years in favour of deeper analysis (quality papers) or constant human interest 'colour' (tabloids) is that these are the only two areas where TV does not have a powerful advantage.

It is incumbent upon TV news to try to speak to the whole nation in a measured, impersonal voice. A successful newspaper, on the other hand, must find a personality and a very specific tone. It should also have at least a rough idea whom it is addressing. The great popular papers of recent history – Beaverbrook's *Express*, Cudlipp's *Mirror* and perhaps even Murdoch's *Sun* – have all displayed the utmost clarity on these points. They also proved, depressingly, that great newspapers are generally run by single-minded, interfering proprietors whose top editorial teams march obediently in step. (Maxwell has proved conclusively at the *Mirror* that to intervene is not enough.)

Shah's *Today* is not seeking an immediate place among the pantheon of great newspapers. But to succeed at all – which means achieving a regular circulation of about 700,000-plus – some respect has to be paid to the traditional rules. Judging from its pre-launch pronouncements, *Today* is, once again, seeking to break most of them.

As a tabloid newspaper wanting to show off its colour capability, it will not have room for more than one major story on the front page. It matters enormously to the sort of paper *Today* will become, and the type of reader it will attract, whether that front page is usually devoted to a human interest story or a serious hard news/political/economic/foreign-news story. It appears that the daily will, like the *Daily Mail*, shift around from day to day and the weekend will stay more serious.

But the *Today* team has been understandably coy about providing too many hostages to fortune and they have, on some issues, honestly admitted that they will not know 'until the day' what the paper will look like. To understand the journalistic and political attitudes that will guide the paper's responses, we thus need to go back to the early discussions between Shah and Mac-Arthur and see how their team was formed.

Considering how many people in the City, industry, and even Fleet Street had heard about Shah's plan during the 'secret year', it is surprising that news about it did not leak out until the end of February 1985. By that time he was already talking to several allies about candidates for the editorship. Among the advisers were Andrew Neil, who had been Shah's first choice as editor, Sir William Rees-Mogg, Brian Nicholson, Charles Wintour and, more interestingly, Bruce Matthews. 'I'm dead without a top-class editor,' Shah was constantly, and rightly, saying.

The consensus finally settled on Brian MacArthur – destined for the second time in his career to be second choice to Andrew Neil, having lost the *Sunday Times* editorship to him two years before. MacArthur is a smooth and surprisingly kind and mild-mannered man to be running a national paper. He is more of the Harold Evans technician editor than the Rees-Mogg intellectual, and was indeed Evans' loyal right-hand man on both the *Sunday Times* and *Times*. There may be doubts about whether he has the presence to act as the paper's front-man or the toughness to stand up to Shah – if he has to – but as a journalist he is a respected professional.

Coincidentally, he was born and brought up fifteen miles from Warrington at Ellesmere Port, the son of an education official, and after the local grammar school went to Leeds University. As a student activist and subsequently full-time president of the Leeds student union in 1962, he learned the organisational skills which he has put to good use over the past year. It was also through national student politics that MacArthur came to know men like Ian Wrigglesworth and Mike Thomas who went on to become Labour – and later SDP – MPS. They were all for Harold Wilson and the 'New Britain'.

Quietly ambitious, MacArthur rose through the *Yorkshire Post*, *Daily Mail* and *Guardian*. In 1967 he joined *The Times* as Education Correspondent and then had his one previous experience of starting a new paper as editor of the rather less significant *Times Higher Educational Supplement*.

After a stretch as news editor of *The Times*, he joined the *Evening Standard* as managing editor and then went to the *Sunday Times* as assistant to Harold Evans in the middle of the 1978–9 lock-out. When Evans took over *The Times* in 1981 – soon after Murdoch bought the paper – he took his chain-smoking, anxious-looking deputy with him to become number three on the daily. Mac-Arthur had already returned to the *Sunday Times* as deputy editor when Evans was traumatically removed by Murdoch. Having been passed over for the *Sunday Times* editorship in 1983, he looked set for a continuing career as a solid number two – until he suddenly left to become editor of the *Western Morning News* in Plymouth. He was a good and popular editor, turning the paper into a provincial *Sunday Times*, but only fourteen months later the move was to provide him, despite his Fleet Street roots, with the provincial tag Shah was looking for in his editor.

When MacArthur met Shah for lunch on 27 March 1985 he was excited at the possibility of editing the first of the new-generation newspapers but he knew it would be a risky project and, like others with liberal politics on the staff of *Today*, he was worried about Shah himself.

He had long since left the Labour Party but had been almost a founder member of the SDP – with his friends from student days – and during his time in Plymouth had drawn close to David Owen, the local MP and SDP leader. He was relieved when Shah turned out not to be the Ghengis Khan he had feared and now says: 'Shah will be closer to my politics than anyone I have ever worked for before.'

MacArthur's appointment provoked a minor drama when Northcliffe Newspapers refused to accept his resignation from the *Morning News* and tried to hold him to his contract. Shah rang him at the Devon Show and told him he had to walk out, which he did, and the matter was later settled without too much malice.

The stage now shifted to a cellar in Covent Garden – *Today*'s first office. It was the basement of the advertising company Wight, Collins, Rutherford, Scott, (WCRS) who had acquired the Shah account through Brian Nicholson. It was here that Shah and MacArthur began to talk about the content of the paper. Shah insisted from the start that it should be politically independent and began to worry when it came to be assumed that it would automatically support the SDP. MacArthur accepts this and has resigned his party membership – but he doubtless intends that, come election-time, *Today* will speak up for the party of 'toughness and tenderness'.

More than independence of party political label, Shah talked about 'breaking up the political blocks' which most papers belong to even in their less explicit news judgements. A paper that appeals to a 'CND-supporting Tory' or 'a trade unionist who supports private education' were his slogans for *Today*. MacArthur chipped in with the concept of non-political middle England: 'The people who Murdoch can never understand because he's too hung up either despising upper England or mimicking lower England.'

Shah drew up a 'Bill of Rights' – the thirteen points to guide the newspaper's coverage:

1. To support true democracy and not the false democracy of collectivism.
2. To operate a truthful and fair free press not influenced by the intimidation and subterfuge of extremists and their ideologies.
3. To remain independent.
4. To produce an attractive and entertaining newspaper without reliance on scandal, sexual and financial titillation and sensationalism.
5. To support freedom of speech and publication.
6. To support freedom from all coercive monopolies.
7. To support freedom of religion and worship.
8. To criticise the law of the land but never to support those who are defiant of the law by use of force, intimidation and subterfuge.
9. To support the right of those who wish to join a trades union as well as those who do not.
10. To protect those who suffer from an irresponsible invasion of privacy.
11. To protect the right to engage in private enterprise and pursue the trade or profession of one's choice without harassment.
12. To protect the freedom of choice in the use of State and private services.
13. To support the right to be defended against the country's enemies.

One can imagine MacArthur, the old pro, blanching initially at the banality of the Bill of Rights. Shah added some even more general hopes: that the paper would try to create a sense of community as his Messenger papers aim to do and which he sees sorely lacking all around him. He believes that somehow 'involvement journalism' – young reporters going out and experiencing life in a hospital or on a picket line – can help instil this community sense. He longs to run a paper that is not constantly sniping at governments and individuals, and if not full of 'good news' at least attractive to look at, with the intelligent use of TV graphics. Finally, Shah wants to support the 'older traditional and more caring ways which we have lost as a nation, thanks in part to the media itself which has helped create a hip, fashionable, slick and faceless society'.

Shah now says he will interfere in the editorial side of the paper only if the original ideals are breached by MacArthur. The vagueness of the Bill of Rights certainly gives him plenty of scope for intervention and few people close to him believe he will be able to resist meddling. Shah's close involvement with MacArthur, Holden and Holborow, the weekday editor, in the paper's editorial birth may make his intervention unnecessary as it will already substantially reflect his own attitudes. If it does not, MacArthur does not seem prepared to resist him for long.

So what are Shah's politics? Despite representing a new departure in almost every sphere of national newspapers, in his own views Shah is a traditional press baron. He cannot abide the comparison but curiously he shares a number of personal traits with the old autocrats; he has the boyishness and vanity of Northcliffe and, like Beaverbrook, is constantly on the telephone spreading gossip or testing out an idea. Tom Clarke's description of Northcliffe is pure Shah: 'He was not a thinker but . . . he arrived at the results of thought without thought itself. His outlook was mainly emotional. He said he knew nothing about politics, art, sport, finance, literature and so on; and when he looked at a picture, or at a game, or a movement in the City, it was not knowledge, but the emotional response in himself, that dictated his attitude.'

Shah may lack the political depth of a Beaverbrook but, like him, he knows more clearly what he is against – the Left, the Establishment, the City, the 'institutions' – than what he is for. He distrusts parliamentarians and bureaucrats and believes he has special access to the thoughts and ideals of 'ordinary people'. He says: 'I believe that people out there basically all think the same things – or at least the big majority do – but often those feelings don't get through because so many of the guys in Parliament – the lawyers and teachers – they haven't experienced anything.'

Hence it is Shah's job as the champion of the little man – the 'people's capitalist' – to represent those views through his paper. It is rather a simple vision at a time when politics is becoming more complex and fragmented. But Shah is unashamedly a 'gut' politician.

One point which certainly distinguishes his politics from the old Tory proprietors is his real concern about the North–South divide in Britain. It is mirrored in the structure of News UK itself with its administrative base in Warrington, although he is starting without a northern editorial base, unlike many other nationals. The Warrington link also, of course, more simply represents Shah's intention to stamp his own authority on *his* company.

At the time of the Messenger dispute he insisted on his 'centrist' politics as a counter to the union-basher image. Soon after the dispute, however, the Messenger Newspaper Group donated £1,000 to the Tory Party – 'more as a thank-you to the local MPs who had helped us than anything else', he now says. Shah insists that he still stands somewhere between the SDP and Tory Party, while critical of both. But any conventional placement on the – admittedly superficial – Left–Right axis would find him a long way to the right on most major issues.

In economics he is an unabashed free marketeer: 'Unions don't take risks. The people that take the risks and create the jobs are the Joes who go out and sell their houses and just have a go, they are the base of British life. And that's where I think Thatcher has failed in not giving even more freedom of movement to encourage people to do that.'

Shah is an 'entrepreneurialist', an English Poujadist, a zealous advocate of the small capitalist and his dreams of the perfect market. In his nostalgia for a lost caring community, he also claims some commitment (like virtually everybody else in public life) to the ideals of the 'old' Labour Party. 'I support the caring society but not socialism – you can't have capital run by politicians – they won't be any good at it,' he says.

Shah is certainly nothing if not a populist. Driving through London recently, he saw a traditionally-dressed senior civil servant with his briefcase and rolled umbrella. He pointed at him and hissed: 'There, those are the guys we've got to get.' He believes his own eclectic views are in tune with the 'spirit of the age' – a disillusionment with Left and Right and advocacy of the caring, socially mobile, free-market society. No wonder the Owenites in the SDP claim him as their own. They doubtless hope that as the *News Chronicle* declined with the Liberal vote in the 1930s, *Today* will rise with the SDP vote in the late 1980s.

But he is also in many respects a 'Thatcherite' hero. Shah opened his typesetting plant in Stockport in 1979 a few weeks after Thatcher's first victory. The Messenger dispute began in July 1983 a few weeks after her second victory. Shah's themes during the dispute chimed in with hers: freedom of the individual against collective pressures of unions and the closed shop; management's right to manage; and a yearning to 'put the Great back in Britain' by unleashing market forces everywhere.

These are mostly long-standing Tory – or simply management – objectives. But in Shah's radical provincialism and populism, there is something of the Thatcher spirit. Shah, while eschewing Thatcherism, does admire Margaret Thatcher. He has met her twice at official functions although they only spoke briefly. Indirectly they have had a fuller exchange of views through Christopher Monkton – an aggressive young Thatcherite who works in the Prime Minister's private policy unit and took Shah out to lunch at Brook's Club nine months before the launch of *Today*.

Shah may think like the old press barons but will he act like them? While he shares the 'outsider' or 'anti-Establishment' epithet with several of the great proprietors – they have usually bought newspapers as a short route to the dining tables of power. Shah remains more ambivalent. He has not exactly objected to his adoption by several leading right-wing businessmen and has enjoyed rubbing shoulders with some of the most powerful men in Britain. But he also says he is determined not to get sucked into the seamy world of London politics and to date he has decided not even to buy a flat in the capital. During the past year his working week has consisted of the first three or four days in London – usually staying at the THF-owned Hyde Park Hotel – with the rest of the week being spent in Warrington. 'I can't bear London,' he is always saying.

Last November in the Pimlico editorial office came a more telling illustration of his attempt to remain aloof. MacArthur asked Shah if he would accompany the senior editorial team to meet Michael Shea, the Royal press officer. Shah's response was: 'No, Brian, you know my position on things like that. I don't want to be part of it. I don't want the cocktail parties.' Knowing he had already over-played his 'I'm just an ordinary chap from the North' role, he presented it as a piece of self-mockery. 'You all know me, just a thick bastard from up North – I haven't got good enough table manners to see the Queen.'

It was clearly not vital from the point of view of Royal coverage that Shah attended the meeting with Michael Shea. But Tony Holden, who through his biography of Prince Charles knows the Royal household better than most, had been told that 'someone important' was interested in meeting Shah. In Royal-talk that could have meant Prince Charles, Prince Philip or even the Queen

225

herself. Holden told Shah – and translated the code –
but it did not change his mind.

The 'shy proprietor' also told MacArthur a few days
later – in a typically immodest display of modesty – that
on *Today*'s grand first night in early March he would not
be sipping champagne and taking the photo-calls in
Pimlico. But, in a gesture at once contrived and sincere,
he said he would be 'with my staff' in one of the printing
plants. The phrase (and the location) had a familiar ring
from the Messenger dispute. The product off the presses
in early March 1986, however, looked very different from
anything the Warrington presses had ever turned out.

At the end of May 1985 Brian MacArthur, in the cramped
Covent Garden basement, was experiencing an editor's
dream come true. Aside from the loose policies laid
down by the proprietor, he had 44 blank pages (or
screens) of a new national paper to fill from scratch
with none of the usual constraints upon a new editor
inheriting the style of his paper and the preconceptions
of its readers.

The process of filling those pages was, over the next
ten months, to be dominated by two still unresolved
debates: first, how do you run a national paper on an
annual editorial budget of only £4.5m. Second, where in
the market is the paper going to slot? Will it be the
Sunday Times, turned daily, tabloid and colour – or will
it be the *Daily Mail* (or even *Mirror*) in colour?

MacArthur's first appointment in early June was a
clear guide to his own preference for an 'up-market'
tabloid. He called his old friend from the Evans era,
Tony Holden. Holden is an urbane figure. After school
at Oundle he went to Oxford, and then made his mark
in national papers as the writer of the Atticus column in
the *Sunday Times*. In 1978 he left to write his best-selling
book about Prince Charles before being lured back to
journalism by the offer of the *Observer*'s Washington
post. After Evans took over *The Times*, he became its

features editor – firmly representing the spirit of the new, liberal *Times*.

Politically he is marginally left of centre – and was until recently a member of the Labour Party. His prejudices are those of the liberal intellectual establishment and as one of his colleagues says: 'Tony wants the paper to be something he does not have to be ashamed of among his friends in Islington.'

After the dismissal of Evans from the *Times*, Holden left at once – in fact he went straight to a TV studio to denounce Murdoch. He then went back to freelance work for the *Sunday Express* magazine and to writing books – a biography of Olivier that he had been working on for years and a *Penguin Guide to Opera* which he was editing with his wife Amanda, a concert pianist.

To underline his own distance from the instincts of mass-circulation tabloid journalism, he tells the story of how, just as MacArthur rang him that May morning, the door bell also rang and there, standing at the door, was Jonathan Miller, freelance man of letters. He had come to pick up the new translation of Mozart's *Don Giovanni* for the English National Opera that Holden and his wife were just completing.

The wide gap between the worlds of Shah and Holden proved no obstacle. 'I warmed to him immediately and what I particularly liked was that – like me – he can't be completely serious for more than about three minutes at a time,' says Holden. He does, however, remain one of the most sceptical and independent members of *Today*'s Inner Cabinet and if the paper takes a turn he doesn't like, he will be readier than most to quit.

At the beginning of June the search began for the daily paper editor and, to balance MacArthur and Holden, it had to be a man from the tabloids. The choice was eventually between Jonathan Holborow, associate editor of the *Mail on Sunday* and Pat Pilton, night editor of the *Daily Express*. Holborow got the job but Pilton's enthusiasm for the new technology had impressed Shah and MacArthur and he was invited to join *Today* as executive production editor.

Temperamentally and journalistically, Holborow occupies a very different space to the two 'nice guys' – MacArthur and Holden. He is self-proclaimedly from the 'orange' school of newspapers – one step up from the yellow, a foot-in-the-door editor.

Holborow, whose brother Paul is a leading figure in the far-left Socialist Workers Party, went to Charterhouse public school and then climbed up the ranks of the *Daily Mail*, a protégé of editor David English, and in 1975 became its news editor. He is an old-fashioned newsdesk shouter and his abrasive style has already made enemies on the paper. In politics and personality he is probably closer to Shah than to MacArthur or Holden. However, he remains firmly behind the latter two in the pecking-order.

MacArthur, Holden and Holborow all talk hopefully about the marriage between the best of the Harold Evans and the David English schools – but with three separate individuals, all of editor rank, jostling at the altar rail, it is a potentially traumatic union.

At the end of June, however, the editorial budget was a more pressing problem than market position. The three editors worked together on different drafts of the budget, which Shah kept rejecting as 'too conventional, too stuck in the Fleet Street rut'. He questioned whether separate staffs were necessary for the daily and weekend papers and at one point even wondered whether sub-editors were needed at all.

Relations between Shah and MacArthur were strained for a time as Shah believed his editor was slipping back into the old ways with his long lunches with old Fleet Street cronies or senior politicians. He even refused to allow MacArthur to put a lunch with David Owen on his expense account.

But it was only a hiccup, as Holden recalls: 'Eddie was very much one of the lads; he was always popping in when we were working on something and we would say, "piss off, we're just plotting how to slip something past you".' The editors won the principle of two separate staffs for the daily and weekend papers (although there will be considerable overlap) but didn't win as much extra money as they wanted.

In early July Jeremy Deedes had joined *Today* as managing editor from the *Evening Standard*. With the brisk manner of a young army officer, he immediately became Shah's aide-de-camp – the most enthusiastic fan of his 'lateral thinking'. And just before Deedes came Gordon Phillips with the task of setting up Britain's first electronic newspaper library, to be staffed entirely by graduate librarians.

At the end of July the senior editorial staff moved into *Today*'s permanent London home – two floors at Allen House, 70 Vauxhall Bridge Road. It is a sensible place to house a new, London-based national paper: closer than Fleet Street to many of the centres of power like Parliament and Whitehall; a good deal cheaper on rent and rates; up the road from Victoria Station; just opposite Pimlico tube and a pleasant little urban village of shops and restaurants.

The advantages were pointed out by Lord Harris whose job consultancy already had offices in the block along with the Boxing Board of Control. The only possible disadvantage was noticed by Lord Harris's son – who pointed out that the next-door office, where the blinds are always down, is occupied by MI6, the intelligence service.

After discovering the identity of his new neighbours, Shah was worried that they might object to such a high-profile company on their doorstep. What temporarily worried him even more was that the day after signing an agreement with the leaseholders in Pimlico, he was offered two floors of Millbank Tower – the grand office block just round the corner on the Embankment, overlooking the Thames. The symbolic journey from

Winwick Quay to Millbank Tower appealed to him but it was too late, and it remains one of his few disappointments of the year.

Jane Reed, former editor of *Woman's Own* and *Woman*, had meanwhile joined as features editor. She had originally been approached by MacArthur to act as an advisor on young talent – but was so attracted by the project that she joined herself. Reed, a rotund, bustling, fluent woman had come from being managing director of the Holborn Group – part of the IPC publishing empire – and was also a full board director of IPC. Despite that weighty background there was some, perhaps rather patronising, anxiety among the other staff – especially Holborow – that her lack of Fleet Street experience might be a problem on a fast-moving daily paper. She responded that her own experience and the relatively high proportion of women on the paper – many in senior posts such as political editor and city editor – will contribute to its individuality. Some see *Today's* market niche becoming predominantly female and Reed's role as potentially central.

Another major appointment was the respected foreign correspondent and former *Sunday Times* journalist Philip Jacobson, to act as world roving reporter. It had been an early ambition of Shah's to have a latter-day James Cameron on the paper. The foreign editor will be Benjamin Pogrund – the former deputy editor of the now defunct South African liberal newspaper, The *Rand Daily Mail*. Initially, foreign staff – apart from Jacobson – will be entirely 'stringers', which could leave the paper exposed if major international stories break before it has its system in working order.

In August everyone – except Shah – went on holiday for most of the month. When they came back in September, a disorganised, living-out-of-suitcases atmosphere still prevailed in Pimlico. This was partly due to the enormous strain on management resources: Roy Dickinson, the production director, was also in effect office manager in London and simply had too much to do. The strain began to show and Shah came to regret having given Dickinson the grand title of publishing director, since this made it difficult to bring in anyone else of equal rank on the production side. Nevertheless, partly due to Dickinson's hard work, the whole project remained remarkably on schedule.

The Hastech equipment arrived in early October and with it another minor crisis. Mary Ann Raymond was sent from Hastech in the US to oversee the introduction of the system and the training of staff on it. But when she arrived at Heathrow her immigration papers were not in order. Lord Harris came to the rescue again with a few calls to his friends in the Ministry.

In October the pace quickened. Shah was seeking and getting an increasing amount of exposure in the media and *Today* became a more solid reality after the advertising presentations in Limehouse. Mike Brown, the 41-year-old former editor of the *Lancashire Evening Telegraph*, joined as the chief sub-editor. Coincidentally, he had been a sub-editor on the Reading *Evening News* in 1965 when it became the first paper in the UK to move from hot metal to photocomposition.

Intense interviewing of journalists now began. There were over 1,000 applicants for approximately a hundred jobs, so Holden and Holborow – who did ten interviews a day for three weeks – had a wide choice. The interviews provided entertaining evidence of the continuing tussle for the soul of the paper.

The two editors liked to devise little news judgement conundrums to test the interviewees' responses. One week after the Tottenham riots, the applicants were asked how they would react if they heard that Bernie Grant, the black leader of Haringey Council, had left his wife for a white Trotskyist lover. Holden was hoping to hear that it was not really relevant to the enormously difficult problem of reporting the crisis in Britain's inner cities, while Holborow clearly wanted some recognition

231

that this was a 'damned good story'. More than one interviewee commented that the two men barely attempted to suppress their own strongly divergent views.

Holden, backed by the advertising agency Wight, Collins, Rutherford, Scott, appeared to be winning his argument for keeping the paper reasonably serious and substantial, but Holborow meanwhile seemed to be getting more of his journalistic allies employed. His view of the paper as 'the *Daily Mail* in colour' was almost literally coming true as about a dozen appointments were made from his old paper. More supporters of his relatively 'down-market' reflexes filled the key newsdesk jobs. Colin Myler, from the *Sunday People*, was appointed news editor.

MacArthur himself took control of the more senior appointments and old friends, usually from quality newspaper backgrounds, like Sue Cameron from the *Financial Times*, helped to redress the balance.

The most daring appointment of all was another poach from the *FT*. The post of city editor appeared set to go to an established figure in financial journalism: someone the outside investors on the board of News UK would feel comfortable with. The head-hunt made little progress until Holden received a tip-off that he need look no further than the bottom of his own street in Islington. Here lived Mary Ann Sieghart, a youthful high-flier on the *FT*'s influential Lex column. They had a long chat and Holden was immensely impressed. He returned to the office and proclaimed that he had found the new Patrick Hutber (the leading financial journalist of the 1960s and 1970s) 'and she is a 24-year-old blonde'. Nobody believed he was serious until he persuaded Jeremy Deedes to ring his father who had employed Sieghart to write leaders for the *Telegraph* at the age of eighteen, and who proceeded to reel off a long list of her qualifications for the job. There was some disquiet on the board about appointing not only the youngest ever city editor, but also the first ever woman in this role. However, the appointment went through.

Representatives of the investors were able to quiz the senior editorial staff about their appointments at the gathering in Warrington on 4 November known as the 'War Games'. This had been planned a long time in advance as a thorough, collective assessment, four months before launch, of the main problems the paper faced – and the kind of response it was likely to provoke from its rivals. Every department was represented – distribution, sales, editorial, advertising, production – and they all delivered short papers.

Sir Richard Storey, now on the board of News UK, asked MacArthur bluntly what his relationship with the board and with Shah would be. MacArthur's reply was that while he as editor-in-chief retained editorial control, he appreciated that Eddie would want a say in the occasional leader article.

Charles Wintour was much more specific. He asked what MacArthur would do if a reporter offered him documentary proof that David Owen was a practising homosexual. It was a particularly acute dilemma for MacArthur because of his real-life friendship with Owen. MacArthur concluded that it would be a suitable case for consulting with Shah. Storey, in an odd role-reversal, butted in and said that on the contrary, it should be entirely the editor's decision – adding with a smile 'even if it is his last'.

Those who have witnessed Shah's journey from the fourth to the first division in newspapers (in one season) have generally assumed that the impulsive Messenger management style would mellow as he surrounded himself with more experienced and substantial business-men. To an extent this has happened. But his elevated status has not changed the essence of his highly personal approach. 'The heart and the power base of News UK and Messenger is myself, Jennifer and Helen,' he says. Both women are forceful and intelligent and – in their different ways – significant influences on Shah, but what he is implicitly saying is 'I am News UK'.

The ten-person board – some of whose members might question that – meets every month. In addition to Helen Graham, Lord Harris, Roy Dickinson and Brian Nicholson, there is usually a representative of THF and Ivory & Sime, John Skeffington from Bricom, James Glen from the Scottish Investment Trust and Sir Richard Storey from Portsmouth and Sunderland. Shah usually dominates proceedings and can still bristle when crossed.

The man who crosses him more than most is Storey – mainly because, as another newspaperman, he asks rather more difficult questions. Relations between them have been strained ever since some of the investors suggested that Storey should become chairman of the company – to Shah's horror. But the tension between the two men was not responsible for PSN's decision at the end of 1985 not to print *Today* under contract in Portsmouth and in Sunderland. 'We didn't see eye to eye on the contract for perfectly sound business reasons on both sides. It was simply not in our interests to take on the extra staff for a print-run which we might only keep for six months,' says Storey. Nevertheless, the management at PSN has expressed remarkably little confidence in *Today* – considering it has a £½m. investment in the paper.

Sir Richard – who could yet come to take the place of Douglas May in the Shah demonology – admits that board meetings are 'more volatile than most I have experienced'. He remains a great admirer of Shah but adds: 'He's like a child, he's ebullient and excitable and it's our job not to trammel him but to examine, restrain and encourage all at once.'

Shah certainly does sometimes take the board's advice. He wanted, for example, to buy cheap, high-quality South African newsprint in the middle of last year despite the nightly scenes of horror on TV. But the board managed to dissuade him.

Although Shah could technically be outvoted on the board, it is almost unthinkable – especially with his block vote of personal friends – and in any case Shah personally owns 60 per cent of the issued share capital of News UK, with Messenger (in which he has at least a 50 per cent share) owning the other 40 per cent.

The investors' £8.5m. does not become share capital until 'conversion' at the beginning of the paper's fourth year of existence. At that point their combined stake converts into a minimum of 55 per cent and a maximum of 88 per cent of the share capital, depending on the profits record over the next three years. The rest is divided between Shah, (10–35 per cent) and the staff, (2–10 per cent). News UK cannot be floated on the stock-market until after 'conversion' and then the decision will rest with the board.

The day-to-day management board – which meets whenever convenient – consists of Deedes, MacArthur, Pritchett, Dickinson and Shah. It will eventually include the News UK finance director but Shah has had difficulty finding a man sufficiently committed to his own unorthodox methods.

In mid-November 1985 he faced a more pressing problem when it looked as if MAN Roland were going to be late delivering the first presses to the Heathrow plant. The media, not for the first time, became Shah's ally. A BBC *Panorama* crew travelled with Shah to Germany and under the TV arc lamps the MAN Roland managing director had to promise that of course the presses would arrive on time – as indeed they did, thanks to some very speedy catch-up work. (The BBC has taken a keen interest in Shah and at one time had two crews following him everywhere – one from *Panorama* and the other from *Forty Minutes*. They did not get on with each other.)

At the end of November the editorial department moved to its final resting-place on the first floor of Allen House and the office started to take proper shape.

Through November and December there was a fresh wave of interest from big-name Fleet Street reporters and columnists. MacArthur joked that he could gauge the morale on different papers each day by the calls he got.

The original problem of budgeting had become even more acute: there was no money left to hire the staff becoming available. The weekend paper had, for example, by December already spent its entire freelance budget for the year ahead on full-time staff. The senior journalists' determination to produce a paper admired by their Fleet Street peers and Shah's desire to change the ground rules of editorial cost remained in amicable tension.

The 'what paper are we?' debate seemed to have become less significant as everyone was swept up into the final surge towards launch. Holden and Holborow accepted an inevitable degree of disparity between their respective weekend and weekday publications.

Columnists now signed up included Melvyn Bragg, Peter O'Sullivan, Joanna Lumley and Derek Jameson, the former *Daily Express* editor who had become another *Today* confidant. Some interest was expressed by Peregrine Worsthorne, the right-wing guru of the *Sunday Telegraph* and briefly by Andrew Alexander, the city editor of the *Daily Mail*. MacArthur welcomed these overtures as a mark of respect of his yet unborn paper, but Shah was not keen on Worsthorne who would have had to be balanced by an outspokenly left-wing columnist such as Ken Livingstone, who was indeed sounded out.

Succumbing to a final bout of gimmickry, Shah decided that all staff cars should be white except his own BMW which was black. He also suggested in mid-December that the leader and feature page – usually about one-third of the way through a paper – should be relegated to the back half. 'People are not interested in all that politics,' he would say wearily. MacArthur, who had learned how to humour him, said it was a very interesting idea and ignored the suggestion.

Since October regular dummy pages had been produced and picked over by designers and editors seeking to avoid that 'blockish' design which can be the mark of screen-based papers. On 24 January came the first full dummy print run at the Poyle plant and soon after, on 10 February they proposed to produce the paper each day until launch. Security had meanwhile tightened dramatically; the electronic newspaper is particularly vulnerable to a few well-placed wire cuts and Shah is still a man with many enemies as the arson attack on the Manchester plant at the end of January showed.

Just before most of the reporters started to arrive in January, the schedule struck its first minor hitch when the German electricians went home for Christmas half a day short of finishing work wiring up the presses, and did not return until January.

But *Today* remained remarkably immune from British labour disruption. The NGA made a token gesture of hostility when it threatened not to connect the paper to the Press Association wire service. The union was not however going to risk another round of heavy court fines over secondary action and quietly made the connection ten days after the threat was first made. The only other potential union lever on Shah is the fact that SOGAT members are scheduled to distribute it – through W. H. Smith's involvement in the provinces – but action is highly unlikely and would again be open to court action.

Despite the big hype the paper is likely, in the end, to be quite conventional, except for its colour content. It may indeed appear rather flat, the product of a compromise between two ultimately incompatible views of the paper's news values. A reasonably strong team has been hired to produce *Today*, but it is considerably understaffed even allowing for initial enthusiasm and could prove an unstable chemical compound. Right up to launch most of the senior executives were continuing to mutter about 'Eddie's learning curve on editorial costs'.

Shah is aware of the possible problem and has indeed accepted the need to train up casual staff on the new equipment in case of staffing trouble. He is also quite happy to drive his staff hard and then see where the gaps really do need filling. Sitting in his new London office on the second floor of Allen House, he says his main regret is not buying several more printing presses for the launch. He adds: 'Of course we will have problems but unlike Fleet Street all our problems will be soluble by the application of a bit of commonsense.' He made it all sound so easy.

13

The Ice Melts: Fleet Street

'Just a few years ago it would have been unthinkable for a Fleet Street employer to open up a custom built, high security, scab printworks just a stone's throw from the Street. Just a few years ago it would also have been unthinkable that you would have been able to read about it in that employers' newspaper.'

Bill Freeman in the London Sogat Post,
December 1985

13

The Ice Melts: Fleet Street

The announcement at the end of February 1985 that Shah intended to take on the national newspaper barons was met initially with derision and later discomfort in Fleet Street boardrooms and chapel offices. Lord Matthews at the Express building pronounced that Shah would be under-capitalised. Bryn Griffiths, the NGA national president, said there was no way that the print unions would allow him to get the paper out.

But as the spring months went by and Shah began to look a more and more serious prospect, the executives of the national newspapers had to start responding. By the end of 1985 Fleet Street had permanently changed. Disentangling the extent to which Shah was directly responsible, or simply a catalyst for a process that was already under way, is perhaps pointless. Undoubtedly Shah was influential, and possibly decisive. But he was just as much a beneficiary as a creator of the new climate. Well before Shah made his announcement, a new calibre of Fleet Street proprietor had arrived in Robert Maxwell, a man willing to kick over the traces from within. Equally, the political and legal changes made it that much easier for men like Maxwell and Murdoch to consider a new offensive against the Fleet Street unions. Those laws had already been used to effect by the provincial newspaper owners such as the Wolverhampton *Express and Star* in their successful attempts to impose direct-input.

It was, one *Daily Express* manager put it, as if 'a series of tributaries had joined up and together had formed a swollen river strong enough to burst the dam that had been blocking change. Eddie Shah was just the final stick of dynamite at the dam's base.' The NGA general secretary Tony Dubbins did not attempt to ignore the confluence, acknowledging in November 1985 both Shah's impact and the longer-term trends: 'The plain fact is that at the moment virtually every employer is using the threat of Shah to put pressure on the unions, bring forward their plans for new investment, new technology, moves to new sites and moves, moreover, where conditions may not be maintained, let alone improved. But even without Shah, I'm afraid to say, I think employers would have a far more acquiescent trade union movement than previously. There is no getting away from that.'

By 1983, the majority of Fleet Street companies, apparently independently, had decided to move their printing, publishing and distribution operations out of their century-old home and into the revitalised East London docklands. Ironically, the decision to leave Fleet Street was made only a little while before it became clear that the balance of power within Fleet Street had finally shifted towards management. Indeed many managers saw the exodus as a symbol of defeat. The failures at the *Mirror*, the *Financial Times* and *The Times*, detailed earlier in the book, suggested that Fleet Street culture and environment were of themselves powerful factors blocking modernisation and greater efficiency.

A move to purpose-built plant with capital grants, cheap land and 'rate holidays' had obvious advantages. For one thing, operating in Fleet Street had meant little or no opportunity to expand floor space to accommodate labour-saving machinery. Although there was no guarantee that such a move could destroy the Fleet Street culture, the view of management generally was that a move to new, less restrictive buildings would raise the chance of negotiating new, less restrictive labour practices. A move at the very least would mean that new printing techniques, unused in Fleet Street, could be more easily installed, including web-offset, new letterpresses and flexography, all of which offered the prospect of colour news pages, better reproduction and a reduction in paper wastage.

So once News International announced in 1979 that it would be moving the *Sun* and the *News of the World* to a new thirteen-acre site in Wapping, Associated Newspapers, the *Daily Telegraph* and the *Guardian* followed suit over the next few years, buying up sites deeper into the docklands, a stretch of land ironically made desolate by the appalling industrial relations in the docks after the war. The only groups that by the end of 1985 had decided to leave their printing operations in Fleet Street were the *Financial Times* and *Express Newspapers*, then owned by Fleet. (At the beginning of 1986 however, the FT too, announced it was joining the exodus).

The capital grants available in the Docklands were sizeable, but it is doubtful that the move eastwards would have been possible, for some of the papers, without the newspaper owners' fortunate discovery in the spring of 1982 that they could float Reuters on the stock-exchange and pick up millions of pounds. 'It was as if they had discovered oil in the back garden,' explained Sir Richard Marsh who, as NPA chairman, had to help umpire the fierce wrangles between the papers over the precise size of their respective shareholdings. For a paper such as the *Guardian*, with few independent resources, the £15m. purchase of land and plant was inconceivable without its 13m. shares worth approximately £40m. Similarly, the *Daily Telegraph*, with a shareholding of the same order, could not have contemplated its fateful move without the support of the Reuters' money.

But the move to the Docklands was dogged with

difficulty. The Wapping plant had been forced to lie idle for two years since its effective completion in 1983, a vivid symbol of the chapels' enduring influence. But changes in the law and the impact of Shah's imminent arrival helped transform the move to the docklands from a sign of defeat into a real opportunity to reassert managerial control to a degree far greater than originally envisaged at the time the move to the docks was first mooted.

The law did not necessarily prove decisive to the outcome of any individual Fleet Street disputes in 1984 and 1985, but it certainly proved a powerful additional bargaining chip for management. As Frank Barlow at the *Financial Times* put it after he had handed out individual writs against his recalcitrant machine room, 'neither party any longer has the monopoly on the use of force'.

Each member of the NPA, for instance, took out in 1983 damages claims totalling up to £4m. against the NGA in compensation for the two days of solidarity strikes held in Fleet Street in protest at the contempt fines imposed on the union in the Messenger dispute. When the NGA claimed that the strikes were spontaneous local reactions, the NPA members responded by starting individual claims against the four London NGA committee members responsible for organising the strikes. (The claims were later dropped as a quid pro quo for other concessions by the NGA.) During disputes in 1984 and 1985 the *Daily Mail*, the *Sun*, the *Guardian*, the *Financial Times* and Mirror Group Newspapers all either secured injunctions against the unions or issued individual writs against strikers. Reuters, for its part, enforced a closed-shop ballot. High Court injunctions, once regarded as the recourse only of the mavericks and ideologues, had rapidly become commonplace in Fleet Street, reflecting a wider psychological shift.

As John Winnington-Ingram, the *Daily Mail*'s managing director put it, 'Whatever you like to say about the woman, Mrs Thatcher has changed the climate. It's very much up to us now.' The bullishness was reflected widely in Fleet Street boardrooms. During 1985, management, long inured to frustration, failure and false dawns, developed a burning conviction that it would never get a better chance to sort 'the union problem' out. For one thing, if they did not act now, a Labour government pledged to restoring union immunities might be returned and the opportunity would be lost. The assertiveness in the boardroom was mirrored by a pessimism on the shop floor. In the words of one Fleet Street electrician, 'We could not go on forever in our ivory tower, pretending that what was happening everywhere else in the country simply did not exist.' If any single event had altered the psychological balance it had been the defeat of the miners. The activists in the Fleet Street production unions had associated themselves totally with the miners' struggle, donating over a million pounds from chapel funds and collections, despatching food convoys up the motorway to the coalfields, assembling miners' right-of-reply newspapers and trying sometimes, backed with industrial action, to push papers such as the *Daily Express*, the *Sun* and the *Daily Mail* into giving space to the miners' case. For a short while proprietorial control over the editorial content of newspapers seemed under siege.

It had become a commonplace assertion among Fleet Street militants – echoing Arthur Scargill – that if the miners lost, the slow erosion of chapel power could not be halted. Once the miners did lose, many of the chapel activists confided: 'Well that's us finished then, it's just a matter of time now.' If the miners with their sheer endurance could not budge their employer or the Government – what chance the Fleet Street unions, who had achieved so much with comparatively little sacrifice? The Praetorian guards had grown flabby under their armour.

However, one of the strongest attacks on the chapels' weakened defences startlingly came from within the labour movement, when the electricians' union, EETPU, injected an entirely new dimension into the drama by announcing in July 1985 that it had signed an outline single-union deal with Eddie Shah. The 1,000-strong branch of Fleet Street electricians had always been an anomaly both within Fleet Street and within its union. Its branch leadership, containing many Communists, had stood out against the ferociously anti-Left attitude that had predominated in the union ever since Frank Chapple had become general secretary in the late fifties in the wake of a communist ballot-rigging scandal. Despite repeated attacks on the branch, Chapple had never been able to bring it under his control. In 1983, amidst rumours that Chapple was willing to 'sell' the branch in frustration, the branch's secretary Sean Geraghty, an electrician at the *Daily Mirror*, led the branch out of the union and into the arms of the London Machine branch of SOGAT. Far from expressing relief at the removal of a thorn in his side, Chapple immediately accused SOGAT of poaching his members and demanded them back. Chapple's hand was strengthened when the branch split over the secession. Some stuck with their old union on the grounds that they had a wider obligation to use the branch's power base to attempt to restore the Left's authority within the union. The TUC for its part threatened to expel SOGAT unless the Fleet Street electricians were returned to Chapple. Bill Keys, the SOGAT general secretary and an elder statesman on the TUC's General Council, understandably buckled.

The EETPU national official responsible for ensuring that the electricians stayed with their old union was a tough former Communist, Tom Rice, ironically an old Irish confederate of Sean Geraghty's. One reason for the intensity with which the electricians fought for the retention of their Fleet Street membership was that they saw in the spread of computers and electronics in newspapers, a golden opportunity to take a new strategic stake in the industry. The way the union first laid claim to that wider stake was quite audacious even by the electricians' standards: soon after Shah had gone public with his plans, the electricians' chief strategists decided to ask Shah if he was interested in a single-union deal.

The electricians have made a speciality of slaying the trade union movement's sacred cows, holding fringe meetings at the CBI, grabbing state cash for union ballots in defiance of TUC policy, inviting Norman Tebbit to their training centre, lambasting the left-led Metropolitan councils and describing the miners' strike as a dispute where lions had been led by donkeys. The union's Japanese-inspired package deal of single union, no-strike deals for employers had, since 1981, been disrupting the traditional multi-union structure, mainly in the electronics industry. However, the union's general secretary Eric Hammond was a more complex politician than his predecessor, Frank Chapple. Hammond argued that the trade union movement's old-fashioned multi-union structure was one reason foreign investors were unwilling to come to Britain. Moreover, even if no-strike agreements were unpalatable, they were preferable to no union presence at all. Nevertheless, to initiate an approach to Shah – the Labour movement's most demonic figure – was to bring a new meaning to the term revisionism.

It was John Grant, a former Labour MP and journalist, now a member of the SDP and the Electricians' Union press officer, who appears to have first had the idea of doing a deal with Shah. He discussed it with Tom Rice who immediately warmed to the idea. Grant rang his fellow SDP member and old acquaintance, Lord Harris, who was interested, but immediately insisted that there must be a no-strike deal and no closed shop – neither was a difficulty for the union. Harris also immediately raised the question of the TUC's Bridlington agreement – which ruled relations between unions and usually prevented the poaching of members who would normally fall into another's patch. Grant, however, pointed out that as Shah's paper was a greenfield site, the union would not be risking expulsion from the TUC under its

Bridlington rules. Anyway, the union had found itself increasingly at odds with the TUC and had been beginning to view expulsion from it with increasing equanimity.

Shah was immediately taken with the idea when Harris mentioned it. He saw it as a way of shaking off the union-bashing tag that he disliked so intensely. Although it was now quite possible to produce a national paper without any union representation, he also recognised that this would attract stigma and a host of avoidable irritations. A deal with the TUC's radical right would not obstruct his project, but might relieve him of those potential troubles. One such minor difficulty was relations with the NUJ – still technically at odds with him over the Messenger dispute. Shah was confident that he could attract adequate staff to his new paper quite happily in the face of an NUJ blacking notice, but he realised that it might restrict his pool of talent, and hoped that a deal with the EETPU might make blacking less likely.

He did not support a deal out of expediency alone. Shah, like many employers, is attracted to the Japanese marriage of single status and consensus in the workplace and wanted to give his backing to the EETPU's new unionism. 'They understand the role of profits,' he said. Playing a small part in transforming the wider industrial relations scene no doubt appealed to his vanity. Shah is also, however, realistic enough to admit that his own interests and those of his employees – or individual workers – might sometimes clash and that 'unions are needed to protect people'. The EETPU deal provides for non-adversarial negotiation on a works council, a no-strike deal and pendulum arbitration under which an arbitrator has to choose between the management's pay offer and the union's pay claim and cannot split the difference. All members on the works council are to be given training in basic accountancy and economics.

It was ironically on 1 May, the Labour movement's traditional holiday, that this unorthodox departure from trade union practice was in effect sealed at a meeting between Shah and the EETPU at the Berkeley Hotel in Piccadilly. Representing the EETPU were John Grant, Tom Rice and Eric Hammond, the general secretary. Hammond, trying to test out Shah, told him frankly that he didn't see why Shah was interested in a deal at all. He also laconically suggested that perhaps Shah should put the deal out to tender to all trade unions. Tom Rice worried that Shah might pick up the idea and intervened, saying of course that would be unnecessary. But the rogue union and the rogue employer had warmed to each other and after that meeting signing a deal looked like a mere formality. When the news of the outline agreement leaked out in July it left the print union leaders speechless. When they had recovered sufficiently, it was in most cases to say that they weren't really surprised.

Both SOGAT and the NGA responded to the electricians' announcement by seeking a meeting with Shah as well, but Shah cut their separate overtures short. 'I'm not going to have lots of different unions in here or else I'll end up like everyone else, spending my whole time negotiating and none of my time running a business,' he said.

The electricians' deal increased not only the likelihood of Shah's paper getting off the ground, but also generally destabilised the print unions. Just as Shah had acted as the interloper disturbing the proprietors' calm, so the sudden coup of the electricians undid the print unions' status quo. As Tony Dubbins put it soon after, 'The danger is that we will soon have a union running round this industry prepared to make deals that we could never consider.' The NGA feared that the electricians' intervention would signal the equivalent of a High Street price-cutting war, with each union scrambling over the other to offer employers cheaper terms. Rumours abounded that SOGAT were willing to offer single-union deals too, and if that happened, the NGA privately warned, they would have to fight dirty as well. As

John Winnington-Ingram of the *Daily Mail* cheerfully observed from the managerial chair, 'We seem to have reached the rather strange situation where the unions are involved in competitive marketing for our benefit.'

In particular, the NGA hierarchy was concerned that the electricians might start to pose as the new craft élite in newspapers and come to some arrangement with the semiskilled SOGAT that would effectively freeze out the NGA.

SOGAT, anyway, had been moving towards a more conciliatory attitude to the employers under the firmly pragmatic leadership of Brenda Dean. For a union that had proved in the past extremely difficult to lead in the face of the fierce independence of the left-led Fleet Street branch committees, Dean had, since becoming general secretary in March, enjoyed a startling influence. As one left-wing member of the executive puts it, 'She can get ideas through the executive and get away with saying things that might have been unthinkable a few years ago.'

Unlike previous recent leaders of either SOGAT or NATSOPA, Dean comes from outside London and this perspective means that she has less instinctive sympathy for Fleet Street workers. She is, for instance, often angered that the many low-paid workers in her 200,000-strong union are assumed automatically to be earning the wages of the tiny Fleet Street élite, the bulk of whom are anyway in the NGA. Leaving school at sixteen, Dean went to work as an office assistant for the Manchester branch of the National Union of Printing, Bookbinding and Paper Workers, one of the founding unions within SOGAT. Between 1972 and 1983 she worked as assistant branch secretary in Manchester and then secretary. The branch was the largest in the union and formed the base from which she won the union's presidency in 1983 and a year later the general secretaryship. Inevitably criticism has been expressed that, as a woman, she does not have the toughness to deal with the rough-and-tumble of Fleet Street. As one London branch secretary put it, 'She has still to learn this is an industrial union. She's got to learn that we have a beer and a cheese sandwich, not a vol-au-vent and white wine.' However, those who have seen her in action with men like Maxwell argue that she has both the mental stamina and adroitness to last the pace.

She takes great care to consult the union's membership, preparing for them lengthy accounts of the history of a dispute and the current state of negotiations, all written out from her word processor. The message that generally streamed from that word processor was that British print unions had to accept technological change if they were to avoid suffering the same mauling as their American counterparts. The union's nine-day study tour of America in May 1985, led by Dean, clearly had a startling impact. The team, including some of the left-wing London branch secretaries, visited four highly modern newspaper houses, including the fiercely anti-union *USA Today*. The lengths to which technology could be put in newspapers, and the extent to which the British press had yet to go to catch up, shook the team. A single electronic library for the whole of Fleet Street, the direct-input of ad copy by the advertisers themselves, franchise distribution, were just some of the possible developments SOGAT foresaw. The report's concluding theme was that 'opposition to technological change was not an option for the printing unions – it was simply a rapid road to deunionisation'. Moreover, resistance to change by one union in order to help another would simply damage both unions in the long term. In a pointed phrase that must have been directed at SOGAT's relationship with the NGA, the report asserted: 'There is little point one union bleeding some to help another bleed less.' The report, published in September 1985, infuriated senior NGA figures who privately likened its tone of appeasement to that of the Munich Agreement.

However, if NGA and SOGAT were falling out, the NGA concurrently were patching up their quarrel with the

NUJ. There had been something of a hiatus in the dealings between the two unions whilst the NUJ elected a new general secretary. Once in situ, the new leader, Harry Conroy, was able to exert some authority over the warring factions within the union. At the same time Lord McCarthy, acting as a TUC conciliator between the two unions, had been able to administer balm on the bruised egos on either side. Above all, neither union could afford to continue their range war throughout the provincial press, from which it was patently obvious that the only beneficiary was the employers.

Under the deal, that with good will could have been struck a year earlier, the NGA conceded that following the introduction of direct-input, NGA members transferred to the editorial area would be represented by the NUJ, although they would have dual-union membership and send all their subscriptions to the NGA. The NUJ agreed that, for a period of five years, its members would not seek to make up or assemble pages. This concession effectively nullified the labour-saving purpose of electronic page make-up, an invention that was being brought into the British newspaper industry for the first time by Eddie Shah's newspaper but which was likely to spread quickly throughout the industry, threatening another wave of job losses amongst NGA members. The deal was endorsed at an unprecedented meeting of two hundred provincial newspaper representatives from the two unions that had the fervour of a revivalist rally. 'It was as if we had stormed the *Achille Lauro*. It got quite embarrassing really,' admitted Aidan White, an enthusiastic supporter of the pact on the NUJ executive.

The deal survived the first three months intact and had an immediate beneficial impact for the NGA in some newspaper houses. But the pressures on the pact remained considerable and by early 1986 there were signs that the NGA were having to face a dignified retreat at some of the big provincial newspaper houses or else face further lock-outs and dismissals. To an extent, all the print unions, save the electricians, were anyway being driven into one another's arms in the face of the onslaught under way in Fleet Street. Having sketched out some of its context, the onslaught can be looked at in a little more detail through Rupert Murdoch and Robert Maxwell, the men leading the charge, and afterwards far more briefly through the changes at the *Daily Telegraph*, the *Daily Mail* and the *Express* newspapers.

Maxwell's 'Miracle'

The considerable shadow of Czech-born Robert Maxwell has been looming over Fleet Street for the past fifteen years. Ever since his failed attempt to outbid Rupert Murdoch for the *News of the World*, his name has cropped up each time a paper has been rumoured to be for sale. So when Reed International announced, in October 1983, that it planned to float the Mirror Group on the stockmarket on the back of its estimated £80m. Reuters stake, severe tremors shot through the Labour Party and union circles. The prospect of Maxwell's domineering and volatile ego gaining control of the Left's only national daily filled the Labour movement with horror.

Certainly by the time of Reed's flotation announcement, Maxwell had the resources to make the necessary bid. He had come to Britain after the war, during which he had been awarded a Military Cross and the rank of captain, and had tumbled from one controversy to another ever since. He started his business career through the specialist publishing business Pergamon Press and increased its profits from £6,000 in 1959 to £500,000 by 1964 when the company went public. A Labour MP between 1964 and 1970, he was condemned, notoriously, in 1971 by the Department of Trade Inspectors as not being, in their opinion, a 'person who can be relied on to exercise proper stewardship of a publicly quoted company'. Recovering from these setbacks, he won control of the British Printing and Communication Corporation in 1981 and turned round the ailing publishing empire in a lightning twelve months. In the face of union opposition, he lopped 3,000 off the 10,500 strong workforce and within three years boosted the profits to £22.1m. However, his most bitter union tangle came in 1983 over the future of his Park Royal plant in West London. It was here that the highly profitable *Radio Times* was printed and typeset for the BBC. Maxwell wanted to replace the ageing presses with new web-offset machinery which would involve major pay and manning cuts that the London print union branches covering Park Royal feared might set precedents in Fleet Street. Maxwell claimed that he was having to pay the London print workers £100,000 a week for work that could be achieved at a fifth of the cost outside the capital. Accusing the workforce of being the 'last outpost of bloody-minded trade unionism in my group', he announced the shut-down of the plant.

Nightmarishly-long, highly theatrical talks ensued, each side bitterly accusing the other of bad faith. It was not uncommon for the union negotiators to wait up to five hours in a room at Maxwell's headquarters penthouse suite, under the illusion that Maxwell was considering their latest offer, only to discover later that he had been asleep all the while. 'A madhouse', was how the then general secretary of SOGAT, Bill Keys, described Maxwell's headquarters. 'He is unique,' another negotiator claims, 'he would promise something one day in front of fifteen people and then totally deny he had said it the next day in front of the same fifteen people.'

In an attempt to force Maxwell to keep Park Royal open, the SOGAT London Central branch, which was responsible for distribution, stopped the circulation of the *Radio Times* in London for eleven weeks. Encouraged by Maxwell, however, the BBC started one of the first court proceedings under the Government's Employment Acts, and SOGAT was faced with a £10,000 contempt fine.

Anxious to avoid following the NGA down the path to sequestration, the union paid up. As Sir Richard Marsh, chairman of the NPA and long-standing friend of Maxwell remarks, 'When it comes to business Maxwell is not a sentimental man. Many people have thought they could call his bluff and ended up being severely bruised in the process.'

By the end of this turbulent episode, Maxwell had closed Park Royal for good, and smashed the presses with a specially-hired crew, equipped with 14-lb hammers.

It was against this background that the print unions viewed the prospect of re-encountering Maxwell in Fleet Street. Their fears seemed assuaged, however, when Reed's chairman, Sir Alex Jarratt, announced that to safeguard the paper's traditions, character and editorial independence, Reed would not accept any offer from a single company, institution or individual. The share-holdings would be spread evenly and no one allowed more than a 15 per cent stake. Clive Thornton, the chairman of Abbey National – a capitalist who had not forgotten his working-class roots – was appointed Mirror Group chairman to oversee the flotation, on the grounds that he could win respect not only with the Left, but also the City. However, his proposals for a share bond scheme, whereby individual readers and employees could take a stake in the company, were not popular with the City investment institutions. They were also dubious about his plans to follow the example of Victor Matthews at Express Newspapers in an attempt to deal with overmanning through an expansion of titles, rather than cuts in staff. By the summer of 1984 the flotation had stalled and Maxwell at last saw his chance.

While Jarratt continued to make promises that Maxwell would not win control of the Mirror Group, on Friday 13 July, on behalf of Pergamon, Maxwell raised his offer to £113m., a sum far in excess of what Reed would earn from the market. It was from *News at Ten* that Thornton heard about the final offer and by the time he reached Jarratt by telephone, the deed was done.

Maxwell had finally won control of a national newspaper and soon began to make up for lost time. If Northcliffe's Fleet Street career had ended in tragedy, Maxwell's began with farce. Anywhere he could interfere he did so – with editorials, with captions, with bingo, with photographs, even in coverage of stories as significant as the miners' strike in which he secured for himself the role of spurned peacemaker. Day after day his papers appeared plastered with his meetings with obscure Eastern European dignatories, the fate of Oxford United – the football club of which he was chairman – or his plans to reschedule complex loans between his myriad companies. One day he would be flying with a Mirror Mercy Mission to feed the starving in Ethiopia, the next, boarding a Mirror Train round Britain to accost innocent victims on platform stations for their views on the *Mirror*.

Maxwell also lost little time in beginning a process of attrition and psychological warfare against the unions. It is a technique for which he has become famous. It was clear from the start that he would not be satisfied with a simple no-disruption agreement – he wanted to slash costs and manpower.

In a long letter to his staff at the beginning of 1985, Maxwell wrote: 'The present inability of the *Daily Mirror*, the *Sunday Mirror* and the *Sunday People* to survive at these high cost levels must cause all of us the gravest concern. The incontrovertible evidence of our present danger is that on a turnover of £260m., we will earn a profit of less than £1m. in 1985, whereas our main rival, News International, made a profit of £32m. on a turnover of £370m. in their business year ending 1984, most of it earned by the *Sun*. While the *Sun* has prospered in recent years, the *Daily Mirror*'s circulation has fallen from 4 million in 1974 to 3,400,000. Meanwhile our labour costs have increased by 70 per cent over the past five years from £70m. to £120m.'

By May, Maxwell began to wave over the heads of his

workforce the imminent competitive threat of Shah, a tactic that was seized on by every other proprietor through 1985. In his annual report as chairman of Pergamon, Maxwell dramatically warned: 'Mr Shah quite unexpectedly, and with quite frightening speed, is implementing his plans to produce early next year a national tabloid in colour seven days a week, competing head on with the *Mirror*. He will have the skilled human resources, capital and equipment to succeed unless we take action: when his paper hits the streets in some nine months' time it will threaten our very survival. We cannot stand head-in-sand like ostriches when the enemy is threatening our very livelihood and the very existence of an institution which has served the people of Britain well in peace and war for over 80 years.'

He announced the purchase of twenty new Web-offset colour presses, which would be ready by 1987, to match Shah's capacity for colour printing. London printing of the papers was to be taken out of the Holborn Circus headquarters within two years, thereby releasing a valuable chunk of real estate. In Manchester, a new print works would be opened or, alternatively, the *Mirror* would buy the contract print works, owned by the International Thomson Organisation, from which 1.3m. copies of the *Mirror* were currently printed for northern distribution. Several thousand jobs, accumulated during the booming years of IPC profitability, would have to go.

The urgency of the inevitable cost-cutting suddenly escalated when a ten-day dispute in August stopped publication of all Mirror titles. The dispute over a relatively minor issue, concerning the typesetting costs of the loss-making *Sporting Life*, appeared to have blown up into the apocalyptic encounter many had predicted between Maxwell and the NGA. Following a disruptive chapel meeting by the NGA compositors about the future of the *Sporting Life*, Maxwell acted on his long-standing threat to shut down his papers in the event of industrial action taken outside agreed dispute procedures. Protective dismissal notices were issued to all staff and Maxwell made an announcement that he would not be reopening for up to eighteen months, by which time his new presses and print works would be ready. The threat, however, did not seem credible. Maxwell surely could not risk being off the streets as Shah came on to the market, nor could his cash flow.

The dispute cost £6m. in lost revenue, but in the wider power struggle between Maxwell and the unions, it was the unions who suffered most. Jobs had been lost and the *Sporting Life*, representing a quarter of the type set in the building, was no longer to be set or printed at Holborn Circus, so freeing the paper from the expensive cost of being produced under national newspaper rates. Although Maxwell had given a commitment to sell the *Sporting Life* within a month, thereby preserving the union's principle that national newspaper proprietors should not be allowed to print national titles without national newspaper rates, the NGA privately accepted that with a man like Maxwell they had no means of enforcing that part of the deal.

The mood of defeatism amongst the NGA was not helped by the fact that, at almost the same time as the *Sporting Life* dispute, with very little publicity, the NGA were having to accept the loss of 675 jobs at Maxwell's Odhams plant in Watford. On 4 September Maxwell had sent a letter to the NGA and the other unions at Odhams, giving them until 5.00 p.m. the next day to accept the redundancies or else see the receiver brought in. The chapels caved in, thus reinforcing Maxwell's authority.

By September it had become public knowledge that the Mirror papers were on a circulation slide. In comparison with the first nine months of 1984, the *Mirror*'s sales in 1985 had fallen by 336,158 to 3,052,105, the *Sunday Mirror* had dropped 440,090 to 3,190,103 and the *Sunday People* had fallen 295,921 to 3,129,208. It seemed beyond coincidence that Maxwell's papers had suffered such a sales drop at the very time Maxwell had assumed such a vulgarly high profile in his own papers. The Liberal journalist, J. A. Spender, once wrote: 'It is an absolute rule among proprietors of newspapers not to write under their own names in their own newspapers. Experience has shown that it does the proprietor no good, for the public invariably discounts what he writes and it does the paper harm since this curious British public seems to have a rooted objection to any newspaper influence which it conceives as personal.' If Maxwell was ever given similar advice, he did not heed it. Instead of the papers' sales increasing in 1985 by the 10 per cent he had predicted at the end of 1984, exactly the opposite had happened, and consequently an immense strain was placed on the papers' revenues.

By some estimates, the slide in sales meant a loss in sales revenue of £20m. The Mirror Group was on course to lose £20m. On 4 November Maxwell felt the skirmishing had to end once and for all. He announced that he had to have union agreement by the end of the month to the loss of a third of the 6,000-strong staff in London and Manchester. Yet again, Maxwell threatened that failure to reach agreement would mean that titles would only resume publication when the colour presses were established in spring 1987. Yet again, he issued dismissal notices to all staff as a precaution against the unions failing to reach agreement by his deadline. At one level Maxwell's repeated bluster was unimpressive – some Mirror Group employees claimed that they had received dismissal notices no less than six times since Maxwell's advent and that Maxwell's editorial interference was the cause of the crisis in the first place – but at another level the repeated confrontations and uncertainty generated an atmosphere of defeatism amongst the workforce.

In private many accepted that in comparison with the rest of Fleet Street, the *Mirror* was grossly overstaffed and had been ever since the mid-fifties and the period of its five million circulation. Maxwell himself produced manning figures comparative to those of the *Sun*, showing that in every *Mirror* editorial and production department there were twice as many as at the *Sun*. Apocryphal or not, stories abounded of seventy-year-olds still on the *Mirror* pay-roll, men who had not worked for years but arrived once a week by taxi to collect their pay-packet.

Maxwell skilfully stoked the 'end-of-an-era' atmosphere by asking Joe Haines, the *Mirror* leader writer and former Harold Wilson aide, to compose a full-page leader declaring that the Fleet Street party was over. In a further move, which probably had far more influence than Haines' rhetorical skills, Maxwell persuaded the Mirror Pension Fund Trustees – one of the few profitable pension funds in Fleet Street – to make £35m. of the £90m. in the fund available as a means of increasing the lump-sum and pension entitlements of those willing to go. Under this arrangement, a man aged fifty-five with fifteen years' service and an annual salary of £23,000 would receive an immediate tax-free lump sum of £28,545, as well as a revised pension of £1,209 per year. Offers of this kind were new to Fleet Street. In short, one of the largest redundancy programmes ever seen in Fleet Street was being promoted through a mixture of bluff, confrontation and cash.

The extent to which the SOGAT leadership was willing to let the wind of change rip in Fleet Street was signalled when the union responded to Maxwell's axe by placing two questions on the ballot paper handed to the union's 3,000 members at MGN. The first question was in the traditional Fleet Street mould, asking their members whether they were prepared to strike if Maxwell refused to withdraw his dismissal notices. But the second question, asking if they were willing to allow their leaders to negotiate voluntary redundancies if the notices were withdrawn, was altogether a more rare specimen in Fleet Street. The membership said 'yes' to both questions and once Maxwell was forced to withdraw the notices, in the face of an effective strike, negotiations on the redundancies and changes in working practices began. Within a month the 2,000 redundancies had been agreed. The likely saving to Maxwell is anything between £25m. and £35m. in a full year. As he himself put it, 'we have become profitable overnight'.

The London Left in SOGAT described the whole episode as a disaster, but in many ways Maxwell had prepared the ground for his 'miracle' too well. Once Maxwell had the bulk of the volunteers he wanted – and many simply wanted to escape his grasp – there was little serious chance of the unions mounting a strike to preserve the *Mirror*'s manning levels. Besides, by the last days of 1985, it was clear that, however radical Maxwell's surgery had been, something more outlandish was being tried by Maxwell's old enemy, Rupert Murdoch.

Barefaced Cheek in Wapping

The Australian Keith Murdoch – who liked to call himself Lord Southcliffe in wry deference to Britain's pioneering newspaperman – died in 1952, leaving to his son Rupert, then a sub-editor on the London *Daily Express*, a small group of Adelaide papers. At the age of twenty-one Rupert Murdoch returned to Australia from England, where he had been educated at Oxford, and over the next fifteen years acquired what became known as his bordello of papers: the *Perth Sunday Times*, the *Sydney Daily* and *Sunday Mirror*, the *Daily* and *Sunday Telegraph*. In his sole and somewhat flawed stab at respectability he founded, in 1964, *The Australian*, the only sober paper under his control.

By 1969 Rupert Murdoch was strong enough to make his first overseas purchase – the British *News of the World* – a transaction which he referred to as 'the biggest steal since The Great Train Robbery'. Murdoch's promise that he 'would travel halfway round the world to throw Maxwell a concrete lifebelt', showed the strength of his affection towards his rival bidder. Six months after edging out the family owners of the *News of the World*, he bought the flagging *Sun* from the Mirror Group, bringing it into his Bouverie Street headquarters off Fleet Street where the *News of the World* was based. The *Sun*, from its relaunch in November 1969, displayed a form of sensationalism that made previous British tabloids look by comparison like staid literary reviews. Circulation at the time was just below a million whilst that of the *Daily Mirror* was just below five million, but Murdoch was not in danger of going broke under-estimating the taste of the British public: within six years of launch, the *Sun* had overtaken the *Mirror*. By the second half of 1985, the daily sales of the *Sun*, of over four million, were roughly 800,000 ahead of the *Mirror*. With 70 per cent of the paper's revenues dependent on sales, as opposed to advertising, the paper had become a gold-mine for Murdoch.

It is ironic that Murdoch's massive expansion in America since 1984 into the field of sophisticated film studios and satellite and cable TV has been financed by such a primitive newspaper, set with Victorian hot-metal technology and printed in a Dickensian basement off Fleet Street. But as Murdoch expanded in the US by taking over 20th-Century Fox and the Metromedia TV stations, a continuing flow of profit from Britain was essential, since his American operations, mainly newspapers and magazines, yielded insufficient funds to finance his investments in that country. In the year ending June 1985, his US companies generated a third of the turnover of Murdoch's Australian-based parent company News Corporation, yet only a third of the return of the UK operations. Murdoch's UK-based subsidiary News International – which includes News Group (publishers of the *Sun* and the *News of the World*) as well as the far less profitable Times Newspapers Ltd (publishers of *The Times* and the *Sunday Times*) contributed just over 45 per cent of the total News Corporation trading profit in 1984–5 of 115m. US dollars. The jewel in Murdoch's crown has been the *Sun* which in the year 1984–5 provided 11 per cent of News Corporation's total worldwide revenues of 1,712m. US dollars. In the three years preceding June 1985, the *Sun* and the *News of the World* made a total profit of nearly £80m, broadly in line with the two paper's success ever since the mid-seventies.

Since the late seventies Murdoch had been seeking to increase still further the return on the *Sun* and the *News of the World* by taking the printing, but not the composing or editorial, operations out of Fleet Street. With a sale of 4.5m., the *Sun*'s print-run is the largest for a single plant outside Japan and almost all its sales came from news-stands as opposed to home deliveries. This fact, plus the sheer size of the print-run and the lack of a northern print plant, had meant that the presses had to start running at 8.00 p.m., two-and-a-half hours earlier than any other Fleet Street paper. Copies of the *Sun* had to be flown to Scotland. Bert Hardy, News International chief executive in 1979, recalls: 'It had become literally physically impossible to expand the business in Fleet Street. Every nook and cranny was taken up. We had even thought of buying the next door pub, knocking down the walls and installing new presses.'

Initially, Hardy had been planning to buy a major site owned by Camden Council just by Kings Cross railway station and therefore ideal for distribution, but the Left-led Council's dislike of Murdoch's politics led to interminable delays and Tower Hamlets Council stepped into the breach, rushing through within six weeks planning permission for a massive site in Wapping, so setting the precedent for the subsequent exodus from Fleet Street to the docklands.

'I had got fed up dealing with middle-class socialists,' Hardy explained, 'and found working-class socialists a lot easier to get on with. It was obvious even then the docklands was going to revive and we got the building for a song, just over £1m. and the rent was a peppercorn.'

The Goss headliner presses installed at Wapping had been bought by Murdoch at cheap rates during the mid-seventies; they were capable of faster speeds, less prone to plate breakages, and it was possible to insert pre-printed pages during the run. At the same time a new £20m. plant was constructed in Glasgow capable of printing 500,000 papers a night, sufficient to make the *Sun*'s airlift unnecessary.

Apart from the printing advantages, management saw Wapping as an opportunity for major cutbacks in staff employed in the machine and publishing rooms. The *News of the World* publishing room, for instance, employed six hundred casuals and Bert Hardy had found their negotiators impossible to deal with. The use of modern stacking and conveyancing systems in Wapping meant that publishing-room staff could be cut by five hundred. In the machine room at Bouverie Street, the newspaper's technical director admitted, 'The paper probably employs between two or three times the manpower which it really needs, effectively on a system where two crews are employed each night (both of which are in any case themselves overmanned), one between 7.30 and midnight, and the second crew thereafter.' The shift to the Wapping plant, which had been completed in 1983, offered the chance of a major renegotiation.

Talks over the terms of the move between Bill O'Neill, Murdoch's chief union negotiator, and the print unions broke down at the end of 1984 after nearly ten months of negotiations which had included the company taking senior chapel officials to newspapers in France and Helsinki to view for themselves the wonders of continental industrial relations. The company proposed that, at least initially, the *Sun* and the *News of the World* would be printed both in Fleet Street and Wapping. However, manning would be considerably lower in Wapping than Fleet Street and pay a little higher. The talks were also stymied by an historical anomaly. Uniquely in Fleet Street, members of SOGAT, rather than the NGA, were employed as machine managers in the *News of the World* machine room whilst the two unions shared the representation equally in the *Sun* machine room. In every other Fleet Street machine room, the NGA represented all the skilled machine managers. If the *Sun* and the *News of the World* were to go to Wapping, the NGA wanted all the machine managers' jobs, something that met with the vehement objection of SOGAT. For their part, SOGAT refused to countenance the kind of manning Murdoch envisaged in the distribution and publishing area. A SOGAT official responsible for distribution quietly told Murdoch's team that he might as well put a bomb under Wapping because it was never going to be used. Nevertheless, the unions still insist that it was Murdoch, not them, who ended the talks, a point with which O'Neill disagrees.

In retrospect, chapel leaders at both the *Sun* and *The News of the World* regretted the breakdown of the talks. The bulk of Murdoch's eighty newspapers around the world are unionised. Head-on confrontation is not necessarily Murdoch's trade mark. Notoriously, in 1978 he pulled his paper, the New York *Post*, out of an employers' pact after eight weeks of a City-wide print strike, called in protest at the publishers' plans to impose 50 per cent cuts in their machine rooms. But Murdoch is also a cold opportunist willing to exploit weaknesses displayed by unions as soon as he sees them. He was able to extract lean manning arrangements when he bought the *Sun* in 1969 and was similarly able to cut a quarter of the workforce following his purchase of *The Times* in 1980 when the unions were still exhausted after the shut-down battle.

In a classic example of this opportunism, Murdoch realised at the outset of 1985 that the collapse of the Wapping talks had occurred at a time when the power balance was visibly shifting in Fleet Street. In the first two months of 1985 Murdoch decided to lay plans for turning his Wapping and Glasgow plants from white elephants, unused due to union boycotts, into priceless technological assets capable of printing all his titles. Murdoch publicly announced that he planned to use Wapping as a plant for the printing of a new evening paper for the capital, the *London Post*, to be expanded later into a national twenty-four hour daily. Unlike the earlier plans for the printing of the *Sun*, the paper would also be written, typeset and composed from Wapping. In private Murdoch prepared his contingency plans for the wholesale transference of all his existing Fleet Street titles to Wapping. In the utmost secrecy Murdoch contacted the American offices of Atex, the leading newspaper computer specialists, and asked them to prepare a direct-input system capable of handling all four of Murdoch's British titles. The UK arm of Atex were to be kept entirely in the dark and a hand-picked team of a dozen US Atex specialists were brought to Britain to prepare the system. By May it had been completed. By the summer however, the absence of any normal journalistic or commercial planning for the *Post* raised some quizzical eyebrows amongst the print unions who began to think that the *Post* might be a blind. As Brenda Dean told a branch union meeting in mid-September, 'It's difficult to distinguish what is a real threat and what is not. There are reports that there are over 200 VDU terminals inside Wapping. We want fo find out what's going on'. The unions began to fear the worst when they heard that Christopher Pole-Carew had been appointed technological consultant at the *Post*. As managing director of T. Bailey Forman, publishers of the *Nottingham Evening Post*, Pole-Carew had confronted the print unions and introduced direct-input in the 1970s.

Throughout the summer rumours grew within Fleet Street that Murdoch was indeed planning to bust the unions in Fleet Street and wreak his revenge for the delay they had caused. Hundreds of members of the electricians' union, EETPU – which already had a no-strike deal with Eddie Shah – had been hired in great secrecy by the union's Southampton district officer. Left-wing activists in the area were not notified of the vacancies. The men, it emerged, met each morning at a car park by the Old Ship Inn on the edge of Southampton where they took a bus for the ninety-minute drive up the motorway to Wapping. Their contracts stipulated that they would certainly work until December, but might be offered further contracts thereafter. The men, picked after rigorous political screening were bound to total secrecy about what they did and saw in Wapping. Nevertheless, manuals acquired by the London print chapels showed that the electricians were being trained to work the presses, even though this was work normally reserved for the NGA and SOGAT. Dummy runs of the *Post* were smuggled out of the plant on 5 September, demonstrating that the electricians now had the ability to run the presses.

When questioned at an emergency Saturday-morning meeting two days later, Murdoch's management insisted that the electricians were merely preparing the presses and undertaking routine maintenance work, but refused to allow print union leaders into the building to see what was going on. Suspicions grew still further when it emerged that, like Shah, Murdoch had commissioned the Australian company, TNT, with which News International had corporate links, to study the possibility of establishing an alternative national distribution network.

Militants at the *Sun* attempted to mount a strike to force the management's hand, but the NGA chapel leaders from News International turned the call down, arguing that it would be better to await the outcome of a meeting arranged with Murdoch for the end of September. A recommendation for a strike from the London SOGAT Machine Branch Committee was rejected 3–2 at a News International mass meeting at Central Hall, Westminster, an unprecedented rebuff from one of the strongest groups of chapels in Fleet Street. Bill Freeman, a member of the SOGAT Branch Committee recalled, 'We put it to them fair and square, no secrets, nothing hidden, but we got turned over. There was a time when the job of a union leadership was to get the members back to work because they insisted on staying out until they had got everything they wanted, but all that's changed and if anything the roles are reversed. A demoralisation has set in.'

The late September meeting with Murdoch had been called at the request of Brenda Dean, who admitted beforehand: 'We want to be in Wapping because it makes sense. The working conditions in Bouverie Street are appalling. If we don't get to Wapping by negotiation, there is no way a man like Murdoch is going to let an £80m. investment fall by the wayside. We have to recognise that this industry is changing. People who don't accept that fact must have their eyes closed. If we don't get an agreement and the *Sun* unions are cracked, it will sweep through the industry like wildfire. There are a lot of people on the sidelines waiting to see what happens and the move to Wapping will prove the benchmark.'

Tony Dubbins, general secretary of the NGA, agreed: 'In the long run the Wapping deal may have wider implications than Shah. Shah may be a one-off, but there are a lot of other employers like Murdoch going to the docklands.'

Neither Dubbins nor Dean could have foreseen the ferocity of the verbal assault Murdoch would mount when the two sides met. At that meeting, Murdoch pulled no punches. 'I have strained myself and my senior colleagues physically, emotionally and financially to build this business and we have met with nothing but cynicism, broken promises and total opposition,' he extravagantly complained. Momentarily forgetting the fantastic profits the *Sun* generated, he continued: 'The story of the *News of the World* and the *Sun* is totally depressing. We bought the *News of the World* in January 1969. It was going downhill rapidly. Ten months later we took over the almost dead *Sun*. We started by giving jobs to about 500 extra people at an average shift rate of £10. Today the *Sun* and the *News of the World* employ 4,700 people at an average weekly wage of more than £300. The vast majority of those people belong to your unions, enjoy a closed shop and all the privileges that go with that. Some of them are dedicated and skilled in their work, whilst, depending on their jobs, many others have little or no skills. And in almost inverse proportion to their skills they work fewer hours. Let us be honest about this. The great majority of night shift workers are at their jobs no more than 20 hours per week, at more than double the national average wage. Furthermore they get from six, eight and in some cases twelve weeks holiday, pensions, sickness and other benefits. We are allowed neither to hire nor fire them.

'Throughout Fleet Street when threats of disruption have been made or disruption takes place, managements have often been forced to choose between extinction and conceding wage and manning levels which are totally uneconomic. The result today is that all national newspaper production departments are overmanned by from 50 to 300 per cent, with working practices that are a continuing disgrace to us all.'

Astutely, Murdoch kept the print unions dangling by insisting that he would only talk about the terms of a union agreement for the transfer of the *Sun* and the *News of the World* once negotiations about the new jobs and agreement for the *London Post* were well under way. Murdoch left it deliberately unclear whether any terms agreed for the *Post* would apply equally to the *Sun*. All the while in the back of the union leaders' minds was the knowledge that the less ideologically inhibited electricians' union, EETPU, was in the wings ready and willing to reach a deal on virtually any terms offered by Murdoch.

The agreement Murdoch tabled with his union negotiator, Bill O'Neill, left the unions dumbfounded. O'Neill told them it was broadly based on an agreement at the *Chicago Sun Times*, but to Fleet Street unions it was as alien as something from the planet Mars. The first clause of the agreement stated: 'The union accepts that laws of supply and demand and technological developments will dictate changes in the skills required from the employees, manning levels and productivity.' The union was to have no closed shop and no control of the supply of labour. All union representatives would have to be elected once a year by a secret ballot of all employees who are union members. Any worker who had been given a disciplinary warning by the company could not stand for or retain any union post. No member of management or supervisory grades could join a union. All new employees would be subject to a six-month probationary period during which time they would not have the right of any internal appeal against dismissal. Employees would undertake their tasks within their competence, but otherwise with complete flexibility. No demarcation lines or minimum staffing agreements would exist.

Any employee taking part in strike action would be liable for immediate dismissal, whilst the union was to commit itself not to 'instigate, sponsor, engage in, finance or condone any strike for any reason whatsoever'. The union was also committed to repudiate immediately any strike action that did occur. Any dispute such as a pay claim would be channelled through a laborious arbitration procedure modelled on Japanese industrial relations practices. Finally, the contract was legally binding, making both company, unions and individual employees liable to legal action if they broke it.

In Britain, unions and companies can sign legally binding collective agreements if they so wish, but unlike the rest of Europe, there is nothing in statute codifying that such agreements must be binding. The one statutory attempt to introduce legally binding contracts – the Industrial Relations Act 1971 – failed. Currently only one agreement in Britain – that between the electricians' union and the Electrical Contractors Association – is legally binding. For unions there are many advantages in ensuring that collective agreements remain only 'gentlemen's agreements'. First, it reduces the role of the judiciary in industrial relations. Secondly, it allows unions to maintain a form of continuous bargaining pressure, effectively backed by the ultimate sanction of speedily-applied strike action. Finally, non-binding agreements place less pressure on union leaderships to police their own memberships to ensure that they do not breach the collective agreement and so leave the union exposed to damages claims. To some, these union objections may seem artificial, but there is a particular aspect to Murdoch's proposal which represents a swing from one extreme in industrial relations to another.

The proposal in Murdoch's document that strikes could only occur legally at the expiry of the contract drew with deliberate selectivity on only one theme of European and American industrial relations' law. Murdoch's package ignored the essential concomitant in European labour law, namely that on the expiry of the contract a worker should have an equally legally binding right to strike without fear of immediate dismissal, a positive right that, for mainly historical reasons, does not exist in Britain. As Murdoch himself showed, with breathtaking certitude, an employer in Britain can sack without compensation any worker on strike, virtually regardless of the strike's cause, on the grounds of a breach of the individual's employment contract.

In short Murdoch's proposals offered unions only the most restrictive parts of British and European labour law. A Murdoch production worker was to have no right to strike without fear of legal retribution save at the expiry of the contract, yet at the same time no statutory protection from dismissal if on the expiry of the contract he did strike.

O'Neill laconically explained: 'We are asking the union to exercise a greater degree of control than they have in the past, otherwise the unions will go on saying "we are not really responsible for our members" and if that's the case, what's the point of having an agreement at all? Probably the only law that applies to Fleet Street at the moment is the law of the jungle. You cannot enforce any agreement that is based only on good intent and honour.' Criticising the Fleet Street culture, O'Neill added: 'It's far more intense here than in America. The workforce is too preoccupied with unionism. I guess some people here follow football, some people collect stamps and some people become chapel officials.'

In an attempt to avoid being accused of intransigence by other unions, notably SOGAT, the NGA responded to Murdoch's proposals by conceding that editorial and classified advertising copy could be input direct, an unprecedented concession to a national newspaper owner by the NGA. O'Neill was nevertheless distinctly unimpressed and stuck to his demands. However, of the five unions with membership in Fleet Street, only the electricians were prepared to countenance a legally binding, no-strike deal.

The extent to which the electrician's union had an inside track with Murdoch was unclear, but it was undeniable that district officers of the union had helped recruit staff for the plant. It was less clear whether the union's national executive knew what the electricians were being trained to do or the extent of Murdoch's plans to circumvent the traditional unions. As one member of the EETPU executive put it, 'We were told in late September, I think it was, that recruitment of electricians was being stopped at Wapping. We all nodded and then nodded off, so to speak. The significance passed us by.'

Undoubtedly, Murdoch could have recruited labour for Wapping without the help of the EETPU, but he had been eager to follow the Shah model and avoid the accusation of being anti-union. Like Shah, Murdoch felt

272

Britain 'had to change to survive' and the EETPU was one vehicle amongst many for that change.

Both Hammond and Tom Rice for their part looked on the increasing use of electronics in news paper printing as a legitimate reason for its members to claim, like the NGA, that they had the right to 'follow the job' into new areas of printing. Hammond had anyway little but contempt for the traditional print union leaders. 'The only thing they have to fear is the consequences of their own actions', he said. He also had personally little time for the TUC's Bridlington principles governing union spheres of influence. Hammond argued that workers should be entirely free to choose which union they joined. The short term consequences might be chaotic, but a free market would force unions to be responsive to the needs and wishes of workers, he argued. However, the TUC was moving in the opposite direction towards tightening up the barriers to unions seeking members in new areas. Indeed, on December 18, 1985 the very day that the TUC General Council decided not to discipline the electricians for stepping out of line by taking state cash for union ballots, the seeds of fresh conflict between the TUC and the electricians had been sown. The General Council banned single union agreements in any industry or company where unions that had traditional bargaining rights had not been consulted. The ban was also to apply to green-field sites. The change in policy had in fact stemmed from a motion promoted by Dubbins at the TUC Congress in September, with the aim of stopping the EETPU's deal with Shah. But its application was just as relevant to Wapping and Norman Willis, the TUC General Secretary, formally advised all five print unions just before Christmas not to reach any agreement with Murdoch without the endorsement of the other unions.

However, by that date Murdoch's plans were in place. His journalists had been softened up, the printing capacity had been tested repeatedly through the Autumn, the TNT contract for distribution was ready and his lawyers were briefed. All that remained was for the unions to fall into the carefully-laid trap and strike, thereby losing their jobs and triggering an overnight decampment from Fleet Street to Wapping.

On the night of Saturday 11 January – before the NGA and SOGAT had completed their strike ballots – Murdoch nearly got his strike. In the second edition of the *Sunday Times* that night, management insisted that an announcement be inserted revealing that the Wapping plant was to be commissioned the following weekend for the production of a new special section of the *Sunday Times*. There had been no consultation with the unions about printing a section of the *Sunday Times* away from Gray's Inn Road. In normal circumstances such a move would have provoked an immediate walk-out. Frantic consultations went on by phone both with Bill Booroff, the NGA regional secretary and Dubbins himself. In the end the compositor was told by his Foc to tap out the copy. 'Don't bloody well read it, just set it', his Foc told him.

Days before the strike began, the print unions under the auspices of the TUC put together an unprecedented package, including binding arbitration triggered by either side, a virtual end to the call system, full flexibilty. Most of the proposals could have been taken line by line from an EETPU single union agreement in the electronics industry. Dubbins enthused, 'It's the best deal offered to any Fleet Street employer ever'. But both the electricians and the company were unmoved. Hammond refused to join the unions' common front. Murdoch simply said 'The horse has now bolted. It's too late. If they had come to us with this package a couple of years ago, they could have had all sorts of things.' Asked if he feared a strike at Gray's Inn Road and Bouverie Street, Murdoch replied triumphantly, 'I've got an alternative printing plant, something no one else on Fleet Street has ever had.' He counselled his readers 'if they strike, hang in there. We may miss for a day or two, but we'll get to you. We have the plans. They just have to be tested and proven up.'

Murdoch did not want just to exclude the old print unions, he also wanted to exclude his old workforce and their culture, preferring instead his own hand-picked workers.

If Murdoch was so clearly relishing a strike why did the unions not sit tight, refuse to strike and wait and see whether Murdoch had in reality ever had plans to start the *London Post* from Wapping in March, as he had always claimed? Such a strategy was put forward within both the NGA and SOGAT, but rejected. In part the unions had been unable to calculate correctly the print capacity in Wapping. Days before the strike occurred Brenda Dean, amongst others, pronounced that 'Mr Murdoch cannot print all his titles in there. He is a good business-man and knows that he needs the cash flow that the *Sun* brings him or else he will be in deep trouble.' So Dean expected the strike to be long, but to bite.

It seemed inconceivable that 5,000 Fleet Street print workers could go out on strike and not stop production of the paper. Moreover, there seemed little point delaying the moment of confrontation with Murdoch. It was bound to occur shortly anyway since Murdoch had already issued notices to his Gray's Inn Road and Bouverie Street workforce stating that their contracts of employment were to be renegotiated in June publicly acknowledging that Shah and the other 'outside' competition – printing at a fraction of his costs – presented a huge and imminent threat.

After the slow year-long build-up to the strike, the ceaseless speculation and torturous manoeuvring, events moved with dramatic speed once the strike started on 24 January. The journalists were within hours faced with the most cynical of ultimatums: go to Wapping or onto the dole queue. They were offered £2,000 to speed their passage. The journalists' illusion that their profession gave them a special relationship with management was shattered. Instead they were revealed as another dispensable production unit, a necessary but highly replaceable extension to the VDU. For some journalists inside Wapping, the building represented nirvana and an end to all the petty restrictions associated with Fleet Street. But for others, Wapping reeked of transatlantic anonymity. The building was described as a plant, journalists as consultants and the men outside on the picket line as obsolete. Constantly at hand were faceless pyschological minders offering environmental adjustment and euphemistic justifications for strike-breaking. The painful and public wrestle between liberal consciences and the need to keep up the hefty mortgage repayments was a repeat of the drama played out in the minds of many American journalists in US print union busting of the mid-1970s.

Outside on the picket line, the men attempted to keep their spirits up as the massive C Registration vans poured down the extraordinary spotlit ramp, past the automatically controlled gates, the lines of barbed wire, the surveillance cameras. 'This is just for show', one picket said on the first Saturday night pointing at the tracks. 'This is mickey mouse stuff. There's nothing in those trucks. They could not drive them that fast if they were full.' But the pickets had no way of telling how wrong they were. The drivers – members of the Left-led Transport and General Workers Union – would not stop and the security surrounding their cargo suggested they were carrying plutonium, rather than newspapers containing naked breasts and monetarism.

Increasingly the crisis over Wapping became not just an unequal trial of strength between Murdoch and the print unions but also a war of nerves between the electricians and the TUC. The conflict was not merely a run-of-the-mill inter-union demarcation row, it was also a conflict between two different philosophies of trade unionism. Splits in the TUC had been predicted before and have come to nothing, but few unions had ever looked on life outside the TUC with such equanimity as the electricians. The revolution in Fleet Street had the potential to be the occasion for a wider revolution in the structure of the British labour movement.

Daily Telegraph

By universal consent, the *Daily Telegraph* has been the most badly managed newspaper in Fleet Street. Despite a sale of 1.2m. – larger than that of the three other quality papers put together – the *Daily Telegraph* has been persistently making a loss. Indeed, apart from a £7m. pre-tax profit in 1984 the company, which had been owned by Lord Hartwell and his family, the Berrys, had made small losses in each of the past four years. The old school management of amiable gifted amateurs had suffered an understandable reluctance to change what had been a winning formula in the shires through the sixties and seventies. However, since 1980 the paper's circulation suffered a slow decline totalling 800,000 over five years. Much of the slippage, according to internal marketing surveys, was due to a dislike amongst potential younger readers of the paper's forbidding and old-fashioned layout. Only 20 per cent of the *Daily Telegraph*'s readers were under thirty-five, the most elderly readership age-profile in Fleet Street but also one of the wealthiest. In addition, the paper had started to lose tranches of the classified advertising market that should never have been going to its competitors. Finally, the paper had not had the resources to indulge in the price-cutting undertaken by *The Times* and the paper's sales suffered accordingly.

Unwelcome as these difficulties undoubtedly would have been at any time, they unfortunately coincided with the *Telegraph*'s decision to combine the purchase of new sites in London and Manchester with a highly expensive switch in typesetting technology. The Berry family simply did not have the resources or managerial skill to compete in the race to modernise. The decision to introduce photocomposition had, in fact, first been announced in 1975, involving a planned cut of 600 in its 1,600 workforce. Little happened.

Instead, in May 1977, the management repeated the 1975 announcement, saying, 'Failure to put our house in order is more likely to produce the man with the scythe rather than a fairy godmother with the wand.' Again nothing happened, save a gradual rise in labour costs until, in 1984, they had reached 46 per cent of total costs.

In a belated attempt to change its cost structure and improve its printing abilities, the company announced that it was erecting two purpose-built printing facilities, one at Trafford Park in Manchester to be ready in 1986, and another at the Isle of Dogs, to be ready in 1987. The total cost would be £108m. Each new web-offset press would be capable of producing 60,000 copies per hour, compared with the 24,000 to 32,000 per hour on the geriatric letterpress machines used in Fleet Street. They would also be capable of full-colour printing and bigger pagination. An additional cost in the move would be an extraordinary £40m. outlay to the printers in redundancy money and the buying-out of their piecework system. In the composing room the redundancy and buy-out terms would amount to £20m. and in the foundry, machine and publishing areas £17.5m. But once the hump of the capital outlay was over in 1990, Lord Hartwell's accountants estimated the paper would be making a profit of £20m. a year.

If the plan was successful, the whole operation would be transformed. With greatly increased pagination and sales far beyond those of its quality rivals, there did seem cause for optimism about the impact colour advertising might have on revenues.

But, in the short term, the *Daily Telegraph* simply did not have the internal resources to finance such an operation, even with its estimated £50m. shareholding in Reuters. Just over £80m. of the capital cost was financed through lease and debt finance, but the balance had to be raised through the issue of £30m. worth of shares, representing 40 per cent of the share capital but still leaving the Berry family in control just as they had been since 1927. Finding businessmen and institutions willing to take up the share capital on this basis proved far more difficult than envisaged. Potential City investors feared they would be unable to offload their shares if things went wrong, and yet unable to influence Hartwell and his management. The merchant bankers, N. M. Rothschild, had to scour the City for investors, threatening the institutions that if they did not take a stake in the *Telegraph*, the bank would make sure they did not get a slice of the action when other more attractive share issues came on the market.

Spurned at every turn, Hartwell was forced to offer a right-wing Canadian businessman, Conrad Black, a 14 per cent stake in the company, a seat on the board and an option to match any other bid for the controlling interest of Lord Hartwell, should the family want, or more likely need, to sell up. Black was a winner on all counts. If the transition to the docklands went well and the company realised profits, Black had made a wise investment: if the docklands project hit problems, he had the opportunity to take control.

However, the cost of modernisation ran away from management in the summer of 1985. Instead of making the estimated projected profit of £5m. in the six months up to September 1985, the paper made a trading loss of £4.6m. – its worst for a long time – as well as suffering extraordinary costs of £11.8m., largely made up of higher than expected costs of buy-outs of the compositors' piecework system. Following the introduction of photo-composition, the weekly earnings of the three-hundred-odd compositors were being cut from around £800 to £400. However, in return for the cut, the compositors were receiving lump-sum payments equivalent to three years' worth of the drop in their salary. The payments could be close to £40,000 per man.

In addition, the NGA linotype operators being trained to work with photocomposition had to be replaced during their retraining by casuals, leading to a total increase in the wage bill. As part of the attempt to encourage redundancies, the company had decided to set up a pension scheme for the first time – previously pensions had been on a basis of grace and favour – and this had been a further extra cost. All in all, the paper did not have the resources to cover such costs, something the management might have foreseen when it negotiated the changes with the NGA. Despite desperate efforts to find other sources of finance, it became horribly clear by autumn 1985 that the only alternative to liquidation was to seek further cash from Conrad Black, even if that meant Hartwell losing control. Other financiers had looked at the *Telegraph*'s books and blanched.

For the paper which exemplified Fleet Street's management inertia better than any other, the years of neglect had caught up. On 8 December 1985 Black became the beneficiary and took control of the *Telegraph*.

Associated – The Mail

Management at Associated Newspapers, publishers of the *Daily Mail*, the *Mail on Sunday* and the London *Standard*, made no attempt to disguise the 'Maxwell factor and the Shah factor' behind their plans to speed up their £100m. move to the docklands. The group, owned by Lord Rothermere, had been originally planning not to move to its Surrey Docks site until 1990, allowing eighteen months for leisurely negotiations with the unions before purchasing the equipment. 'That was a long time for negotiations,' admitted John Winnington-Ingram, the man responsible for the move, but Associated had been reluctant to sign contracts until it was first sure that it had the right manning agreements.

But the pressure from Shah and his colour printing

led to a sudden announcement by the paper in June that it planned to start building its print works in 1986 with a view to moving all the printing to the Surrey Docks by early 1988. The telescoped timetable meant that Associated had to make £10m. worth of investment before securing union agreement – money that will be thrown away if the terms for the move are not right. 'We had to move quickly if we were to remain competitive. We will possibly be eighteen months after Shah with colour and just a few months after the *Telegraph*.'

As a necessary part of the move, the *Daily Mail* will switch from hot-metal production to photocomposition by the autumn of 1986, involving the buy-out of the London Scale of Prices. A Koenig Bauer press of the kind to be installed in the Surrey Docks will be installed at the *Mail*'s current Fleet Street building, also in 1986, in order that the machine room can learn the flexographic printing method that will be used in the new building. Cuts of up to a third in the machine and publishing areas are envisaged.

In explaining why the Group is moving downriver with a lot more brio than before, Winnington-Ingram admitted: 'If we were going to move, we had to get on with it. We simply could not afford to wait until 1990 to be fully competitive and to watch our market position being gradually eroded in the meantime. Shah has made everyone realise that there is a necessity for change. There is a new mood. We have also concentrated on talking more and more directly to our staff, instead of negotiating through the branch level where there are both some obstructive people and also some people that are actually working for the competition.'

Unlike the *Telegraph* under Hartwell, Associated has the resources to finance the move from within the Group. The Group owns seventeen regional newspaper companies, extensive North Sea oil and gas interests through Blackfriars Oil, a 50 per cent share in the London *Standard*, a highly successful American publishing company,

13–30 Group. On a turnover of £357m. in 1984, it made a pre-tax profit of £21m., broadly in line with the previous five years. With the major loss-maker, the *Mail on Sunday*, beginning to trade profitably, the whole Group faces no difficulty in financing the move to the docklands.

Daily Express

Examining the *Daily Express* today, it is hard to grasp the pre-eminence Lord Beaverbrook's flagship enjoyed in the fifties. In 1955 the paper sold an astonishing 4,036,000 copies, representing a 27 per cent share of the total popular nationals' circulation. As late as 1965, despite a small drop in actual sale of the paper, the *Express*'s market share had risen to 29 per cent, due to a total fall in the total sale of the populars. However, by the late sixties decay had set in and for the first time the *Express* started losing sale faster than the other populars until, in 1973, the *Express* conspicuously continued its slide as the other populars recovered their balance and put on sale. At the top end of the popular market, the *Daily Mail* had benefited from going tabloid six years before the *Express* whilst at the bottom end, the *Express* had not been able to slug it out with the *Sun* for fear that it would alienate its large white-collar readership. In an attempt to fend off the predators eating away at both ends of its market share, the *Express* raced up and down market with a rapidity that must have left its ageing and by now dizzy readership increasingly anxious over what they were going to be offered from one day to the next. Six different editors occupied the helm ranging from a former editor of the *Economist*, Sir Alistair Burnett, to Sir Larry Lamb, the inventor of the 'soaraway' *Sun*.

Between 1976 and 1985 the paper's sales fell in every year but two. By 1985 its sales stood at 1,883,322, only 60,000 more than the *Daily Mail*, representing a fall of nearly 28 per cent from its 1975 figure. Over the same ten year period the *Sunday Express* lost 30 per cent of its sales with half the loss occurring in the final three years, presumably due to the growing popularity of the *Mail on Sunday*, launched in 1982 as a direct challenge to the *Sunday Express* and its massive advertising revenues.

Ever since Fleet Holdings, owners of Express Newspapers, had been hived off from Trafalgar House in 1982, the Group had been vulnerable to predators. The failure of Lord Matthews as chairman to halt the circulation slide left Fleet even more exposed. Matthews could fairly point out that Fleet had been profitable overall, making £22m. in the year ending June 1984 (including £4.6m. from the sale of Reuters' shares) and a further £26m. in the following year. Its market value had also risen dramatically in the space of three years. Even Fleet's national newspapers – the *Express*, the *Sunday Express* and the *Daily Star* – turned in surpluses. However, a third of the newspaper division's profits derived from a lucrative contract to print the London *Standard* on the presses of the *Express*. Moreover, over half the Group's total profits came from Morgan Grampian, the specialist magazine company.

In the City a strong feeling existed that Lord Matthews had become a soft touch for the unions. Ironically, Matthews had taken over at the *Express* in 1977 and had been immediately hailed as the saviour of Fleet Street. The cause of the inordinate celebration was that Matthews had won a costly victory against the maintenance staff over a differential pay claim. However, subsequently Matthews appeared to lose the initiative, an impression strengthened by the Group's decision to keep printing in Fleet Street. Even though the recently equipped press hall and profitable *Standard* contract were both sound reasons for staying put, critics claimed that Matthews had lost his drive. The impression was not dispelled when Matthews himself admitted, on the day of United Newspapers' takeover bid in March 1985, 'Of course we'd like to see a substantial saving in the labour force, but under the present terms in which we employ our staff, given away many years ago by proprietors, long before my time, it is impossible in fact to do anything very serious.'

Throughout its gruelling bid for Fleet, David Stevens, United Newspapers' aggressive chairman, repeatedly asserted that he had managed to cut 20 per cent of its staff in the Group's northern regional newspaper chain. He insisted that the same proportion could be excised from the 6,800 *Express* staff in London and Manchester. Matthews replied that shedding staff in the provinces is not quite as complex as in Fleet Street. Moreover, the *Daily Express* was introducing photocomposition in Manchester by the end of 1985 and a little later in London, so jobs would be going.

However, in the end, the respective abilities of the two managements in wielding the axe was not the decisive factor in United's takeover. United had diversified and expanded in a way that Fleet had not. Stevens, by purchasing the Link House publishing group and a series of retail and publishing interests, drastically reduced United's reliance on newspapers for its profits. In 1981 72 per cent of United's profits came from newspapers, falling to only 17 per cent by the end of 1984. The expansion had given United the resources to make a bid that the shareholders, including Lord Matthews, could not turn down.

Since taking over, a new management team has been brought in and there have been promises of 20 per cent job cuts within twelve months, a new upmarket image for the *Daily Express* and a clean broom. Probably no paper is more directly threatened by the arrival of Shah's paper than the *Express*. The battle is likely to be intense.

14

The Politics of Information

'The newspaper is of necessity something of a monopoly, and its first duty is to shun the temptations of monopoly.'

C. P. Scott, 1926

14

The Politics of Information

The limited store of geological and topographical meta-
phors has already been thoroughly ransacked over the
past few months in attempting to describe the radical
change in Fleet Street upon which Shah has had such
a quickening effect. Tributaries have joined together,
icebergs have cracked, seismic shifts have been recorded,
avalanches have started tumbling, dams have burst and,
of course, sea changes have rolled.

But a nagging doubt remains that the man who has
unleashed all these natural disasters may find that his
own plans are flooded out. It has long been a commonplace observation that Shah is just 'a stalking horse' for
the other Fleet Street employers, and that once he has
outlived his usefulness as a bogeyman to frighten the
unions he will be crushed. Such a view under-estimates
the genuine good will there has been for Shah at the
highest level in Fleet Street, especially from Rupert Murdoch whose papers are at least clear of Shah's mid-
market focus. Even titles more directly in *Today*'s market
range, like the *Mail* and *Express*, are in two minds about
the newcomer.

No quarter could be given to Shah, however, at the
time of *Today*'s launch, and many of the other newspaper
groups planned to have special offers, temporary colour,

discounts and even new papers on display. One paper is said to have had a reporter digging up evidence for the past four months on the several skeletons that undoubtedly clatter about in Shah's cupboard. A leading merchant bank has compiled a dossier on Shah's personal finances for another proprietor.

Today should survive such an onslaught, but it will have a genuine struggle establishing itself as a successful newspaper; it is here that the pioneer may perish. The media market is an unusual one, hedged about with imponderables, and the recent experience of high-profile media launches has been one of almost unmitigated failure. From *Now!* magazine, which closed after eighteen months, to the *Mail on Sunday*, which had to be relaunched after five months, to tv-am which had to be saved by Roland Rat – the precedents are not encouraging.

Shah is determined not to go down in history as a courageous failure. But he has repeated some of the same mistakes. He has, for example, like James Goldsmith at *Now!*, raised expectations too high. A few months before *Now!* closed it was regularly selling 180,000 copies a week – a satisfactory enough, if loss-making, figure which could have been built on but which looked poor in relation to the projections of a quarter of a million. Similarly, with *Today* anything less than a readership of one million will now disappoint, even if it can make considerable profit on 700,000.

As with tv-am, *Today* was probably pitched too far up-market in the early stages of its conception. It is also a risk of any new glittering enterprise that the individual stars who have been thrown together may fail to form the kind of unit that Shah is hoping for. Shah's own personality, too, although the driving force behind the project, could become its worst enemy if things turn out badly. Technologically the paper should work but in the event of the inevitable hiccups, all systems, except the printing presses, are duplicated. Although both the colour advertising and news content will remain an advantage for only about eighteen months before the rest of Fleet Street has caught up, the appeal to advertisers should last unless circulation slumps. But there has been some disquiet in the advertising world that Shah's rates, while remarkably low, are too inflexible. Most papers, if they have not sold a half-page advertising slot for the next day's paper, will discount heavily. Shah says his rates are not negotiable even in those circumstances, and if the space is not sold he will fill it with editorial.

Despite the considerable doubts, even those Fleet Street executives who were amongst the most sceptical when the plan was first announced are now conceding that it can work, although they believe it is likely to be stuck at a circulation of about 500,000. The sceptics have always focused doubts on distribution and editorial quality. The distribution problem has been largely dealt with by the W. H. Smith deal; as regards editorial quality, everything remains to be seen.

Shah's new cost structure will of course give him far more room to manoeuvre than conventional Fleet Street papers – particularly with his low break-even circulation point. And if, as some rivals have suggested, he does turn out to be under-capitalised, some of the investors, including Bricom, have said they will be prepared to make more funds available if it shows itself to be a going concern. The two Australian newspaper moguls – Fairfax and Packer – have also told Shah they are ready to bail him out if necessary.

But assuming *Today* is successful and claims the 1m plus readers that wcRS have told Shah he needs for long-term credibility with advertisers, what effect will that have? In addition to the wider catalytic effect the new paper has already had on Fleet Street a successful *Today* may have an even more directly disruptive effect on papers like the *Daily Express* and the *Mail*, from whom it aims to take about one third of their readers. A 500,000 sales loss could be fatal to either of those papers in the circulation war that Shah may be about to unleash.

Today's success would also probably encourage many more outsiders to follow Shah's example. If they do, what kind of papers will they produce? Will they aim as *Today* proclaims 'to colour the newspaper not the news'? Will their politics be any different from those of the people currently running newspapers?

Few observers of any political persuasion need convincing that there is an imbalance in our national press. At present, opinion polls indicate that 60 per cent of the population do not support the Conservative Party, yet only two newspapers, the *Guardian* and the *Daily Mirror*, consistently oppose the Conservatives. Minority groups, left-wing trade unionists and non-conformists in society are all regularly treated in the national press with a cavalier disrespect. Standards of accuracy and fair play have plummeted. Investigative reporting is dismissed as passé and a bore. Sensationalism and show-biz journalism is at a premium.

In the past ten years newspapers may have been taken over but the only result has been one proprietor in a pin-stripe suit succeeding another. The new owners duly announce that they are taking their investment up or down market, but along the more important horizontal political axis there is very little sign of movement, save a slow shuffle to the Right. Lord Thomson is replaced by Murdoch, Sir Alex Jarratt by Maxwell, Lord Matthews by Stevens and Lord Hartwell by Black. And as with any game of musical chairs, the number of people left in, playing the proprietorial game, continues to diminish.

Attempts to prevent by law the concentration of press ownership, by referring takeovers to the Office of Fair Trading, have been tried and have so far transparently failed. Since 1965, when the takeover law came in, the big press chains have, as James Curran has pointed out, bought over eighty newspaper companies entirely unhindered by anti-monopoly legislation. The five major regional press chains have over the same period doubled their market share, whilst Rupert Murdoch has become a dominant influence at both the top and bottom ends of the daily and Sunday newspaper scene. No new national paper has been launched from outside the existing newspaper empires since the *Daily Worker* in 1930. The only new papers to be successfully launched since 1945 – the *Daily Star*, the *Sunday Telegraph* and the *Mail on Sunday* – have come from inside existing stables. In 1983, the TUC dropped its plans to start a new daily paper printed outside London with a capital base of £6.7m. It could not raise the cash.

As long ago as 1957, Francis Williams in his *Dangerous Estate* bemoaned the impregnability of Britain's monolithic press. 'The journalistic tragedy of our time,' he said, 'is that the risk of trying something new has become too great to be taken.' He argued that the capital investment involved in establishing a plant prohibited 'the launch of any new popular daily of large circulation'. The industry needed a technological revolution similar to that which occurred in the nineteenth century and which had led 'to an immense burst of activity in founding new newspapers'. Only with a further technological revolution, Williams asserted, 'can costs be brought down to a level at which it will once again be economically possible to publish general-interest national newspapers with an optimum circulation of a million or less'. He said no such large-scale technological revolution was yet in sight and if it were, 'it would probably be resisted by strongly entrenched interests on both sides'.

Hitherto the Left has not made the rapid introduction of new technology one of its priorities for the reform of Fleet Street. It has instead taken its cue from the major print unions which have resisted technology on the industrial grounds that it constitutes a threat to existing jobs, wages and unionisation. One left-winger within SOGAT, Barry Fitzpatrick, a leader of the clerical chapel at *The Times* during the lock-out, did canvass the notion that the print unions' industrial and political interests need not necessarily conflict. He argued that in bargaining with the newspaper employers, unions could link concessions on technology with changes in press ownership. The unions would make specific concessions on technology, so long as the employer accepted that a proportion of the consequent savings were placed in a fund to help establish more newspapers. The notion that unions could have some say over the industry through collective bargaining was denounced as a utopian impracticality and the idea quietly died.

Blocked off by the unions' opposition to technological change, organisations such as the Campaign for Press and Broadcasting Freedom have concentrated their efforts on pressing for government intervention to reduce the distortions caused by unfettered market forces and to spread newspaper ownership by law. Since the 1970s it has lobbied for wider access to printing facilities through national and local printing corporations; a launch fund for new publications funded by an advertising levy; a statutory right of reply; a fairer distribution system; and strict limits on the number of newspapers a single proprietor can sell each day. The Left's shopping-list of reforms is by now familiar, a tribute in itself to the failure to shift government opinion. The immediate outlook hardly looks more hopeful. The chance of a Conservative government which is built on free market principles and sustained by its cheerleaders in Fleet Street, sponsoring such changes, is about as great as the Government appointing Bernie Grant head of the Metropolitan Police.

Yet as Shah has crept closer to his launch, a new orthodoxy is starting to spread, remarkably similar to the views of Francis Williams. Far from Eddie Shah being a force for evil, he is being portrayed as a harbinger of a rebirth of a politically diverse press. Briefly, the proponents of the new orthodoxy claim that printers' wages and extravagant manning have become the modern equivalent of the nineteenth-century stamp duty. Whilst stamp duty artificially inflated the price of newspapers to ensure that seditious ideas and knowledge did not penetrate the working-class, so the wages of the modern Fleet Street worker have artificially inflated the natural economic cost of starting and running a newspaper, thereby preserving newspaper ownership for the rich and the Right. For many years both the proprietors and the printers have had a self-evident mutual interest in continuing this arrangement. For the proprietor, it usefully discourages outsiders from starting newspapers; for the worker it helps finance an extension to the Billericay bungalow. Eddie Shah may have stung the NGA for £2m., but many of the Left are privately delighted at his exposure of 'the Fleet Street conspiracy'. From the ashes of the NGA, they hope, will arise a socialist daily press.

It is argued that the cut in costs made possible by technology would allow a host of small-scale specialist papers to be set up and chip away at the circulation of the big-sale dailies. These papers, with their specialist markets, could charge a higher cover price than general papers and may be able to attract specialist advertising. With extensive use of colour, it might also be possible for the newspaper industry to claw back markets seized by the astonishing recent proliferation of magazines. A traditional stumbling-block of the small-sale papers – the reluctance of wholesalers to carry such papers – might also be overcome by the growth of the alternative distribution franchise network which has been established by Shah, and which will be eager to find other papers besides Shah's to distribute.

The political press, amongst others, could too enjoy a renaissance after decades on the margins of weekly and monthly journalism. In recent years, the only daily newspapers explicitly run by political parties are the Trotskyist Workers Revolutionary Party's *Newsline* and the Communist Party's *Morning Star*. Both papers are subsidised from abroad, and both have anyway been riven with factional disputes. However, on a break-even sale of 100,000 the Labour Party, the Alliance and even the Green Party could consider converting their present palsied propaganda sheets into something more substantial.

Eddie Shah himself shares the view that his own long-term impact will be the permanent establishment of more newspapers. 'Everybody is waiting to see what we do,' he asserts, 'but once we are up and running the environment will change. Once we have done it, others psychologically will be prepared to follow because they will realise that it's profitable to run papers with much lower circulations. We are the first and therefore the most expensive. The people that follow can afford to do it more cheaply. If you are producing a paper at contract printers it will soon be possible to be profitable on a 60,000 sale.'

But Shah is not waiting to be overtaken by the new-wave competition. Such is his confidence in the revolution he has partly inspired, that he is already working on quite detailed plans for several more titles after *Today*. The plans encompass a daily sports paper, a mass circulation popular paper, a specialist financial paper and even possibly a new quality paper – all of which could be printed on extra presses at his existing plants. In Shah's words: 'It's like the free newspaper industry, it was easy to hit the sluggish paid-for press at first, but after a while they caught up with us. That's why we are already planning the new national papers now, we're not going to be caught out.'

If these ambitions are realised, it may be that the old-technology Fleet Street monopolists will simply be replaced by a few new-technology monopolists. Yet the promise of the new technology and its economics is precisely that such domination will become more difficult, and there is evidence that Shah will not have the field to himself. At the end of 1985 news leaked out of the first major post-Shah non-Fleet-Street national newspaper project, organised by Andreas Whittam Smith, former city editor of the *Daily Telegraph*, and Douglas Long, former chief executive of the *Mirror*. Although the proposed broadsheet paper, targeted at young quality newspaper readers, is up-market of *Today*, it has leaned heavily on Shah's example. Whittam Smith acknowledges that it was the announcement of Shah's project early in 1985 which gave him the idea.

First, however, he did try to interest the management of his own, ailing paper with a plan to raise finance by asking readers to invest through the Business Expansion Scheme. 'The plan was properly done and verified by City specialists. If only 12,000 *Telegraph* readers had put up the minimum £500 each it would have raised £6m.,' he says. In fact he believes that £40m. to £50m. could have been raised and the subsequent need for a change of ownership at the paper avoided. Lord Hartwell, chairman and editor-in-chief of the *Telegraph*, rejected the plan on the grounds that it would be wrong to mix up readers with investors.

A few weeks before Whittam Smith had had a secret breakfast meeting with Shah at the Hyde Park Hotel and received some useful advice and contacts. The two men have subsequently kept in touch and Whittam Smith, on Shah's advice, considered hiring the company which designed the *Today* newsroom, Peter Pozzoni.

Whittam Smith's paper is, like Shah's, aiming to use the newest direct-input technology and may try to conclude a deal with the EETPU. Unlike Shah, however, Whittam Smith and Long are planning to contract-print their hoped for 400,000 daily sales (break-even 300,000) at provincial groups around the country.

This may prove difficult as provincial managements may be reluctant to take on extra staff for a project which may collapse after three months. To circumvent this problem they will probably have to promise hefty down-payments to contract printers which is why they are aiming to raise £17m. or £18m. – only a little less than

Shah's total – nearly half of which has been spent buying expensive printing presses.

About £2m. of the pre-funding money had already been raised before Christmas 1985 through venture capital specialists Stephen Rose Partners and the prospects for raising the rest look good. Indeed the new paper found that of the first six investment institutions it approached at the end of 1985 all but one agreed at once to back it, a remarkably good record for any new business. It appears that Shah, despite his own relatively frosty reception by the financial institutions, has broken the ice and the City is now prepared to back the newspaper revolution.

The paper, due to launch in October, may prove the point that it is easier to follow the Shah example in the up-market bracket where income from sales is less important than advertising revenue. The founders – three of whom are former *Telegraph* journalists – are clearly aiming to exploit the *Daily Telegraph*'s vulnerability, but they also point to the fact that the overall quality newspaper readership figures have been rising for several years. As with *Today*, their estimated profit figures make mouth-watering reading for the money men and, even if they are only half-realised, will banish the notion that national newspapers are doomed to poor profitability. If successful the Whittam Smith paper the *Independent* could also start a new commercial trend towards splitting the publishing of newspapers from the more costly printing.

However, the argument that Shah and those following him will have an unprecedented competitive edge over the existing mass-sale papers, and will therefore be able to break the long-standing tendency in the industry towards monopoly, needs qualification. For one thing, the extent to which technology cuts costs has to be kept in proportion. In a typical Fleet Street newspaper, newsprint would represent over 30 per cent of total costs, all wages and salaries around 40 per cent and the remaining expenses just under 30 per cent. As a proportion of total operating costs, production, as opposed to editorial, wages would represent around a quarter of total costs. A leanly staffed, fully-electronic newspaper might be able to cut those labour costs by four-fifths, but even this would represent only a 20 per cent cut in total operating costs.

But even if costs can be cut spectacularly, the underlying tendency for the big newspapers to drive out the small is likely to remain. As the Royal Commission on the Press pointed out in 1961: 'Where competition is severe, a general reduction in costs, though manifestly desirable from a wider point of view, does not necessarily have the effect of strengthening the position of the weak newspapers as against the strong. Unless the weak receive some benefit that is not equally given to the strong, what they gain from reduced costs is counterbalanced by what they have to do to keep pace with the increased attractions which comparable savings will have enabled their stronger rivals to offer without any increase in price.'

Putting this argument in a contemporary context, Shah's technological and labour revolution may cut costs, but the other existing newspaper empires are moving quickly to win the same reductions and re-establish the built-in advantages of their greater resources. Shah and the new generation of proprietors – assuming there will indeed be one – are unlikely to be able to claim for long any monopoly on the reduction in costs.

Alan Hayling, the acting editor of the proposed new left-wing Sunday paper, *News on Sunday*, has had direct experience, like Shah, of trying to raise capital to start a paper. He and his colleagues are currently seeking £6m. for a contract-printed paper budgeted to make an annual profit of around £1m. a year. Unlike Shah, the *News on Sunday* team cannot rely on political good will in the City to raise capital. Although part of the *News on Sunday* team insist that direct-input must be an integral part of their plans if City institutions are to have confidence in them, Hayling claims that direct-input does not dramatically alter the sums involved in starting a paper. For instance, technology does not alter newsprint costs or the crippling requirement for capital to finance the first seventeen weeks when newspaper retailers do not return the cover price revenue to a newspaper.

Hayling argues that the long-term profitability of newspapers, post-Shah, remains a matter for speculation. 'It depends on how the industry reacts. If Shah and the other existing papers reduce production costs and in the meantime can retain traditional advertising and cover-price levels, then profitability will rise sharply. There could be new opportunities for more newspaper projects to raise capital in the City or amongst trade unions and other possible sources of finance. The newspaper industry will become known as a high-return industry. But it is just as likely that free market forces will mean that the rest of the industry will respond to Shah by cutting their own advertising rates and cover price. In such a situation we, at *News on Sunday*, would have to cut our planned cover price and revenue in order to compete and our profitability would be cut. We would be a no more nor less attractive proposition for investors than before.'

In other words, the cut-throat competition in the mainstream general newspaper section of the industry is such that the benefit from the cost reductions will not necessarily be enjoyed by the producers, but by the consumer in the form of lower advertising rates and cover price. Such reductions might, it is true, create more two-newspaper households and increase the 4 per cent annual growth in newspaper advertising already expected over the next two years (unless undermined by advertising on the BBC). But there is some evidence that demand for newspapers in Britain is close to its peak and may not be coaxed higher by a cut in cover price. In gross terms, only Japan and the United States sell more copies than Britain, but proportionately more people read newspapers in Britain than almost any other developed country.

According to the European Institute for the Media, Britain sold on average in 1985 more national and regional papers (both daily and weekly) per 1,000 inhabitants than any other country apart from Australia and Canada. The British public bought 727 copies per 1,000 inhabitants, Australia 877, Canada 745, Japan 717, USA 542, Germany 411, Austria 356, Holland 306, France 184 and Italy 92. However, the British newspaper industry is uniquely a national industry. In Britain, 590 copies of national papers are bought per 1,000 inhabitants compared with a figure for the USA of 37 or for Germany of 148. By contrast, only 137 copies of regional papers are bought per 1,000 inhabitants in Britain compared with 505 in the USA, 263 in Germany or 353 in Japan. Out of the twenty countries surveyed, only three countries sell fewer regional papers per head than Britain whilst no country sells as many national papers.

The current strong orientation in Britain towards a national industry has meant that the country has a peculiarly class-based set of papers, divided between the low-sale qualities containing high levels of advertising and the high-sale populars containing less advertising. Papers that don't head towards one of these two areas tend to disappear into the industry's Bermuda Triangle.

By contrast, the regional-based industry on the Continent is forced to offer a more bland product in order to appeal to a cross-section of the regional community. Crucially, the continuing existence in Britain of the quality-popular dichotomy is likely to reduce the extent to which cost-cutting technology can help create new papers, especially in the politically important field of mass-sale papers. Papers aimed at working-class audiences have had to go for sale in order to attract advertising. They have operated on the basis that advertisers will find low-income readerships attractive to reach only if they are massed together in millions. Inevitably, these mass-sale papers are the most expensive and hazardous commercial ventures. To launch a mass-sale paper from outside an existing national or local newspaper chain, the sceptics argue, would still be a fiendishly expensive proposition. J. S. Elias, later Viscount Southwood, attempted it with the *Daily Herald* in the 1930s at great expense and with indifferent commercial results.

So, even with the cost-cutting technology can bring, a paper for the less wealthy will continue to be driven harder and harder after sale in order to survive, as was Southwood in the thirties. A general-interest newspaper with a sale amongst 500,000 working-class readers will still have the odds stacked against it. Advertisers will remain indifferent to a low-income audience of such a size so long as other mass papers are able to boast sales in the millions. The point is crudely illustrated by an apocryphal story of Rupert Murdoch pleading with a space-buyer from Bloomingdale's, one of New York's most exclusive department stores. Murdoch had proudly pointed out that the *Post* – one of the less restrained tabloids in the Murdoch stable – had hit a new sales record and told the space-buyer that it was time he started taking out ads in the paper. The buyer replied, 'But Rupert, your readers are my shoplifters.'

Nevertheless, the fact that newcomers to the national press without huge resources behind them will still find it hard to break into the mass-circulation market, should not detract from the prospects of greater diversity that now exist. Lower production costs *will* make the small circulation, specialist, paper more feasible. If it is aimed at the relatively affluent it should be able to tap the slow but steady growth in total advertising spend that is projected over the foreseeable future. However, if an audience of 100,000 is loyal enough on political or special interest grounds, a paper should also be able to survive with very little advertising. Eddie Shah, the one-time freesheet entrepreneur, may ironically have given a fillip to the specialist, cover-price-funded, national and weekly press.

Probably more significant, the newspaper revolutionaries are even promising to overcome the British press's Bermuda Triangle. They claim that regional printing of national papers could slowly break the national paper 'quality–popular' polarity and create a new generation of semi-serious, mid-market papers with a mix of local and national news similar to the few remaining provincial morning papers or the better US and continental provincial/nationals.

Today is itself stepping into the Triangle and if it does not disappear there are plans to acquire many more regional printing bases and start serious local editionalising.

The experience of the newspaper revolution in the rest of the world has only limited application to Britain because of its uniquely national industry. However, evidence recently compiled by the Economist Intelligence Unit suggests that a certain scepticism towards the more exuberant theorists of 'let a thousand flowers bloom' is justified. Again, there is no doubt that the introduction of direct-input in the US and on the continent has increased the number of new titles – especially suburban and small-commuinity newspapers. In the US the sale of morning daily newspapers has risen by nearly two per cent per annum in the ten years to 1982. In Germany sales of newspapers fell steadily between 1954 and 1979 but have now stabilised. In the Netherlands the sale of local papers has risen but the number of national papers has fallen. In Japan where direct-input is less advanced, partly due to the complexities of the Japanese language, sales have also risen – a reminder that technology is only one factor among many determining growth.

On the even more important question of the industry's post-revolutionary employment prospects, the message from abroad remains mixed. British newspaper employers repeatedly claim that the unnecessary production jobs which they are cutting will be more than replaced both by new jobs in the editorial and advertising departments of particular papers and by the general increase in the number of newspaper titles. It may be little consolation for a 45-year-old male compositor to know that from his lost job will be created two part-time jobs for young women – but the employers' argument is probably half correct.

In the short term shake-out there will clearly be a reduction in jobs, especially in the national newspaper industry. Eddie Shah may be creating 600 jobs but his net effect, taking into account Fleet Street's rapid shedding of labour, will be to take several thousand jobs out of the industry. In the medium and longer run the foreign experience suggests many of these will return, albeit in very different form. In the US employment levels in the industry have risen from 345,000 in 1965 to 443,000 in 1984; in Germany employment has also risen by 3 per cent a year since 1979. In Holland, however, total employment has actually fallen since the introduction of new technology.

Although the changes now under way appear gargantuan, particularly after decades of ossification, there are still more to come. Television, videotext and other electronic media will become the dominant means whereby hard instant news is presented, but there will always be a need for interpretation, analysis and perspective – dimensions of news coverage that television can only provide laboriously. If anything, as leisure time and incomes continue to rise, the demand for the printed word both for interpretation and entertainment will continue to rise.

Printing of the product, however, is likely to continue moving closer to the point of consumption, allowing later deadlines as well as giving advertisers greater flexibility. Eventually, newspaper printing is likely to be taken to its most logical extension and will start to be electronically distributed direct to the home via the cable TV or computer. The subscriber will be able to view the range of stories available on the screen and have them printed out in the home. It should eventually be possible to construct your own newspaper from the range of stories available. Increasingly, the communications empires being built by men like Murdoch, merging cable and newspapers, will themselves start to merge the two media through the advent of the electronic newspaper. But for the foreseeable future the permanence, portability and flexibility of the printed word suggests that it will retain its status as the primary means of communication. And for the foreseeable future, anyway, the British newspaper industry already has one revolution to be coming to terms with.

A Royal Mail service in association with the Book Marketing Council & The Booksellers Association.
Post-A-Book is a Post Office trademark.